Mastering
SIMULINK 2 ®

The MATLAB Curriculum Series

Dabney/Harman, *Mastering Simulink 2*
0-13-243767-8 ©1998

Dabney/Harman, *The Student Edition of Simulink: Dynamic System Simulation for MATLAB User's Guide*
0-13-659699-1 1998

Etter, *Engineering Problem Solving with MATLAB, 2/e*
0-13-397688-2 ©1997

Garcia, *Numerical Methods for Physics*
0-13-151986-7 ©1994

Hanselman/Littlefield, *Mastering MATLAB 5: A Comprehensive Tutorial and Reference*
0-13-858366-8 ©1998

Marcus, *Matrices and MATLAB: A Tutorial*
0-13-562901-2 ©1993

McClellan, et. al., *Computer-Based Exercises for Signal Processing Using MATLAB 5*
0-13-789009-5 ©1998

McClellan/Schafer/Yoder, *DSP First: A Multimedia Approach*
0-13-243171-8 ©1998

Ogata, *Solving Control Engineering Problems with MATLAB*
0-13-182213-6 ©1994

Polking, *Ordinary Differential Equations Using MATLAB*
0-13-133944-3 ©1995

Roughgarden, *The Primer of Ecological Theory*
0-13-442062-4 ©1997

Van Loan, *Introduction to Scientific Computing*
0-13-125444-8 ©1997

Hanselmann/Littlefield, *The Student Edition of MATLAB, Version 5 User's Guide*
0-13-272550-9 ©1997

Mastering
SIMULINK 2®

James B. Dabney
Thomas L. Harman

The MATLAB® Curriculum Series

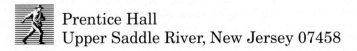

Prentice Hall
Upper Saddle River, New Jersey 07458

Library of Congress Cataloging-in-Publication Data
Dabney, James
    Mastering Simulink 2: dynamic simulation for MATLAB /
James B. Dabney, Thomas L. Harman.
      p.   cm. — (MATLAB curriculum series)
    Includes bibliographical references and index.
    ISBN 0-13-243767-8
    1. Computer simulation. 2. Simulink 3. MATLAB.   I. Harman,
    Thomas L., 1942– . II. Title.   III. Series.
QA76.9.C65D32   1998
003'.353042—dc21dc21   97-47332
                                                  CIP

Publisher: Tom Robbins
Editorial / Production Supervision: Ann Marie
    Longobardo
Editor-in-Chief: Marcia Horton
Managing Editor: Bayani Mendoza de Leon
Vice President of Production and Manufacturing:
    David W. Riccardi
Manufacturing Buyer: Julia Meehan
Manufacturing Manager: Trudy Pisciotti
Editorial Assistant: Nancy Garcia
Copyeditor: Marjorie Shustak
Composition: RDD Consultants, Inc.

RESTRICTED RIGHTS LEGEND

Use, duplication, or disclosure by the Government is
subject to restrictions as set forth in subdivision
(b)(3)(ii) of the Rights in Technical Data and
Computer Software clause at 52.227–7013.

The software described in this document is
furnished under a license agreement. The software
may be used or copied under the terms of the license
agreement.

© 1998 by Prentice-Hall, Inc.
Simon & Schuster / A Viacom Company
Upper Saddle River, New Jersey 07458

MATLAB and Simulink are registered trademarks
of The MathWorks, Inc. Other product and company
names mentioned are trademarks or trade names of
their respective companies.

The author and publisher of this book have used their best efforts in preparing this book. These efforts
include the development, research, and testing of the theories and programs to determine their
effectiveness. The author and publisher make no warranty of any kind, expressed or implied, with regard to
these programs or the documentation contained in this book. The author and publisher shall not be liable in
any event for incidental or consequential damages in connection with, or arising out of, the furnishing,
performance, or use of these programs.

Printed in the United States of America

10 9 8 7 6

ISBN 0-13-243767-8

Prentice-Hall International (UK) Limited, *London*
Prentice-Hall of Australia Pty. Limited, *Sydney*
Prentice-Hall Canada, Inc., *Toronto*
Prentice-Hall Hispanoamericana, S.A., *Mexico*
Prentice-Hall of India Private Limited, *New Delhi*
Prentice-Hall of Japan, Inc., *Tokyo*
Simon & Schuster Asia Pte. Ltd., *Singapore*
Editora Prentice-Hall do Brasil, Ltda., *Rio de Janeiro*

The MathWorks, Inc.
24 Prime Park Way
Natick, Massachusetts 01760-1500
Phone: (508) 647-7000
Fax: (508) 647-7001
E-mail: info@mathworks.com
http://www.mathworks.com

To Beth

Contents

Preface

We intend for this book to serve both as a tutorial for new users of Simulink®
and as a reference for experienced users. The book covers all of the important
capabilities of Simulink, including subsystems, masking, callbacks, and S-
Functions. The book is meant to be used with Simulink 2. The examples were
produced with Simulink Version 2.1.

Simulink is a programming language specifically designed for simulating
dynamical systems. Therefore, in order for you to use Simulink effectively, you
should have the appropriate mathematical preparation. We assume you have a
good understanding of the concepts usually covered in the introductory courses
in calculus and differential equations. However, as many new users of
Simulink may be unfamiliar with block diagram notation, we have included a
chapter that introduces the notation.

Using the book

The authors have developed a software supplement to *Mastering Simulink*.
This software is available free of charge via file transfer protocol (ftp) from The
MathWorks' world wide web site. The files may be found at

ftp://ftp.mathworks.com/pub/books/dabney/

The software supplement includes many of the Simulink examples explained
in the text. All of the MATLAB M-files and C source files discussed in the text
are also included. This software will allow you to experiment with the examples on your own computer. You may also use the examples in the software supplement as a starting point for your own simulation projects.

Here, we offer suggested reading sequences for new users of Simulink, for
users experienced with a previous version of Simulink, and for advanced users
ready to take advantage of all of the power of Simulink.

New Users

It is possible to model fairly complex systems with basic proficiency with Simulink. The fastest way to gain this basic proficiency is to adhere to the following sequence:

1. If you are new to block diagrams read Sections 2.1 and 2.2. These sections introduce block diagram notation and illustrate using block diagrams to model scalar continuous systems.

2. Carefully work through all of the examples in Chapters 3 and 4 to master the mechanics of building and running models.

3. Read Sections 5.1, 5.2, and 5.4 and experiment with the examples. After completing this material, you should be comfortable building and running models of scalar continuous systems.

4. As you gain proficiency with Simulink, complete Chapter 2, then work through the rest of Chapter 5 and Chapter 6.

Experienced Users

If you are experienced with a previous version of Simulink, or if you are a new user, after you have acquired basic proficiency, we suggest you proceed as follows:

1. Read Section 3.4. The new Block Browser provides detailed on-line documentation for all Simulink blocks. We believe that you will find the Block Browser to be easy to use and to be a real time-saver.

2. Review Chapter 4. The Simulink 2 user interface has many improvements over the previous version of Simulink. Pay particular attention to Section 4.8 concerning selecting and configuring a solver.

3. Scan Chapters 5 and 6. Pay particular attention to Section 5.2.1. The Integrator block has been improved and has a new dialog box.

4. Read Sections 7.1 and 7.2, then work through Sections 7.3 and 7.4 in detail. You will find that masking has been improved significantly. Additionally, learning to use conditionally executed subsystems will allow you to build very efficient models.

5. Read Chapter 8, even if you don't plan to use the analysis capabilities right away. You may well discover that the analysis tools will make your use of Simulink much more productive.

6. Review Chapter 12. An understanding of the numerical issues can allow you to build models that are both faster and more accurate.

Advanced Users

If you are already experienced with Simulink 2, we suggest you proceed as follows:

1. Scan Chapter 4 to review the basics of model building and Chapter 12 to review the numerical issues.

2. Read Chapters 7 and 8 to review subsystems, masking, and Simulink analysis tools.

3. If you intend to build graphical user interfaces or interactive animations, read Chapter 9 and study the examples.

4. Review Chapter 10, particularly Sections 10.1-10.4. Even if you don't need to use S-Functions right away, understanding the capability will allow you to recognize situations in which S-Functions are appropriate.

5. Review Chapter 11 and experiment a little with the Animation Toolbox.

Acknowledgments

We wrote this book with a tremendous amount of help. The MathWorks® was very supportive. In particular, we wish to acknowledge Jim Tung, Rick Spada, Loren Dean, Kevin Kohrt, Paul Holway, Liz Callanan, and Naomi Bullock. We are also grateful for the assistance of Jeanne Lesley at the University of Houston—Clear Lake and Nancy Garcia of Prentice Hall for administrative support. We wish to thank Ann Marie Longobardo for ably managing production.

The following reviewers provided many helpful suggestions:

Diane Kennedy, Ryerson Polytechnic University
Jonathan Locker, University of Illinois—Urbana-Champaign
Paul H. Lewis, Michigan Tech

Finally, we wish to acknowledge the continuous support and encouragement provided by our editor, Tom Robbins. Tom provided a great deal of helpful advice, solved every administrative problem we encountered, and made sure we had all the resources we needed to complete the project.

Introduction

In this chapter, we will explain what Simulink is and why it's important. Next, we will look at some industry applications of Simulink. Then, we'll discuss two important approaches to using Simulink: rapid prototyping and rapid application development. We'll then discuss factors you should consider when selecting a simulation environment. Chapter 1 will conclude with a preview of the remaining chapters.

1.1   What Is Simulink?

Simulink is an extension to MATLAB that allows engineers to rapidly and accurately build computer models of dynamical systems using block diagram notation. Using Simulink, it is easy to model complex nonlinear systems. A Simulink model can include both continuous and discrete-time components. Additionally, a Simulink model can produce graphical animations that show the progress of a simulation visually, significantly enhancing understanding of the system's behavior.

In the past, a common approach to developing a computer model of a dynamical system was to start with a block diagram. Next, the block diagram was translated into the source code of a programming language. This practice involved duplication of effort, as the system and controller had to be described twice—once in block diagram form, and then again in the programming language. It also introduced the risk that the translation from block diagram to source code may be inaccurate. A difficult problem in debugging a control system design was determining the location of an error. The error could be in the design (block diagram world), in the program (programming language world), or in the translation from block diagram to program. With Simulink, the duplication of effort in rewriting the model in a programming language is eliminated, and the fact that the "program" is the block diagram itself eliminates the risk that the program may not accurately implement the block diagram.

The potential productivity improvement realized from this block diagram approach to programming is dramatic. As an example, consider the simple spring-mass system of Figure 1-1. A Simulink model of this system is shown in Figure 1-2. Table 1-1 provides a comparison of programs modeling this system in 8086 assembly language using 16-bit integer arithmetic and simple Euler integration, in FORTRAN using floating-point arithmetic, in MATLAB using matrix arithmetic, and in Simulink. For the Simulink program, we list the number of blocks rather than program statements, and we include the number of mouse clicks with the number of keystrokes. As there is a strong correlation between the number of lines of code required to produce a program and the time required to write the program, it is clear that Simulink provides the opportunity for significant productivity improvements.

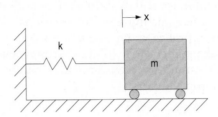

Figure 1-1   Spring-mass system

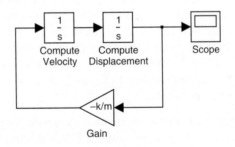

Figure 1-2   Simulink model of spring-mass system

Table 1-1   Program size comparison

Programming Language	Lines of Code (Blocks)	Approximate Keystrokes
8086 Assembly Language	92	1540
FORTRAN	14	240
MATLAB	3	90
Simulink	4	25

1.2 Simulink Examples

Simulink is now widely used in industry. Two examples of Simulink use in industry are the modeling of a steel rolling plant and the modeling of internal combustion engines. We'll look at examples of each application next.

1.2.1 Steel Rolling Plant Modeling

Our first example of industrial use of Simulink is in the simulation of a steel rolling plant [1]. The steel rolling process begins with flat-cast 25-ton slabs that are fed into the rolling mills at 1200 C (2200 F). The slabs move through the mills at the rate of 20 slabs per hour, exiting the rolls at 10 meters per second. The objective of the plant control system is to maximize the rate of production while maintaining the desired material properties and thickness of the finished product.

It is not economically feasible to experiment with the plant controls to evaluate control strategies to increase production. Consequently, the plant engineers developed a high-fidelity Simulink simulation of the plant and the control system. Using the Simulink model, controller parameters are fine-tuned off line, and new control algorithms are evaluated. Additionally, the Simulink model is used as a training tool for new engineers. The advantages of Simulink use in this case are the ease with which the Simulink model may be modified, and the fact that the Simulink model is nearly self-documenting.

1.2.2 Automotive Engine Modeling

Simulation is an important tool in the development of automotive engines. A Simulink model of a port fuel-injected internal combustion engine was developed by Simcar.com [3]. This is a complex, hierarchical model that accounts for nonlinear air, fuel, and exhaust gas recirculation dynamics in the intake manifold, as well as internal process delays. A top-level view of the Simulink model is shown in Figure 1-3.

The engine model is used in several ways. It is used as a non-real-time engine model for testing engine control algorithms and engine sensor and actuator models. It is also used as a real-time model for testing prototype controllers. It may also be used as an observer embedded within a control algorithm, or as an engine subsystem model embedded in a powertrain or vehicle dynamics simulation. It has been found that the ability to rapidly evaluate new strategies in Simulink permits engineers to try ideas in minutes or hours, instead of the days or weeks previously required to test the ideas on an actual vehicle [3].

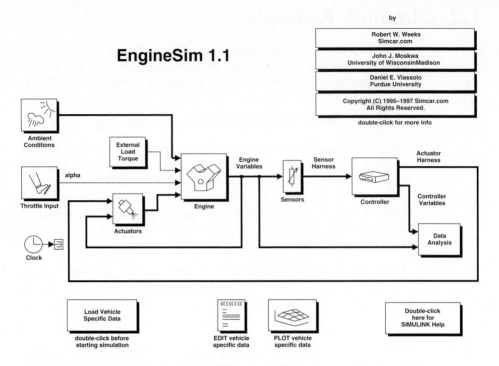

EngineSim 1.1

by

Robert W. Weeks Simcar.com
John J. Moskwa University of WisconsinMadison
Daniel E. Viassolo Purdue University

Ambient Conditions

External Load Torque

Engine Variables

Sensor Harness

Actuator Harness

alpha

Throttle Input

Engine

Sensors

Controller

Controller Variables

Actuators

Clock

Data Analysis

Load Vehicle Specific Data

double-click before starting simulation

EDIT vehicle specific data

PLOT vehicle specific data

Double-click here for SIMULINK Help

Figure 1-3   Simulink automotive engine model

1.3   Simulink Employment Strategies

So far, we have looked at the evolution of engineering programming languages, and the improvements in productivity that Simulink offers. In this section we will discuss the two principal strategies for Simulink employment: rapid prototyping and rapid application development (RAD). Rapid prototyping is the application of productivity tools to develop working prototypes of control systems in the minimum amount of time. Rapid prototyping methods are optimized for development speed, rather than execution speed or memory use. RAD is an extension to the rapid prototyping methodology in which the final computer program is the Simulink model, or is derived automatically from the Simulink model.

1.3.1   Rapid Prototyping

Digital control systems are built using either general-purpose computers or embedded microprocessors. In both cases, it is very expensive and time-consuming to develop and debug controller software using the target physical system. In some cases, such as aircraft autopilots, it would be not only expensive, but also quite dangerous to attempt to develop the controller software using the target computer and physical system. The most common approach to developing controller software is to first develop a software model of the plant to be controlled, and then use this model to develop a simulation of the control system. A common development strategy is to design the controller on paper using block diagrams, then to implement the design in the desired programming language and integrate the controller with the plant model. Next, parameters of the controllers are tuned through repeated runs of the combined controller-plant simulation. If the controller proves unsatisfactory, or if alternative designs are to be evaluated, the design and programming cycle is repeated. Rapid prototyping provides a means to streamline the design of a controller by delaying the translation from block diagram to computer program until the design is complete and verified.

The rapid prototyping process begins with the development of a simulation of the physical system to be controlled. The simulation can be a Simulink model, or it can be a model developed in MATLAB or C. Next, the controller is developed using Simulink and perhaps MATLAB toolboxes such as the Optimization Toolbox. This phase is really a combination of the requirements and design phases of traditional software development cycles. During the prototyping phase, a detailed set of test cases is executed to verify that the design satisfies all performance requirements. Alternative designs may be tried, and controller parameters tuned as well.

Once the Simulink prototype has been thoroughly tested, the controller software is coded in a programming language compatible with the target computer. The program is then loaded into the target computer, and tests are run using the operational controller to control the computer model of the plant. This testing verifies that the operational program correctly implements the design that was verified using the Simulink model. Last, the operational controller is tested using the actual plant.

There are several advantages of the rapid prototyping approach. One advantage is that the time-consuming process of developing controller software using a traditional programming language is performed only once. A second advantage is that alternative designs may be tried relatively inexpensively, promoting innovation. Finally, having the design verified before programming begins facilitates debugging during the programming phase, as the likelihood of errors being in the design rather than in the program is low.

1.3.2 Rapid Application Development

RAD extends the rapid prototyping idea by eliminating altogether programming in a traditional language. In cases in which the controller is a computer compatible with Simulink, Simulink can be used as the final programming language. In the steel rolling mill application discussed earlier, the Simulink model is used operationally as the training simulation for new engineers.

Often, the Simulink model of the controller is not suitable for deployment directly. In some applications, the Simulink controller does not respond fast enough. In many applications, the controller computer is an embedded microprocessor that is not compatible with Simulink. Both of these types of applications are candidates for automatic code generation using The MathWorks' Real-Time Workshop. Real-Time Workshop automatically converts the Simulink block diagrams into C language programs that may be compiled for the target computer. The automatically generated controller code may then be linked with off-the-shelf real-time executive[1] and interface code to produce an operational control system for embedded microprocessors. In applications where the Simulink model is not fast enough, translating the Simulink controller into C using Real-Time Workshop will provide substantial speed improvements, particularly when run on high-speed simulation hardware available from dSPACE, Applied Dynamics, and a number of other vendors.

1.4 Selection Considerations

Simulink is a very powerful tool for modeling and control system design, and, like every powerful tool, it is better suited to some tasks than to others. Sometimes, it's better to use other special-purpose tools. For example, although it's possible to model electronic circuits using Simulink, there are special-purpose software packages designed for that specific task. Of course, many programming tasks are best handled with general-purpose programming languages. There are three key questions which must be answered in choosing a tool for an engineering design task:

1. Is the tool suitable to the task? Simulink is designed to model dynamical systems using block diagram notation. If simulation is a significant part of the project, Simulink should be considered.

2. What are the schedule implications? Time is an important factor in every engineering project, both in the university and in industry. If Simulink is suitable for the task at hand, it can save a significant amount of time.

3. How will the choice of development tools affect the total project cost? It has been estimated that it can cost from 10 to 100 times as much to correct a software error found in operational software than to correct the same error in the design stage. [2] A Simulink model can be thought of as an executable software design document. Thus, whether Simulink is used for rapid prototyping or rapid application development, it has the potential to save significant development costs.

---

[1] A real-time executive is a special type of computer operating system for computers in control systems. The real-time executive ensures that important tasks are performed on schedule.

1.5   Outline of Text

This text is intended to supplement the principal text for courses in control systems, dynamics, or simulation, and is also meant to be a tutorial and reference for practicing engineers. Chapter 2 provides an overview of block diagrams for continuous and discrete systems. Chapter 3 provides a quick introduction to basics of model building, followed by detailed coverage in Chapter 4. Chapter 5 discusses modeling continuous systems, and Chapter 6 discusses discrete-time systems. Chapter 7 shows how to model more complex systems using hierarchical block diagrams and custom blocks called masked blocks. Chapter 8 discusses the use of Simulink analysis tools, including the linearization and trim functions. Callback functions, discussed in Chapter 9, provide a means to add functionality to Simulink models using MATLAB M-files. S-Functions, discussed in Chapter 10, allow you to create new Simulink blocks using either the MATLAB language or C. Chapter 11 shows how to add animations using S-Functions and the Animation Toolbox. Finally, Chapter 12 discusses numerical issues of concern in Simulink modeling.

1.6   References and Further Reading

1. "Simulink Helps BHP Steel Achieve World-Class Production," *Application Note*, The MathWorks, 1994.

2. *Software Independent Verification and Validation*, AFSC AFLC Pamphlet 800-5, Department of the Air Force, DC, 1988, p. 2.

3. Weeks, Robert W., and Moskwa, John J., "Automotive Engine Modeling for Real-Time Control Using MATLAB/Simulink," *Vehicle Computer Applications: Vehicle Systems and Driving Simulation*, SP-1080, Society of Automotive Engineers, 1995, pp. 123–137.

Block Diagrams

This chapter is devoted to an introduction to block diagrams. We start with primitive blocks used to describe simple continuous systems, and progress to discrete and hybrid systems. We will also discuss the state-space concept and development of state-space models from the describing differential and difference equations. For each block discussed, we will show the standard block diagram notation and the equivalent Simulink block. Several examples illustrate the use of the block diagram components and the relationship between the block diagrams and differential and difference equations.

2.1 Introduction

In Chapter 1, we looked briefly at the uses of Simulink and some example Simulink programs. Before we proceed to explore Simulink, we will introduce block diagrams for both continuous and discrete systems. We will examine the most common blocks for both types of systems. More specialized blocks will be introduced in later chapters.

Block diagram notation is a graphical means to represent dynamical systems. The notation has been used for many years. While block diagrams originally were used to represent linear time-invariant continuous systems, the notation has been extended to represent complex nonlinear systems containing both continuous-time and discrete-time components. A continuous system is a system that may be represented using differential equations. A discrete system is represented using difference equations. A hybrid system contains both continuous and discrete components. A typical hybrid system would consist of a continuous process controlled by a digital computer. Today, the hybrid system is the most common.

Block diagrams bear a superficial resemblance to computer program flow charts, but they are conceptually quite different. A flow chart describes a sequence of operations, so only one block in the flow chart is active at a time. A block diagram describes a set of relationships that hold simultaneously. All blocks in a block diagram may be active at once, so a block diagram may be thought of as representing a set of simultaneous equations. Thus, a computer program that models a dynamical system would evaluate each block in the block diagram repeatedly.

9

We will start our discussion of block diagrams with continuous systems. We will look at typical components of a continuous block diagram and their Simulink representations. Next, we'll show how the blocks may be composed to model simple continuous systems. In later sections of this chapter, we'll examine block diagrams for discrete and hybrid systems.

2.2 Continuous Systems

Most physical systems are modeled as continuous systems, since they can be described using differential equations. The simplest models are linear and time-invariant. Although few physical systems are truly linear or time-invariant, much useful insight can be gained using linear time-invariant models. Additionally, the blocks used to model such idealized systems are also needed to model the behavior of nonlinear and time-varying systems.

Four primitive blocks are used to represent continuous linear systems. These are the *gain block*, the s*um block*, the *derivative block*, and the *integrator*. Any system that can be described using linear differential equations may be modeled using these four primitive blocks. In addition to the four primitive blocks, the transfer function block is also frequently used in the modeling of physical systems and controllers.

2.2.1 Gain Blocks

The simplest block diagram element is the gain block. The output of the gain block is the input multiplied by a constant. Thus, the block represents the algebraic equation

$$y = kx \tag{2-1}$$

Figure 2-1 illustrates the conventional representation of a gain block and its Simulink counterpart. Note that the output follows the input continuously.

| (a) Gain block | (b) Simulink Gain block |

Figure 2-1   Gain block

A simple physical example of a gain block is the force balance of a lever. Refer-ring to Figure 2-2, the lever in equilibrium can be represented by the equation

$$F_{out} = a F_{in} \tag{2-2}$$

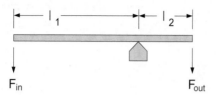

F_{in} F_{out} **Figure 2-2**   Lever force multiplication

where a is the length ratio,

$$a = l_1/l_2 \tag{2-3}$$

Other physical examples that would be represented using gain blocks are the linear model of an electrical resistor and the linear spring. The equation for the linear resistor is

$$v = RI \tag{2-4}$$

in which the input is the current I, the gain is the resistance R, and the output is the voltage v. The behavior of a linear elastic spring is represented by the equation

$$F = kx \tag{2-5}$$

where the input is the spring deflection x, the gain is the spring constant k, and the output is the force F.

2.2.2 Sum Block

The sum block permits us to add two or more inputs. The output of the sum block, shown in Figure 2-3, is the algebraic sum of the inputs. Each input is labeled with a plus sign (+) or a minus sign (−) to indicate whether the input is to be added or subtracted. Thus, the sum block in Figure 2-3 represents the algebraic equation

$$c = a - b \tag{2-6}$$

A sum block must have at least one input and exactly one output. While there is in general no limit to the number of inputs, too many inputs makes the block diagram difficult to read. When the number of inputs to a sum block begins to make the diagram difficult to read, it's better to cascade several sum blocks.

(a) Sum block   (b) Simulink sum block

Figure 2-3   Sum block

2.2.3 Derivative Block

The derivative block computes the time rate of change of its input. The block represents the differential equation

$$y = \frac{dx}{dt} \tag{2-7}$$

Figure 2-4 shows two common representations of the derivative block and the Simulink representation. The second representation (the block containing s) is due to the fact that the Laplace transform of the derivative of a function (ignoring initial conditions) is

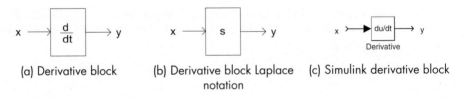

(a) Derivative block   (b) Derivative block Laplace   (c) Simulink derivative block
                            notation

Figure 2-4   Derivative block

$$L\left(\frac{dx(t)}{dt}\right) = sL(x(t)) \tag{2-8}$$

where L represents the Laplace operator and s the Laplace domain complex frequency variable. We will use the representation of Figure 2-4(a) for consistency with Simulink. A derivative block has a single input and a single output.

A physical example of a system component that could be represented using a derivative block is a dashpot as depicted in Figure 2-5.

The force equation of the dashpot is

$$F = c\frac{dx}{dt} \tag{2-9}$$

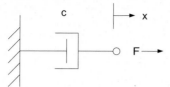

Figure 2-5   Dashpot model

where F is the damping force and c is the damping coefficient.

2.2.4 Integrator

The integrator block computes the time integral of its input from the starting time to the present. Integrator blocks are shown in Figure 2-6, along with the Simulink equivalent.

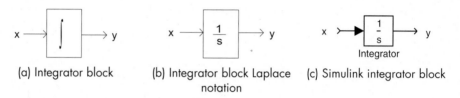

(a) Integrator block   (b) Integrator block Laplace   (c) Simulink integrator block
                                        notation

Figure 2-6   Integrator Block

The integrator block represents the equation

$$y(t) = y(t_0) + \int_{t_0}^{t} x(\tau)d\tau \tag{2-10}$$

The Simulink 1/s label is a reference to the Laplace transform representation of integration: recall that integration in the time domain corresponds to multiplication by 1/s in the Laplace complex frequency (s) domain. In fact, it is now probably more common to see the 1/s representation in block diagrams than the integral sign representation. We will use the 1/s notation for consistency with Simulink.

An example of a physical component that could be represented using an integrator block is the capacitor, as shown in Figure 2-7. The input to the block is the current divided by the capacitance, and the output is the voltage across the capacitor plates.

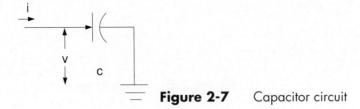

Figure 2-7 Capacitor circuit

2.2.5 Simple Physical Models

The primitive block diagram components we've defined so far may be used to model any physical system that may be described completely using linear differential equations. To see how we build block diagrams using these components, consider the simple cart shown in Figure 2-8. Ignoring friction, the equation of motion of this system is

$$\ddot{x} = \frac{F}{m} \qquad (2\text{-}11)$$

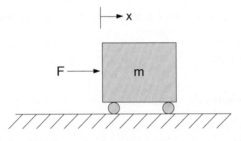

Figure 2-8 Cart

(Note that we use the notation $\dot{x}$ to represent the time derivatives, thus $\ddot{x}$ is equivalent to d^2x/dt^2)

This system may be represented by the block diagram shown in Figure 2-9. We can expand this block diagram to compute the cart position. In Figure 2.10, we have added two integrators. The first computes the cart velocity, the second computes displacement.

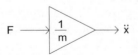

Figure 2-9 Block diagram of cart equation of motion

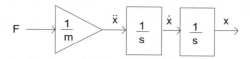

Figure 2-10   Block diagram of cart position computation

2.2.6 Transfer Function Block

Transfer function notation is frequently used in control system design and system modeling. The *transfer function* can be defined as the ratio of the Laplace transform of the input to a system (or subsystem) to the Laplace transform of the output, assuming zero initial conditions. Thus, the transfer function provides a convenient input-output description of the system dynamics. As we'll see, the transfer function block is a compact notation for a composition of primitive block diagram components.

Consider the spring, mass, dashpot system depicted in Figure 2-11. Ignoring friction, the equation of motion of this system is

$$m\ddot{x} + c\dot{x} + kx = F \tag{2-12}$$

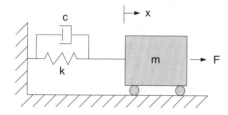

Figure 2-11   Spring, mass, dashpot system

Taking the Laplace transform and ignoring initial conditions yields

$$m s^2 X(s) + c s X(s) + k X(s) = F(s) \tag{2-13}$$

Figure 2-12 depicts this system using primitive block diagram components.

The ratio of the Laplace transform of the output ($X(s)$) to the Laplace transform of the input ($F(s)$) is the transfer function ($G(s)$),

$$G(s) = \frac{X(s)}{F(s)} = \frac{(1/m)}{s^2 + \dfrac{c}{m}s + \dfrac{k}{m}} \tag{2-14}$$

Figure 2-13(a) represents the same system in transfer function form. The transfer function representation is more compact, and it is useful in under-

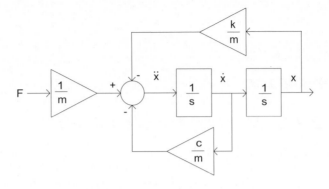

Figure 2-12 Block diagram of spring, mass, damper system

standing the system dynamics. The denominator of the transfer function is the characteristic equation of the system, and thus the roots of the denominator are the eigenvalues of the system. (See Harman et al. [2] for a detailed discussion of eigenvalues.)

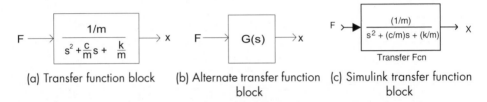

(a) Transfer function block   (b) Alternate transfer function block   (c) Simulink transfer function block

Figure 2-13 Transfer function representations of a spring, mass, damper system

While the transfer function of a dynamical system is unique, the differential equation that describes a dynamical system is not unique. Thus, if we need access to internal variables, such as $\dot{x}$, we can't use transfer function notation. For the same reason, if we need to specify initial conditions, we can't use transfer function notation.

Figure 2-13(b) shows an alternate notation for the transfer function block. This representation treats the transfer function symbolically, and is commonly used in diagrams with multiple transfer function blocks. A common convention is to represent the transfer function of the plant as $G(s)$, and the transfer function of the controller as $H(s)$. Figure 2-13(c) depicts the Simulink representation of the same transfer function block.

Block Diagrams   Chapter 2

2.3   State-Space Block

The *state-space block* is an alternative to the transfer function block. Like the transfer function block, the state-space block provides a compact representation of the system or subsystem dynamics. However, the state-space block also permits us to specify initial conditions, and can provide access to internal variables. Another advantage of the state-space block is that it allows us to conveniently model systems with multiple inputs and multiple outputs, whereas the transfer function block accommodates only one input and one output.

2.3.1   The State-Space Concept

Before we explain the definition of the state-space block, we will first discuss the concept of state variables, then show how the state-space model of a system is developed.

A *state vector* is a set of *state variables* sufficient to describe the dynamic state of a system. The general form of the state-space model of a dynamical system is

$$\dot{x} = f(x, u, t) \tag{2-15}$$

where x is the state vector, u the *input vector,* and t time. Equation (2-15) is called the *system state equation*. We also define the system output to be

$$y = g(x, u, t) \tag{2-16}$$

Equation (2-16) is called the *output equation*.

Note that we will use lowercase boldface type to distinguish vectors and uppercase boldface type to distinguish matrices.

The so-called *natural state variables* are physical values such as position, velocity, temperature, or electrical current. For a mechanical system, the natural state variables are positions and velocities. For electrical circuits, the natural state variables could be voltages or currents. The natural state variables are not the only set of state variables we can choose. In fact, any independent combination of a valid set of state variables is also a valid set of state variables. Example 2-1 illustrates the selection of state variables for a single-degree-of-freedom system.

Example 2-1

Consider the pendulum of Figure 2-14.

Figure 2-14 Pendulum model

A natural set of state variables would be the deflection angle and the rate of change of deflection:

$$x_1 = \theta$$

$$x_2 = \dot{\theta}$$

The state-space approach becomes very useful as the complexity of a system increases. Example 2.2 illustrates selection of state variables for a system with two degrees of freedom.

Example 2-2

The two-mass system in Figure 2-15 has two degrees of freedom, each of which is described by a second-order differential equation, so we need four state variables to specify the dynamic state of the system. A natural set of state variables would be

$$w_1 = x_1$$
$$w_2 = \dot{x}_1$$
$$w_3 = x_2$$
$$w_4 = \dot{x}_2$$

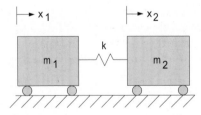

Figure 2-15 Two mass system

Another equally valid set of state variables is

$$z_1 = x_1$$
$$z_2 = \dot{x}_1$$
$$z_3 = x_2 - x_1$$
$$z_4 = \dot{x}_2 - \dot{x}_1$$

2.3.2   Linear Single-Input, Single-Output Systems

The state variable approach is particularly useful in modeling linear systems because we can take advantage of matrix notation to describe very complex systems in a compact form. Additionally, we can compute the system response using matrix arithmetic. In this section we will use the state-space approach to model linear systems with one input and one output.

The natural state variables of a mechanical system are position and velocity. Consider the spring, mass, dashpot system of Figure 2-11. This is a second-order system with one degree of freedom, so we must choose two state variables. Choosing

$$x_1 = x$$
$$x_2 = \dot{x} \tag{2-17}$$

the time rates of change of the two state variables are

$$\dot{x}_1 = x_2 \tag{2-18}$$

$$\dot{x}_2 = -\frac{k}{m}x_1 - \frac{c}{m}x_2 + \frac{1}{m}F$$

These equations can be written in matrix notation

$$\dot{x} = Ax + Bu \tag{2-19}$$

where

$$x = \begin{bmatrix} x_1 \\ x_2 \end{bmatrix} \tag{2-20}$$

$$A = \begin{bmatrix} 0 & 1 \\ -\dfrac{k}{m} & -\dfrac{c}{m} \end{bmatrix} \tag{2-21}$$

$$u = F \tag{2-22}$$

$$B = \begin{bmatrix} 0 \\ \dfrac{1}{m} \end{bmatrix} \tag{2-23}$$

Matrix A is frequently called the *system matrix*. The system matrix is always square. Matrix B is the *input matrix*. The number of rows in the input matrix is the same as the number of state variables, and the number of columns is the same as the number of inputs. Equation (2-19) is the matrix form of the system state equation for a linear system. Note that the system and input matrices are not characteristics of the system. Different choices of state variables will result in different system and input matrices.

The state variables we have defined may be considered internal states of a system. The state variables are not necessarily the system outputs. The outputs may consist of a subset of the states, or may consist of a linear combination of the system states and the inputs. The output equation for a linear system is

$$y = C x + D u \tag{2-24}$$

If we choose the output of the system depicted in Figure 2-11 to be the position of the mass (x), referring to Equation (2-17),

$$y = x_1 \tag{2-25}$$

we have

$$C = \begin{bmatrix} 1 & 0 \end{bmatrix} \tag{2-26}$$

and

$$D = 0 \qquad (2\text{-}27)$$

C is called the *output matrix*. D is called the *direct transmittance matrix* because if it is non-zero, the input is transmitted directly to the output.

The complete specification of a state-space block consists of the four matrices and the initial values of the state variables. The state-space block is frequently depicted as three blocks, as shown in Figure 2-16(a) (see, for example, Kuo [3]),

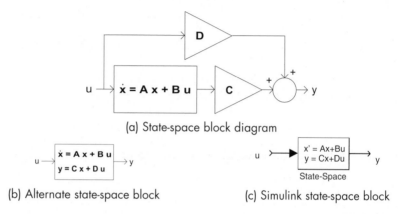

(a) State-space block diagram

(b) Alternate state-space block

(c) Simulink state-space block

Figure 2-16   State-space block

with the direct transmittance block (D) omitted if there is no direct transmittance. The representation in Figure 2-16(b) is also common (see Middleton [5]). The Simulink representation is shown in Figure 2-16(c). Note that the state-space block solves the vector differential equation and therefore contains an integrator for each element of the state vector.

Example 2-3

Consider the electric water heater shown in Figure 2-17. We wish to model the heat loss to outside air as discussed in Middleton [5]. The heat capacity of the tank is C, and the ambient air temperature is T_0. Heat leaves the tank at the rate

$$heat\ out = k\,(T - T_0)$$

and enters (via the heater) at the rate

$$heat\ in\ =\ \frac{1}{CR}u^2$$

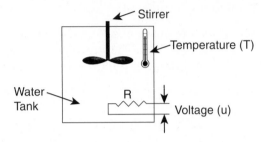

Figure 2-17 Electric water heater

This is a single-degree-of-freedom first-order system, so only one state variable is required. We choose the state variable to be the temperature difference,

$$x\ =\ T - T_0$$

and to avoid the nonlinearity due to u^2, we define

$$p\ =\ u^2$$

Thus,

$$\dot{x}\ =\ \frac{k}{C}x + \frac{1}{CR}p$$

The output is our state variable,

$$y\ =\ x$$

In this example, all the matrices are scalar; they have only one element:

$$\boldsymbol{A}\ =\ -\frac{k}{C}$$

$$\boldsymbol{B}\ =\ \frac{1}{CR}$$

$$\boldsymbol{C}\ =\ 1$$

$$\boldsymbol{D}\ =\ 0$$

Example 2-4

In this example, we will find state-space models for both sets of state variables defined in Example 2-2. Referring to Figure 2-15, we see that there is no input to this system. Therefore, we know that $\boldsymbol{B}$ and $\boldsymbol{D}$ may be ignored. Let's define the output to be the position of the right block (m_2). The force in the spring is

$$f_1 = k(x_2 - x_1)$$

and is positive acting on m_1 and negative acting on m_2. Therefore, for the first set of state variables

$$\dot{w}_1 = w_2$$

$$\dot{w}_2 = \frac{k}{m_1}(w_3 - w_1)$$

$$\dot{w}_3 = w_4$$

$$\dot{w}_4 = \frac{k}{m_2}(w_1 - w_3)$$

so

$$\boldsymbol{A} = \begin{bmatrix} 0 & 1 & 0 & 0 \\ -\dfrac{k}{m_1} & 0 & \dfrac{k}{m_1} & 0 \\ 0 & 0 & 0 & 1 \\ \dfrac{k}{m_2} & 0 & -\dfrac{k}{m_2} & 0 \end{bmatrix}$$

$$\boldsymbol{C} = \begin{bmatrix} 0 & 0 & 1 & 0 \end{bmatrix}$$

For the second set of state variables ($\boldsymbol{z}$), the force in the spring is dependent only on z_3. This makes the system matrix even simpler. However, as the output is no longer a state variable, the output matrix must extract the position of the right block from z_1 and z_3:

$$\dot{z}_1 = z_2$$

$$\dot{z}_2 = \frac{k}{m_1} z_3$$

$$\dot{z}_3 = z_4$$

$$\dot{z}_4 = -k\left(\frac{1}{m_1} + \frac{1}{m_2}\right) z_3$$

so

$$A = \begin{bmatrix} 0 & 1 & 0 & 0 \\ 0 & 0 & \dfrac{k}{m_1} & 0 \\ 0 & 0 & 0 & 1 \\ 0 & 0 & -k\left(\dfrac{1}{m_1} + \dfrac{1}{m_2}\right) & 0 \end{bmatrix}$$

The output is

$$y = x_2 = z_1 + z_3$$

so the output matrix is

$$C = \begin{bmatrix} 1 & 0 & 1 & 0 \end{bmatrix}$$

2.3.3 Multiple-Input, Multiple-Output Systems

The system state equation (2-19) for a linear system is not limited to a particular number of inputs, nor is the output equation (2-24) limited as to the number of outputs that may be defined. Many physical systems have numerous inputs and outputs, and the state-space block is a convenient means of representing such systems. Rather than show each input and output as a separate line, it is common to use vector lines to represent a set of signals, such as the input vector and the output vector. Vector lines are shown as either thick lines or double lines. Figure 2-18 depicts both common representations and the Simulink equivalent. Example 2-5 illustrates the development of a state-space model for a multiple-input, multiple-output system.

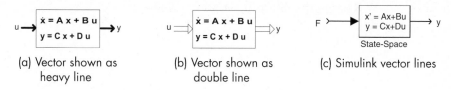

(a) Vector shown as heavy line

(b) Vector shown as double line

(c) Simulink vector lines

Figure 2-18   Multiple-input, multiple-output state-space block

Example 2-5

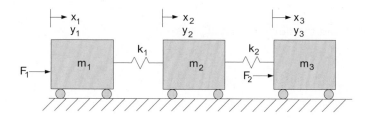

Figure 2-19   Three-mass system with forcing functions

Consider the system depicted in Figure 2-19. There are two inputs to the three-mass system. The outputs are the positions of each block. We'll choose as state variables the positions and velocities of the blocks. The accelerations of the blocks are

$$\ddot{x}_1 = \frac{1}{m_1}(k_1(x_2 - x_1) + F_1)$$

$$\ddot{x}_2 = \frac{1}{m_2}(k_1(x_1 - x_2) + k_2(x_3 - x_2))$$

$$\ddot{x}_3 = \frac{1}{m_3}(k_2(x_2 - x_3) + F_2)$$

The input vector is

$$u = \begin{bmatrix} F_1 \\ F_2 \end{bmatrix}$$

We choose the following state variables:

$$z_1 = x_1$$

$$z_2 = \dot{x}_1$$

$$z_3 = x_2$$

$$z_4 = \dot{x}_2$$

$$z_5 = x_3$$

$$z_6 = \dot{x}_3$$

and the output variables are

$$y_1 = z_1$$

$$y_2 = z_3$$

$$y_3 = z_5$$

Thus the system matrix is

$$
\boldsymbol{A} =
\begin{bmatrix}
0 & 1 & 0 & 0 & 0 & 0 \\
-\dfrac{k_1}{m_1} & 0 & \dfrac{k_1}{m_1} & 0 & 0 & 0 \\
0 & 0 & 0 & 1 & 0 & 0 \\
\dfrac{k_1}{m_2} & 0 & -\dfrac{(k_1+k_2)}{m_2} & 0 & \dfrac{k_2}{m_2} & 0 \\
0 & 0 & 0 & 0 & 0 & 1 \\
0 & 0 & \dfrac{k_2}{m_3} & 0 & -\dfrac{k_2}{m_3} & 0
\end{bmatrix}
$$

and the input matrix is

$$
\mathbf{B} = \begin{bmatrix} 0 & 0 \\ \dfrac{1}{m_1} & 0 \\ 0 & 0 \\ 0 & 0 \\ 0 & 0 \\ 0 & \dfrac{1}{m_3} \end{bmatrix}
$$

The output matrix is

$$
\mathbf{C} = \begin{bmatrix} 1 & 0 & 0 & 0 & 0 & 0 \\ 0 & 0 & 1 & 0 & 0 & 0 \\ 0 & 0 & 0 & 0 & 1 & 0 \end{bmatrix}
$$

and the direct transmittance matrix is zero.

$$
\mathbf{D} = \begin{bmatrix} 0 & 0 \\ 0 & 0 \\ 0 & 0 \end{bmatrix}
$$

To complete the definition of the state-space model, we must specify the initial value of each state variable (z_i).

2.4 Discrete Systems

A discrete system is a system that may be represented using difference equations, and that operates on discrete signals. A discrete signal can be represented as a sequence of pulses, as shown in Figure 2-20.

A discrete system takes as its input one or more discrete signals, and produces one or more discrete signals as its output. A discrete-time system is a discrete system which may change only at specific instants of time (Ogata [6]). In the majority of discrete-time control systems, the signals are not inherently discrete. In these systems, the discrete signals are extracted from continuous signals by a process known as *sampling*. Figure 2-21 illustrates the sampling process.

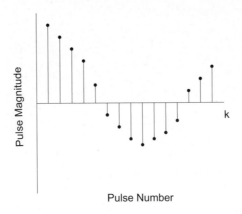

Figure 2-20   Discrete signal

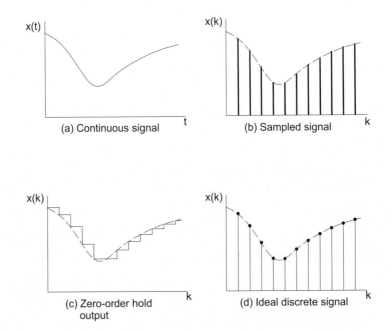

Figure 2-21   Sampling a continuous signal to produce a discrete signal

The type of sampling illustrated in Figure 2-21 is performed using two devices: a *sampler* and a *zero-order hold*. The sampler periodically closes a switch for an instant. Each time the switch is momentarily closed, a pulse of very short (theoretically zero) duration, and equal in magnitude to the input signal, is produced (Figure 2-21(b)). The spacing between the pulses is the *sampling period*. The zero-order hold follows the sampler and clamps its output at the last value of its input, producing a stairstep signal as shown in Figure 2-21(c). A discrete controller requires a sequence of numbers as its input. The *analog to digital (A/D) converter* is a device that converts the stairstep signal of Figure 2-21(c) into a sequence of numbers, as represented by the pulse sequence shown in Figure 2-21(d). The combination of the sampler and zero-order hold block is illustrated in Figure 2-22 along with the Simulink equivalent.

(a) Sample and zero-order hold   (b) Simulink zero-order hold

Figure 2-22   Sample and zero-order hold

We refer to signals that vary with time using the notation $x(t)$. The corresponding notation for discrete signals is $x(k)$, where k is the pulse number. The mapping from continuous time to sample space is

$$x(k) = x(kT) \qquad (2\text{-}28)$$

where T is the sample period.

We will now discuss the discrete counterparts to the continuous system block diagram components discussed in Section 2.2. These discrete components may be physically realized as either digital circuit elements or as computer instructions in microprocessor based controllers.

2.4.1   Discrete Gain Block

The discrete gain block is identical in appearance to the continuous gain block described in Section 2.2.1 and illustrated in Figure 2-1. The discrete gain block represents the algebraic equation

$$y(k) = a x(k) \qquad (2\text{-}29)$$

so the output is the present input multiplied by the gain.

2.4.2   Discrete Sum Block

The discrete sum block is identical in appearance to the continuous sum block shown in Figure 2-3. The output of the sum block is the algebraic sum of its inputs.

2.4.3 Unit Delay

The *unit delay* is the fundamental discrete-time block. The unit delay is also called a *shift register* or *time-delay element*. The output of the unit delay block is the input at the previous sample time. The unit delay represents the difference equation

$$y(k) = x(k-1) \qquad (2\text{-}30)$$

Figure 2-23 shows two common representations of the unit delay and the Simulink equivalent.

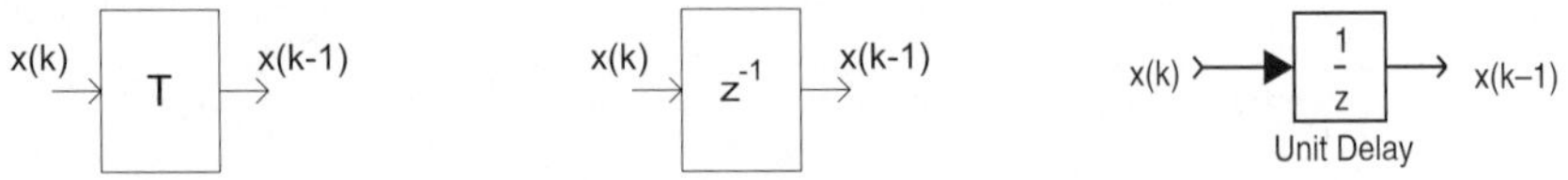

(a) Unit delay block   (b) Z-transform notation   (c) Simulink unit delay block

Figure 2-23   Unit delay block

2.4.4 Discrete-Time Integrator Block

The output of the discrete-time integrator block is an approximation of the time integral of the input signal. That is, it is a discrete approximation of a continuous integrator. Thus, the output of the discrete-time integrator block approximates

$$y(k) = y(k-1) + \int_{T(k-1)}^{Tk} u(t)dt \qquad (2\text{-}31)$$

where $u(t)$ is the input to the integrator, $y(k)$ is the output, and T is the sample period.

Three standard implementations of the discrete-time integrator block are: *forward Euler integration* (also known as *forward rectangular integration*), *backward Euler integration* (*backward rectangular integration*), and *trapezoidal integration*. All three implementations approximate the area under a curve as the sum of the areas of a finite number of rectangles.

Note that you will sometimes see the definitions of forward and backward Euler integration reversed from the Simulink convention, which is used here. For example, Kuo [3] refers to the method Simulink calls forward Euler integration as backward rectangular integration, and the method Simulink calls backward Euler integration as forward rectangular integration.

Forward Euler

Forward Euler integration is based on the approximation $u(t) = u(T(k-1))$. Thus, forward Euler integration approximates

$$y(k) = y(k-1) + Tu(T(k-1)) \tag{2-32}$$

Taking the Z transform of Equation (2-32),

$$Y(z) = z^{-1}Y(z) + Tz^{-1}U(z) \tag{2-33}$$

Rearranging terms, the Z transfer function of the forward Euler integrator is

$$\frac{Y(z)}{U(z)} = \frac{T}{z-1} \tag{2-34}$$

This is graphically depicted in Figure 2-24.

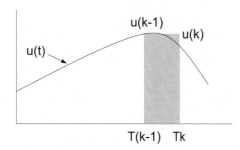

Figure 2-24   Forward Euler integrator

Backward Euler

Backward Euler integration is based on the approximation $u(t) = u(Tk)$. Thus, backward Euler integration approximates

$$y(k) = y(k-1) + Tu(Tk) \tag{2-35}$$

The corresponding Z transfer function is

$$\frac{Y(z)}{U(z)} = \frac{Tz}{z-1} \tag{2-36}$$

This is graphically depicted in Figure 2-25.

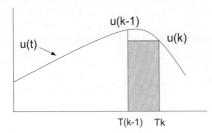

Figure 2-25 Backward Euler integrator

Trapezoidal Integration

Trapezoidal integration is based on the approximation

$$u(t) = \frac{u(Tk) + u(T(k-1))}{2} \qquad (2\text{-}37)$$

Thus, trapezoidal integration approximates

$$y(k) = y(k-1) + \frac{Tu(Tk) + Tu(T(k-1))}{2} \qquad (2\text{-}38)$$

The corresponding Z transfer function is

$$\frac{Y(z)}{U(z)} = \frac{T(z+1)}{2(z-1)} \qquad (2\text{-}39)$$

The rule for trapezoidal integration is illustrated in Figure 2-26.

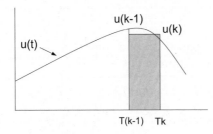

Figure 2-26 Trapezoidal integration

Discrete-Time Integrator Blocks

Figure 2-27 shows forward and backward Euler integrator blocks, and the Simulink Discrete-Time Integrator block. Simulink's Discrete-Time Integrator block can be set to use either of these methods or trapezoidal integration. Forward and backward rectangular integration are probably equally common in practice; trapezoidal is somewhat less common. All three produce approximately the same results when used properly. As with continuous integrators, the complete system specification includes the initial value of the integrator output.

Block Diagrams   Chapter 2

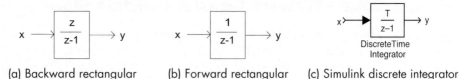

(a) Backward rectangular integration

(b) Forward rectangular integration

(c) Simulink discrete integrator

Figure 2-27   Discrete integrator block

2.4.5 Simple Discrete System Models

The discrete blocks we've described so far may be used to build a model of any linear discrete system. Example 2.6 illustrates the development of a block diagram for a simple economic problem.

Example 2-6

In this example we will model the amortization of an automobile loan. At the end of each month, the loan balance $b(k)$ is the sum of the balance at the beginning of the month ($b(k-1)$) and the interest for the month ($i\,b(k)$), less the end-of-month payment $p(k)$. Thus, the balance at the end of month k is

$$b(k) \;=\; rb(k-1) - p(k)$$

where $r = 1 + i$, and i is the monthly interest rate.

The block diagram in Figure 2-28 will model this system. Note that the complete system specification includes the initial loan balance.

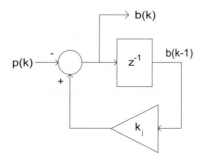

Figure 2-28   Block diagram of loan amortization

2.4.6 Discrete Transfer Function Block

The *discrete transfer function* is analogous to the continuous transfer function we discussed in Section 2.2.6. The discrete transfer function is the ratio of the Z-transform of the input to a system or subsystem to the Z-transform of the output. Like the continuous transfer function, the discrete transfer function provides a compact notation for the input-output relationship of a system. We'll illustrate the definition with a simple example.

Example 2-7

Consider the loan amortization problem discussed in Example 2-6. The difference equation describing the loan amortization is

$$b(k) = k_i b(k-1) - p(k)$$

Taking the Z-transform,

$$B(z) = k_i z^{-1} B(z) - P(z)$$

Rearranging terms, we get the transfer function

$$\frac{B(z)}{P(z)} = -\frac{z}{z - k_i}$$

As with the continuous transfer function, the denominator of the transfer function is the characteristic equation of the system. The roots of the characteristic equation are the eigenvalues of the system. The discrete transfer function block is depicted in Figure 2-29 along with its Simulink equivalent.

(a) Discrete transfer function block   (b) Simulink discrete transfer function block

Figure 2-29 Discrete transfer function block

2.5 Discrete State-Space Block

The state-space concept discussed in Section 2.3 for continuous systems is also useful for modeling discrete systems. Whereas the state variables in continuous systems represent derivatives or algebraic combinations of derivatives, the state variables in discrete systems represent portions of sequences or algebraic combinations of portions of sequences. Thus the discrete equivalent to equation (2-15) is the general form of the discrete state-space model of a dynamical system:

$$x(k+1) = f(x, u) \qquad (2\text{-}40)$$

where as before x is the state vector and u the input vector. The corresponding output equation is

$$y(k) = g(x, u) \qquad (2\text{-}41)$$

The matrix notation for linear discrete systems is similar to the model for continuous systems. The same four matrices (system matrix, input matrix, output matrix, and direct transmittance matrix) are used. Thus the system equation is

$$x(k+1) = Ax(k) + Bu(k) \qquad (2\text{-}42)$$

The output equation is

$$y(k) = Cx(k) + Du(k) \qquad (2\text{-}43)$$

Example 2-8 illustrates the definition of a linear state-space model and Example 2-9 illustrates a more complex model.

Example 2-8

Consider a system that can be described by the difference equation

$$y(k+1) = y(k) - 2y(k-1) + u(k)$$

Define state variables

$$x_1(k) = y(k-1)$$
$$x_2(k) = y(k)$$

The state equations are

$$x_1(k+1) = x_2(k)$$
$$x_2(k+1) = x_2(k) - 2x_1(k) + u(k)$$

In matrix form we have

$$x(k+1) = \begin{bmatrix} 0 & 1 \\ -2 & 1 \end{bmatrix} x(k) + \begin{bmatrix} 0 & 1 \end{bmatrix} u$$

so the system matrix is

$$A = \begin{bmatrix} 0 & 1 \\ -2 & 1 \end{bmatrix}$$

and the input matrix is

$$B = \begin{bmatrix} 0 \\ 1 \end{bmatrix}$$

There is no direct transmittance, so D is zero. The output variable is $y(k)$, so

$$C = \begin{bmatrix} 0 & 1 \end{bmatrix}$$

Example 2-9

Suppose a linear system can be described by the difference equation

$$y(k+1) + 5y(k) + 3y(k-1) = u(k) + 2u(k-1)$$

We choose the following state variables to make $u(k-1)$ implicit:

$$x_1(k) = y(k-1) - \frac{2}{3}u(k-1)$$
$$x_2(k) = -3x_1(k) - 5x_2(k) + u(k)$$

The state equations are

$$x_1(k+1) = x_2(k) - \frac{2}{3}u(k)$$
$$x_2(k+1) = -3x_1(k) - 5x_2(k) + u(k)$$

The system matrix is

$$A = \begin{bmatrix} 0 & 1 \\ -3 & -5 \end{bmatrix}$$

and the input matrix is

$$B = \begin{bmatrix} -\dfrac{2}{3} \\ 1 \end{bmatrix}$$

The output matrix is

$$C = \begin{bmatrix} 1 & 1 \end{bmatrix}$$

and the direct transmittance matrix is zero:

$$D = 0$$

2.6 Nonlinear Blocks

The block diagram concept can be generalized to include a wide variety of blocks in addition to the linear systems blocks we've defined so far. Normally, a block is labeled with text or a picture that makes it easy to understand the purpose of the block. Some of the more common blocks are listed below, although this list is far from complete.

- Product—product of two scalar input signals
- Abs—absolute value of the input signal
- Logical operators (AND, OR, NOT)
- Relational operators (>, <)
- Sign—signum nonlinearity
- Saturation function
- Transport delay
- Table lookup (interpolate in a table)

2.7 Hybrid Block Diagrams

A *hybrid system* contains both discrete and continuous components. The most common hybrid system consists of a continuous physical process that is controlled using discrete logic components or a microprocessor. Figure 2-30 illustrates a hypothetical hybrid system adapted from Ogata [6] in which the controller includes continuous and discrete blocks. We'll describe each block in Figure 2-30. Referring to the letters (a, b, etc.) in the blocks, we'll proceed clockwise starting with the continuous process block.

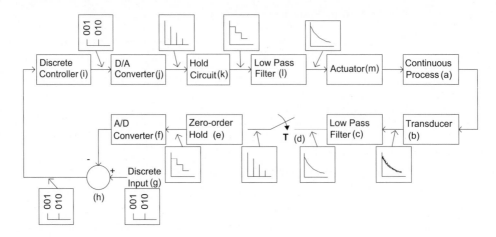

Figure 2-30 Hybrid system

a The continuous process could be any physical process, such as a chemical plant tank heater, an aircraft autopilot, or a robot arm. We are interested in controlling a particular parameter of the process, such as the temperature of the tank contents, the aircraft pitch attitude, or the angle of one of the robot arm rotary joints.

b The transducer is a device that maps each possible value of the parameter we're controlling to a unique value of the output signal. For example, a temperature transducer may consist of a thermocouple that produces a voltage proportional to the temperature. The aircraft pitch transducer may produce a voltage proportional to a gyroscope gimbal angle, and the robot joint angle transducer might consist of a voltage signal produced by a potentiometer.

c Transducers frequently produce output signals that contain noise. To reduce the noise from the signal before the signal is sampled, it is common to follow the transducer with a lowpass filter. In this application, the lowpass filter is frequently called an anti-aliasing filter. The block diagram representation of the lowpass filter is usually a transfer function block, although the filter could be described using the primitive blocks described in Section 2.2 or a continuous state-space block as described in Section 2.3.

d The sampler is the first step in producing the discrete signal. It produces a sequence of pulses as described in Section 2.4.

e The zero-order hold clamps the sampler output to create the stairstep signal. Up to this point, the signal is a physical quantity, such as voltage or current.

f The A/D converter produces a sequence of numbers that correspond to the stairstep input signal. Frequently, the zero-order hold and A/D converter are combined in a single device.

g The discrete input is the desired numerical value (the set point) of the parameter being controlled. This could be a value input at a computer console, or it could be a value set by positioning a bank of switches.

h The discrete summer computes the difference in the desired value of the parameter and the measured value. This difference is the error in the controlled parameter, and is the input to the discrete controller.

i Based on the input sequence, the discrete controller produces an output sequence intended to cause the controlled parameter to reach the desired value (g). The discrete controller could be built using the primitive blocks described in Section 2.4, a discrete transfer function block, or a discrete state-space block. The controller could also be a microprocessor-based controller, or even a general purpose computer.

j The *digital to analog (D/A) converter* transforms an input sequence of numbers into a corresponding output sequence of pulses.

k The hold circuit, usually a zero-order hold, transforms the discontinuous input pulse sequence into a continuous output sequence. In this example, a zero-order hold produces a stairstep signal. In practice, the zero-order hold is usually incorporated in the D/A converter device.

l A lowpass filter smooths the stairstep signal. It is frequently necessary to smooth this signal to prevent damage to physical components or to conserve the energy consumed by the actuator. For example, a series of step inputs to an aircraft autopilot could produce a rough ride for the passengers.

m The actuator is a device that changes a characteristic of the controlled process. For the tank heater, the actuator could be a steam valve. The aircraft autopilot would control the elevator position. The robot joint control might use a variable voltage regulator that controls drive motor torque.

An endless number of variations of hybrid controllers is possible. The controller can be simplified considerably if the transducer is a digital device. For example, pulse encoders are a popular means of sensing the position of a rotary joint.

2.8 Summary

In this chapter, we have discussed the most common block diagram elements for both continuous and discrete systems. We have discussed the construction of simple block diagrams of linear systems using primitive blocks, transfer function blocks, and state-space blocks. We briefly mentioned the many possible nonlinear blocks. Finally, we discussed hybrid systems, and looked at the block diagram of a hypothetical hybrid system.

2.9   References and Further Reading

1. Dorf, Richard C., *Modern Control Systems*, 7th ed., Reading, Mass., Addison-Wesley Publishing Company, Inc., 1995. This introductory text in control systems uses MATLAB extensively. The book presents numerous examples of models of dynamical systems, many including block diagrams.

2. Harman, Thomas L., Dabney, James, and Richert, Norman, *Advanced Engineering Mathematics Using MATLAB 4*, Boston, Mass., PWS Publishing Company, 1997, pp. 149-194. This book presents a practical approach to advanced engineering mathematics. MATLAB is used in many examples and in the extensive set of worked problems at the end of each chapter.

3. Kuo, Benjamin C., *Automatic Control Systems,* 7th ed. Englewood Cliffs, N.J., Prentice Hall, 1995, p. 274. An excellent basic text on control systems.

4. Lewis, Paul H., and Yang, Charles, *Basic Control Systems Engineering*, Upper Saddle River, N.J., Prentice Hall, 1997. This text provides an introduction to control systems analysis and design, and includes a brief introduction to Simulink. Simulink is used in many of the examples.

5. Middleton, Richard H., and Goodwin, Graham C., *Digital Control and Estimation: A Unified Approach*, Englewood Cliffs, N.J., Prentice Hall, 1990, pp. 13–14. An advanced text on digital control systems. This text provides a balanced mixture of theory and applications.

6. Ogata, Katsuhiko, *Discrete-Time Control Systems*, 2nd ed., Englewood Cliffs, N.J., Prentice Hall, 1994, pp. 5–7. An excellent text on discrete control systems. Many examples are presented with MATLAB solutions, and there are many block diagrams that can be easily converted into Simulink models. This text is very readable, and would be particularly useful for self-study or as a reference.

7. Phillips, Charles L., and Nagle, H. Troy, *Digital Control System Analysis and Design*, 3rd ed., Englewood Cliffs, N.J., Prentice Hall, 1995. This book provides a comprehensive coverage of discrete-time control systems analysis and design. It presents many practical examples, and makes good use of MATLAB.

3

Quick Start

In this chapter we will discuss the basics of building and executing Simulink models. We will start with a simple first-order system. Next, we will build a more complex model that includes feedback and illustrates several important procedures in Simulink programming. Finally, we will discuss the Simulink Help system.

3.1   Introduction

Simulink is a very powerful programming language, and a big part of that power is its ease of use. In this chapter, we will introduce Simulink programming by building and executing two simple models. Our purpose here is to cover the basics of model building and execution. We will discuss these topics in more detail in later chapters.

The examples shown in this chapter (and the rest of the book) were produced using Simulink 2.1 and MATLAB 5.1 in the Microsoft Windows 95 environment. There are very few differences between using Simulink in the Windows 95 environment and using it in the Macintosh or X Windows environment; we will point out those differences where necessary.

3.1.1   Typographical Conventions

Before we build the first model, we need to establish some typographical conventions.

Computer Type

All computer input, output, variable names, and command names are shown in sans-serif font.

Using Menus

The Simulink user interface is based on four pull-down menus located on a menu bar at the top of the Simulink window. To facilitate discussion of the various menu choices, we will use the convention: [**Menu bar choice**]:[**Pull-**

down menu choice]. For example, choosing "File" followed by "Save As" (as shown in Figure 3-1) will be written **File:Save As**.

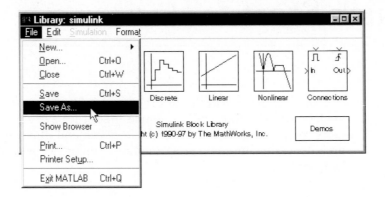

Figure 3-1   Menu selection

Dialog Box Fields

Simulink makes extensive use of dialog boxes to set simulation parameters and configure blocks. Dialog box fields are indicated in **bold** type. For example, choosing **File:Save As** opens the dialog box shown in Figure 3-2. The fields in this dialog box are **Save in**, **File name**, and **Save as type**.

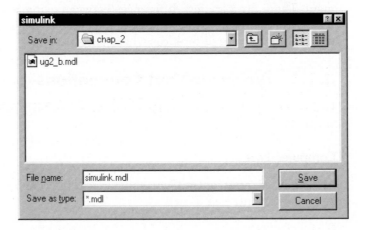

Figure 3-2   **File:Save As** dialog box

3.2 Building a Simple Model

Let's start by building a Simulink model that solves the differential equation

$$\dot{x} = \sin(t) \tag{3-1}$$

where $x(0) = 0$.

Simulink is an extension to MATLAB, and it must be invoked from within MATLAB. Start Simulink by clicking the Simulink icon on the MATLAB tool bar (Microsoft Windows or Macintosh), as shown in Figure 3-3 or by entering the command `simulink` at the MATLAB prompt. On an X Windows system, enter the command `simulink` at the MATLAB prompt.

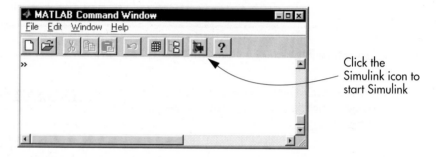

Click the Simulink icon to start Simulink

Figure 3-3   Starting Simulink

Two new windows will appear on the screen. The first window is the Simulink block library, shown in Figure 3-4. The second window (Figure 3-5) is an empty model window, named `untitled`, in which you will build the Simulink model.

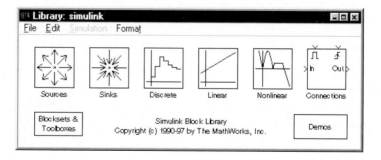

Figure 3-4   Simulink block library window

Figure 3-5 Empty model window

Double-click the Sources icon in the Simulink block library, opening the Sources block library.

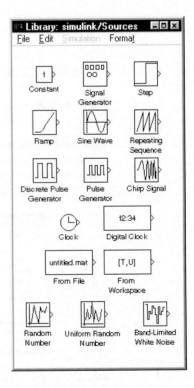

Drag the Sine Wave block from the Sources block library to the model window, positioning it as shown. A copy of the block is placed in the model window. Note that, in the figure, we have resized the model window to save space.

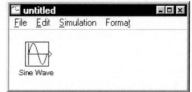

Open the Linear block library and drag an Integrator block to the model window.

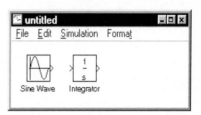

Open the Sinks block library and drag a Scope block to the model window.

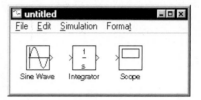

Next, connect the blocks with signal lines to complete the model:

Place the cursor on the output port of the Sine Wave block. The output port is the > symbol on the right edge of the block. The cursor changes to a cross-hair shape when it's on the output port.

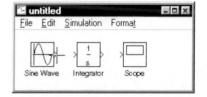

Drag from the output port to the input port of the Integrator block. The input port is the < symbol on the left edge of the block. As you drag, the cursor retains the cross-hair shape.

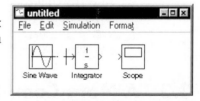

Now the model should look like this. The signal line has an arrowhead indicating the direction of signal flow.

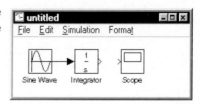

Draw another signal line from the Integrator output port to the Scope input port, completing the model.

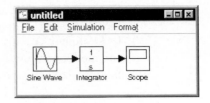

Double-click the Scope block, opening a Scope window as shown in Figure 3-6.

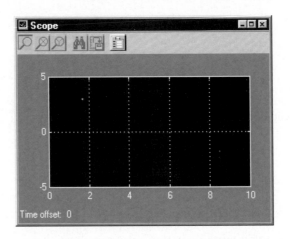

Figure 3-6   Scope window

Choose **Simulation:Start** from the menu bar in the model window (not the Simulink block library window). The simulation will execute, resulting in the scope display shown in Figure 3-7.

To verify that the plot shown in Figure 3-7 represents the solution to Equation (3-1), you can solve Equation (3-1) analytically, with the result $x(t) = 1 - \cos(t)$. Thus, the Simulink model solved the differential equation correctly.

3.3 A More Complicated Model

So far, we've shown how to build a simple model. There are a number of additional model building skills that you'll need to acquire. In this section we use a model of a biological process to illustrate several additional skills: branching from signal lines, routing signal lines in segments, flipping blocks, configuring blocks, and configuring the simulation parameters.

Scheinerman [1] describes a simple model of bacteria growth in a jar. Assume that the bacteria are born at a rate proportional to the number of bacteria

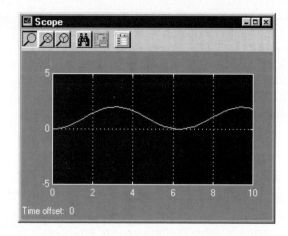

Figure 3-7   Scope display after executing the model

present, and that they die at a rate proportional to the square of the number of bacteria present. If x represents the number of bacteria present, then the bacteria are born at the rate

$$\text{birth rate } = bx \tag{3-2}$$

and they die at the rate

$$\text{death rate } = px^2 \tag{3-3}$$

The total rate of change of bacteria population is the difference between birth rate and death rate. This system can therefore be described with the differential equation

$$\dot{x} = bx - px^2 \tag{3-4}$$

Let's build a model of this dynamical system assuming that b = 1/hour and p = 0.5 /bacteria-hour. Then, we'll compute the number of bacteria in the jar after 1 hour, assuming that initially there are 100 bacteria present.

If you haven't closed Simulink yet, open a new model by choosing **File:New** from the Simulink block library window menu bar or clicking the Simulink icon in the MATLAB window menu bar (Windows 95 or Macintosh). Otherwise, open a new model window as discussed earlier.

This is a first-order system, so one integrator is required to solve the differential equation. The input to the integrator is $\dot{x}$, and the output is x. Open the Linear block library and drag the integrator block to the position shown. Don't close the Linear block library yet.

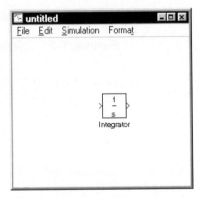

Drag two Gain blocks from the Linear block library and place them as shown. Notice that the name of the second Gain block is Gain1. Simulink requires each block to have a unique name. We'll discuss changing the name later.

Drag a Sum block from the Linear block library, then close the Linear block library.

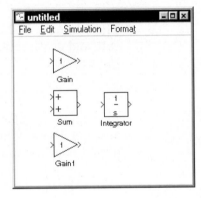

Open the Nonlinear block library and drag a Product block to the position shown. We will use the Product block to compute x^2.

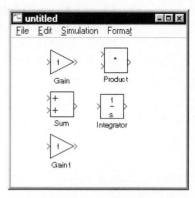

Open the Sinks block library and drag a Scope block to the model window as shown.

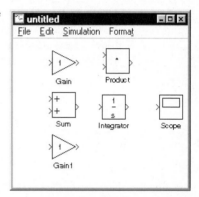

The default orientation of all the blocks places input ports on the left edge of the block and output ports on the right edge. The model will be much easier to read if we flip the Product block and the Gain blocks so that the input ports are on the right edge and the output ports are on the left edge. Starting with the Product block, click the block once to select it. Notice the handles that appear at the four corners of the block, indicating that it is selected.

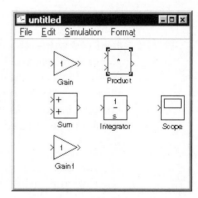

Choose **Format:Flip Block** from the model window menu bar. Now the inputs are on the right and the output is on the left. Repeat the flipping operation for each Gain block.

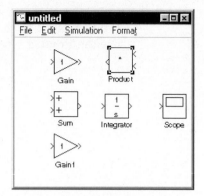

Draw a signal line from the output of the Sum block to the input of the Integrator block, and another from the output of the Integrator to the input of the Scope block.

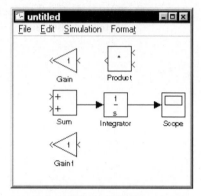

Next, we need to branch from the signal line connecting the Integrator and Scope block to feed the value of x to the lower Gain block. Press and hold the Control key (Windows 95, X Windows) or Option key (Macintosh) and click on the signal line. The cursor will change to a cross-hair shape. Continue to depress the mouse button and release the key.

If the mouse has two or three buttons, clicking and dragging using the right mouse button is equivalent.

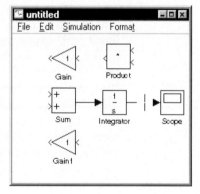

Drag directly to the input port of the Gain block. Notice that the signal line is dashed, and the cursor changes to a double cross-hair when it is on the input port of the gain block. Simulink automatically routes the signal line using 90-degree bends.

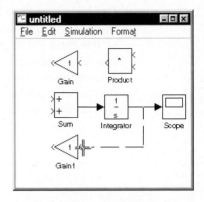

In a similar manner, branch from the signal line connecting the Integrator and Scope blocks to the top input port of the Product block.

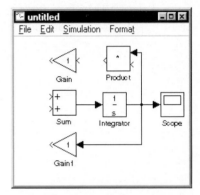

Branch from the signal line entering the upper input port of the Product block to the lower input port of the Product block. Thus, the output of the Product block is x^2. Connect the output of the Product block to the input of the upper Gain block.

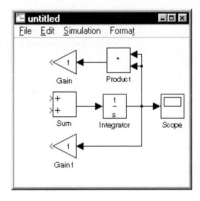

3.3   A More Complicated Model

Draw the signal line from the output port of the upper Gain block to the upper input port of the Sum block in segments. To draw the line in segments, start by dragging from the output port to the location of the first bend. Release the mouse button. The signal line will be terminated with an open arrowhead.

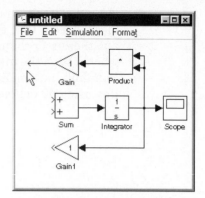

Next, drag from the open arrowhead to the upper input port of the Sum block.

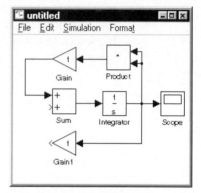

In a similar manner, draw the signal line from the output of the lower Gain block to the lower input of the Sum block.

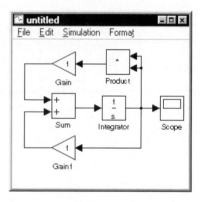

The model is now complete, but several of the blocks must be configured. Currently the value of gain for both Gain blocks is the default value of 1.0. The Sum block adds its two inputs instead of computing the difference. Finally, the initial value of the integrator output (the initial number of bacteria, x) must be set, as it defaults to 0.0. Start with the Gain blocks.

Double-click the upper Gain block. The Gain block dialog box will be displayed. Change the default value in field **Gain** to 0.5. Click **Close**.

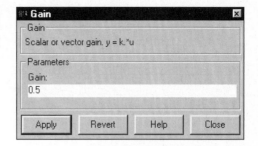

Notice that the value of gain on the block icon is now changed to 0.5.

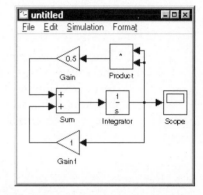

Double-click the Sum block, opening the Sum block dialog box. Set **List of signs** to –+ (a minus sign (–) followed by a plus sign (+)). Click **Close**.

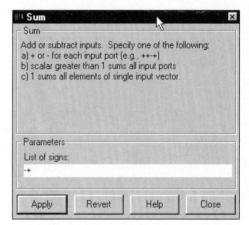

Now the Sum block is configured to compute the value of $\dot{x}$ according to Equation (3-4), after substituting in the values of b and p.

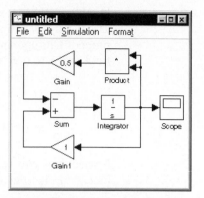

The final configuration task is to set the initial value of number of bacteria (x). Double-click the Integrator block, opening the Integrator dialog box. Set **Initial condition** to 100. Click **Close**.

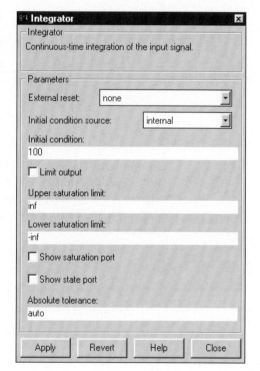

The simulation start time defaults to 0, and the stop time defaults to 10.0. To change the stop time to 1, open the Simulation parameters dialog box by choosing **Simulation:Parameters** from the model window menu bar. Set **Stop time** to 1, then **Close**.

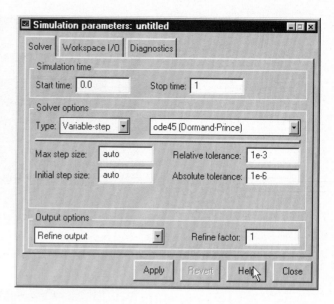

The model is now complete and ready to run. It's always a good idea to save a model before running it. To save the model, choose **File:Save** from the model window menu bar, and enter a file name, say examp_2, without an extension. Simulink will save the model with the extension .mdl, and change the model window name from untitled to the name you entered.

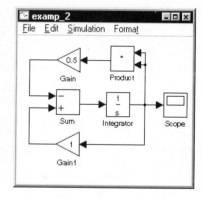

Open the Scope by double-clicking the Scope block. Then choose **Simulation:Start** to run the simulation. The scope display will be as shown in Figure 3-8. Click on autoscale button ![binoculars icon]. The scope will resize the scale to fit the entire range of values, as shown in Figure 3-9.

3.4 The Simulink Help System

Simulink includes an extensive on-line Help system. The Help files are designed to be viewed with an Internet Web browser such as Netscape Navigator or Microsoft Internet Explorer. Detailed on-line documentation for all of the blocks in the Simulink block library is available through the Block

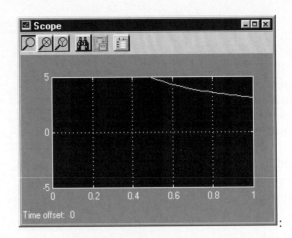

Figure 3-8   Scope display after running the bacteria growth model

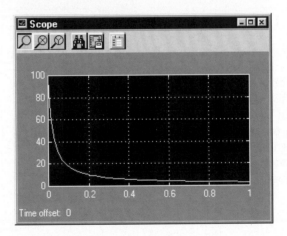

Figure 3-9   Scope display after rescaling

Browser, shown in Figure 3-10. Additionally, on-line help is available by clicking the **Help** button in the dialog box for **Simulation:Parameters**.

3.4.1   Opening the Block Browser

The procedure for opening the Block Browser for a particular block is as follows:

Double-click a block,

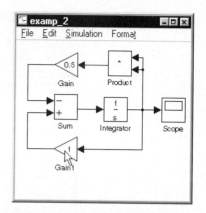

opening the block dialog box. Click the **Help** button.

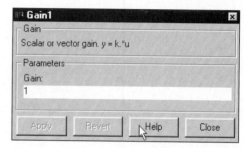

The Web browser (Netscape in Figure 3-10) will open to the Block Browser page for the block you selected.

3.4.2 Block Browser Window

There are three frames to the Block Browser window. The top frame contains an icon for each block in the Simulink block library. The icon currently selected (the Linear block library in Figure 3-10) is highlighted with a drop shadow. Select a different block library by clicking its icon in the top frame.

The lower left frame contains the icons for all blocks in the block library currently selected in the top frame. Click a block in this frame to open the corresponding Block Browser page.

The right frame contains the Block Browser page for the currently selected block. This is detailed documentation that explains how the block is used and how it is configured.

The top frame of the Block Browser also contains a field to request a search for a particular block. You can use this search capability to quickly locate a Block Browser page if you're not sure which library a block is in.

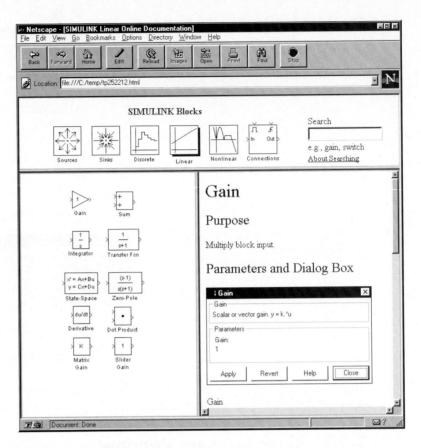

Figure 3-10 Simulink Block Browser

3.5 Summary

In this chapter, we have presented the basic steps for building and executing Simulink models. We have also described the Simulink Help system. Using the procedures discussed in this chapter, it is possible to model a wide variety of dynamical systems. Before proceeding further, you may find it beneficial to build a few simple models to gain proficiency in the skills discussed thus far. You may also find it interesting to explore some of the Simulink demonstrations in the Demos block library.

3.6 Reference

1. Scheinerman, Edward C., *Invitation to Dynamical Systems*, Upper Saddle River, N.J., Prentice Hall, 1996, pp. 22–24.

Model Building

In this chapter we will explain the mechanics of model building in detail. The procedures discussed here will enable you to build models that are easy to interpret. You will also learn how to select and configure a differential equation solver and how to print a Simulink model and embed a model in a word processing document.

4.1 Introduction

In Chapter 3 we discussed the basics of building and running a Simulink model. Using the procedures discussed there and the on-line Block Browser, you can build extremely complex models. However, as models get more complex, they become more difficult to interpret. The procedures discussed in this chapter will enable you to make your models easier to understand. First, careful arrangement of blocks and signal lines can make the relationships easier to follow. Next, naming blocks and signal lines and adding annotations to the model can make the purpose of the model elements easier to understand.

We will also describe the **Simulation:Parameters** dialog box, which provides extensive options for selecting and configuring the differential equation solver used to perform model simulation. In addition to selecting a solver most appropriate to your problem, you can control the spacing of output points and the generation of error and warning messages, and even send internal simulation data to the MATLAB workspace.

Finally, we will explain how to print your models. You can either print directly to a printer, or embed an image of the model in a word processing document.

Our purpose in this chapter is to explain the mechanics of model building: manipulating blocks, drawing and editing signal lines, annotating the model, and so on. Once you have mastered these mechanics, you will be ready to begin building models using the procedures covered in the subsequent chapters.

4.1.1 Elements of a Model

A Simulink model consists of three types of elements: *sources*, the *system* being modeled, and *sinks*. Figure 4-1 illustrates the relationship among the three elements. The central element, the system, is the Simulink representation of a block diagram of the dynamical system being modeled. The sources are the inputs to the dynamical system. Sources include constants, function generators such as sine waves and step functions, and custom signals you create in MATLAB. Source blocks are found in the Sources block library. The output of the system is received by sinks. Examples of sinks are graphs, oscilloscopes, and output files. Sink blocks are found in the Sinks block library.

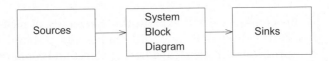

Figure 4-1   Elements of a Simulink model

Frequently, Simulink models lack one or more of these three elements. For example, you might wish to model the unforced behavior of a system initially displaced from its equilibrium state. Such a model would have no inputs, but it would have system blocks (Gain blocks, Integrators, etc.) and probably sinks. It is also possible to build a model that has sources and sinks, but no system blocks. Suppose that you need a special signal composed of the sum of several functions. You could easily generate the signal using Simulink source blocks and send the signal to the MATLAB workspace or to a disk file.

4.2   Opening a Model

In Chapter 2 we discussed creating a new model by choosing **File:New** from the Simulink menu bar or by clicking on the Simulink icon in the MATLAB tool bar. We also discussed saving a model using **File:Save**. To use an existing model, choose **File:Open** from the menu bar of the Simulink window and select the file.

The default directory will be the current default directory in the MATLAB session from which you started Simulink. If you change to a different directory using the Simulink file menu, the default directory will not change. It will remain the same as the current directory in the MATLAB session, so if you wish to open another model in the same directory as the model you previously opened, and that model was not in the directory currently active in the MATLAB session, you will have to navigate once again to the appropriate directory. Therefore, it is frequently convenient to change to the directory containing the Simulink model in the MATLAB session (using the cd command), then open the model using the Simulink **File:Open** menu choice.

Although it is not necessary, we recommend that you set up a directory for your Simulink models separate from the MATLAB directory structure. This will make it easier to keep track of your files. It will also eliminate the possibility of overwriting or deleting your files if you upgrade MATLAB and Simulink in the future.

An alternative method to open an existing model is to type the name of the model as a command at the MATLAB prompt. MATLAB will search for the model via the MATLAB path, starting in the current directory. For example, if the model is named `examp.mdl`, enter the command `examp` at the MATLAB prompt.

4.3 Manipulating Blocks

In Chapter 2, you learned how to drag a block from a block library to a model window and to flip a block. In addition to those basic operations, you can resize, rotate, copy, and rename blocks. In this section we will discuss these and several other block manipulation operations. To prepare to practice the operations illustrated here, start Simulink, or, if Simulink is already started, open a new model window.

4.3.1 Resizing a Block

Frequently, resizing a block can improve the appearance of a model. To resize a block, proceed as follows:

Open a block library, and drag a block to the model window. Here, we're using a Gain block from the Linear block library. We've set block parameter **Gain** to the value 1227.86. Since this value won't fit on the block icon, the displayed value is -K-.

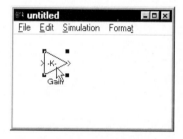

To resize a block, first select the block, causing the handles to appear.

Click the desired handle, and, continuing to depress the mouse button,

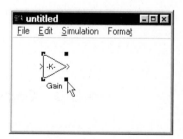

drag the handle to resize the block. Notice that the cursor changes shape, confirming that you have "grasped" the resize handle.

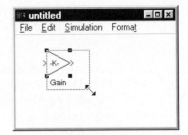

Release the mouse button. Now, the block icon is large enough to display the value of **Gain**.

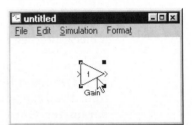

4.3.2 Rotating a Block

Occasionally, you will want to rotate a block. Select the block, then choose **Format:Rotate**.

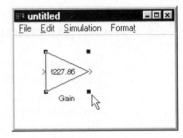

The block will rotate 90 degrees clockwise.

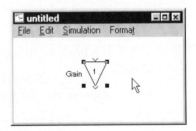

4.3.3 Copying a Block within a Model

You will frequently want to copy a block from within a model. For example, after you have resized a block, you will probably want all similar blocks to appear identical. Rather than attempting to resize each block, you can copy the block you resized.

To copy a block within a model, depress and hold the Control key (Microsoft Windows or X Windows) or Option key (Macintosh), then click the block.

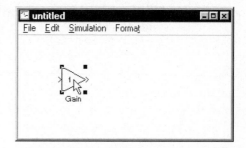

Drag the copy to the desired position.

If you have a two- (or three-) button mouse, dragging by using the right mouse button is equivalent.

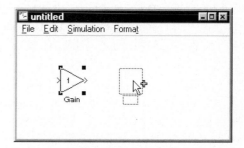

Release the mouse button, completing the copy operation.

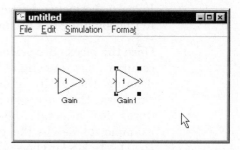

An alternative is to click the block, select **Edit:Copy** (or press Control-C in Microsoft Windows or X Windows, Apple-C on Macintosh), then **Edit:Paste** (or press Control-V in Microsoft Windows or X Windows, Apple-V on Macintosh).

4.3.4 Deleting Blocks

To delete a block, select the block and then press the Delete key. An alternative is to select the block, then choose **Edit:Clear** from the model window menu bar. Choose **Edit:Cut** to delete the block and save it on the Clipboard.

4.3.5 Selecting Multiple Blocks

You can select multiple blocks and move, copy, or delete them as a group. There are two ways to select multiple blocks. The first is to depress and hold the Shift key while clicking each block in the group. The other method is to use a bounding box as follows:

Click and hold the mouse button outside the blocks.

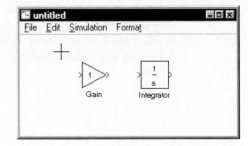

Drag the bounding box that appears so as to enclose all the desired blocks.

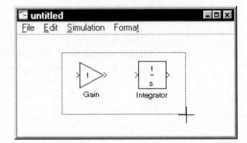

Release the mouse button. All blocks in the bounding box are now selected.

Once the blocks are selected, the procedures for moving, copying, or deleting the entire group are the same as the corresponding procedures for a single block. So, for example, to delete the group, press the Delete key or choose **Edit:Cut** or **Edit:Clear** from the model window menu bar.

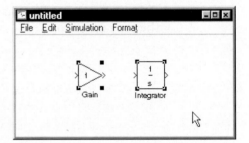

4.3.6 Changing a Block Label

Simulink supplies a default label for each block as you place the blocks in the model window. For example, the first gain block will have the default name "Gain," the second gain block will be labeled "Gain1," and so on. Change the block label as follows:

Click the block label. An editing cursor will appear. You can position the cursor anywhere in the label by clicking, and you can move the cursor by using the cursor movement keys.

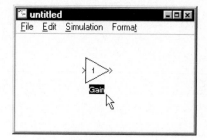

To replace a label, select it, then double-click it. The label will be highlighted as shown here.

Enter the new label.

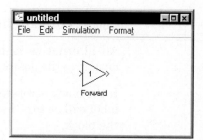

To create a multiple-line label, press Return at the end of each line.

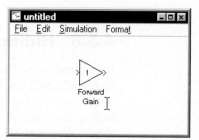

Click away from the block to accept the label.

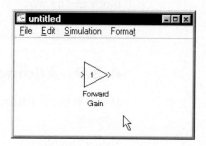

Each block must have a unique name of at least one character.

4.3.7 Changing Label Location

You can move the block label from below to above the block as follows:

Select the block.

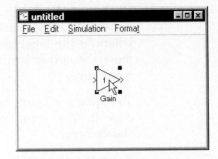

Choose **Format:Flip Name**.

An alternative is to click the name and drag it to the desired position.

If the block is rotated 90 degrees, the block label will be to either the left or the right of the block.

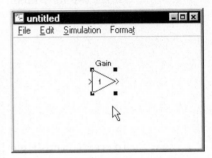

4.3.8 Hiding a Label

It is sometimes desirable to hide the name of a block. For example, since the shape of a gain block uniquely identifies the purpose of the block, and the value of the gain is displayed on the block, a cluttered model might be improved by hiding the names of the gain blocks. To hide the name, select the block and choose **Format:Hide Name.** Note that this does not change the name of the block in any way—it simply makes the name invisible. If the name of a block is hidden, when the block is selected, **Format:Hide Name** is replaced by **Format:Show Name** on the **Format** pull-down menu.

4.3.9 Adding a Drop Shadow

If you want to call special attention to a block, you can apply a drop shadow as follows:

Select the block.

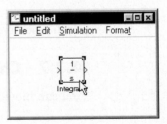

Choose **Format:Show Drop Shadow** from the model window menu bar. If a block is configured with a drop shadow, the menu choice will change to **Format:Hide Drop Shadow** for that block, permitting you to remove the drop shadow if desired.

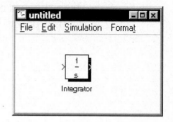

4.3.10 Configuring Blocks

In Chapter 3, we discussed setting block parameters. In the example in Chapter 3, the numeric parameters were set to constants. However, configuration parameters do not have to be constants. They can be any valid MATLAB expression, and may use variables that will be defined in the MATLAB workspace when the model is executed. This is a very useful capability. Later, we'll discuss executing a Simulink model from a MATLAB script. By making certain parameters variables, the parameters can be changed by the script.

4.4 Signal Lines

In Chapter 3 we discussed drawing signal lines using Simulink's automatic routing capability and drawing signal lines in segments. In this section we'll discuss drawing signal lines in an arbitrary direction and editing signal lines.

4.4.1 Drawing Signal Lines at an Angle

Recall that if you drag directly from an output port of one block to an input port of another block, Simulink will automatically route the signal lines in horizontal and vertical segments. If you override the automatic routing and draw a signal line in segments, the segments will still be horizontal and vertical. You can override this feature and draw signal lines at any arbitrary angle as follows:

Depress and hold the Shift key, then click and hold on the output port.

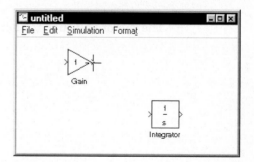

Drag the end of the signal line to the desired point.

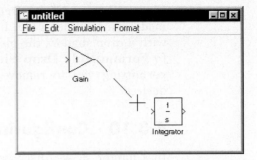

Release the mouse button and Shift key.

To draw in segments, release the mouse button momentarily at the end of each segment, then continue drawing the next segment, all the while continuing to depress the Shift key.

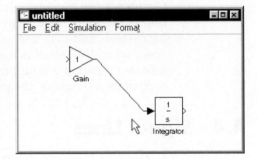

4.4.2 Moving a Segment

To move a line segment, click the segment.

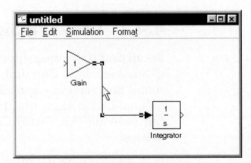

The cursor will change shape.

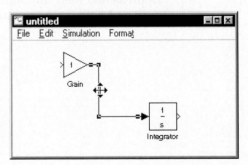

Keeping the mouse button depressed, drag the segment to the desired location.

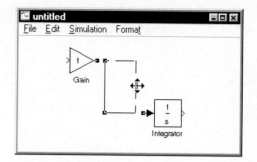

Release the mouse button.

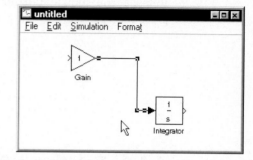

4.4.3 Moving a Vertex

To move a vertex, start by clicking the vertex.

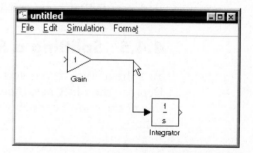

The cursor will change shape to a circle.

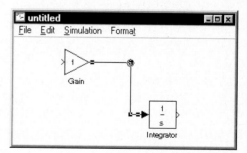

Drag the vertex to the desired location.

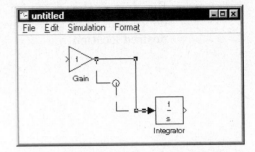

Release the mouse button to complete the operation.

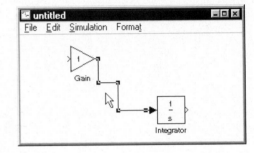

4.4.4   Deleting a Signal Line

To delete a signal line, select the signal line by clicking it. Press the Delete key, or choose **Edit:Clear** or **Edit:Cut** from the model window menu bar.

4.4.5   Splitting a Signal Line

To split a line, first select the line. Depress the Shift key, then click the line at the point at which you wish to split it.

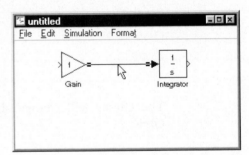

The cursor will change shape to a circle and the segment will split into two segments.

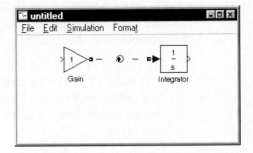

Drag the new vertex to the desired location.

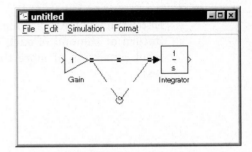

Release the mouse button to complete the process.

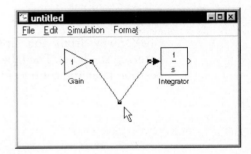

4.4.6 Labeling a Signal Line

Each signal line may have a label. The label can be positioned at either end of the signal line, and on either side. Signal line labels, unlike block labels, do not have to be unique.

To add a label to a signal line, double-click the line, causing an editing cursor to appear near the line.

Be sure that you click the line itself, not just near the line. Double-clicking away from a line will result in an annotation (to be discussed later) rather than a signal line label.

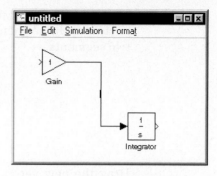

Enter the label. As with block labels, press Return at the end of each line to enter a label consisting of more than one line of text.

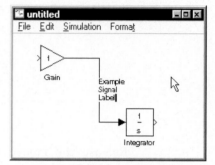

Click away from the line to complete entering the label. The label will snap to a position near the center of the line.

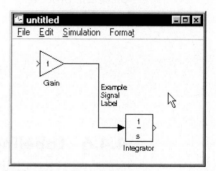

4.4.7 Moving or Copying a Signal Line Label

You can move a signal line label to either end or the middle of the signal line.

To move a signal line label, click the label.

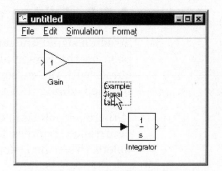

Drag the label to the desired location near the signal line.

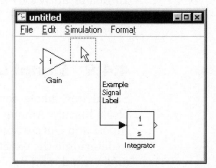

Release the mouse button. The label will snap into position.

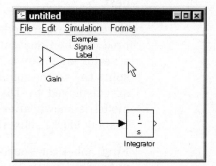

To copy a signal line label, depress the Control key (Microsoft Windows or X Windows) or Option key (Macintosh) while dragging the label to the new position.

If your mouse has two or three buttons, dragging with the right mouse button is equivalent.

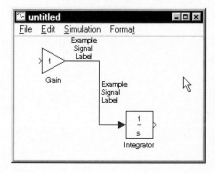

4.4.8 Editing a Signal Line Label

To edit a signal line label, click the label. An editing cursor will appear. You can position the cursor anywhere in the label by clicking, or you can move the cursor with the cursor movement keys. Click away from the label when you're finished editing it. All occurrences of the label will be changed.

If there are multiple occurrences of a signal line label, you can delete a single occurrence. Depress the Shift key, then click on the occurrence you wish to delete. Press the Delete key to complete the process.

To delete all occurrences of a signal line label, delete all characters in one instance of the label. When you click away from the label, all occurrences will be removed.

4.4.9 Signal Label Propagation

Signal line labels can propagate through several blocks in the Connections block library. Among these are the Mux and Demux, Goto and From, and Inport and Outport blocks. Signal line propagation provides an accurate means to determine the exact content of a signal line. This can make a model easier to understand, and can also be useful in debugging. The process is illustrated next.

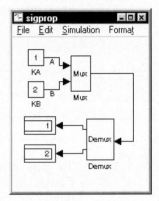

Here, we have a model in which two scalar signals produced by Constant blocks are combined to form a vector signal by a Mux block. The Demux block splits the vector signal into two scalar signals that are displayed by Display blocks. Notice that the model is shown after running the simulation (the Display blocks show the signal values).

First, label the source signal lines. Here, the outputs of the constant blocks KA and KB are labeled A and B.

Label each signal line onto which you want the labels propagated with the single character <. Here, we have configured all three signal lines to propagate the labels.

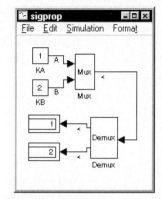

Choose **Edit:Update Diagram** from the menu bar of the model window. Here, the signal line leaving the Mux block contains two signals, so the label is changed to <A,B>, showing both. The Demux block separates the vector signal into components, so the signal lines leaving it each contain only one signal, as shown by the labels. In both cases the propagated labels are enclosed in angle brackets to distinguish them from simple labels.

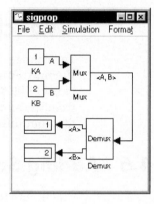

4.5   Annotations

You can add annotations to a model to make it easier to understand. You can also change the font used in an annotation to add emphasis.

4.5.1   Adding Annotations

Double-click at the location where you want the center of an annotation to be. An editing cursor will appear.

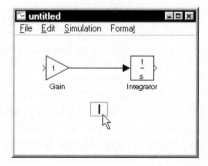

Enter the annotation. Press Return at the end of each line of a multiple-line annotation. Click away from the annotation to complete the process.

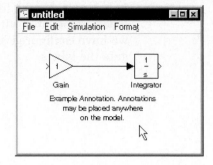

You can move and copy annotations using the same procedures used to move and copy blocks.

4.5.2 Changing Annotation Fonts

To change the font of an annotation, select the annotation. Choose **Format:Font** from the menu bar of the model window. A font selection dialog box will be displayed. Select the desired font, then press **OK**; then click away from the annotation. All characters in a particular annotation will be the same font, but different annotations can be in different fonts.

4.6 Adding Sources

The inputs to a model are called sources, located in the Sources block library. A source block has no inputs and at least one output. Detailed documentation for each block in the Sources block library is available via the Block Browser. In this section, we will mention several of the more commonly used blocks in the Sources block library. Then, we will briefly discuss From Workspace and From File blocks, which allow you to create any signal you can describe mathematically in MATLAB and then use that signal as a Simulink input.

4.6.1 Common Sources

Many of the input signals used in modeling dynamical systems are available in the Sources block library. The Constant block produces a fixed constant signal, the magnitude of which is set in the block dialog box and displayed on the block icon. The Step block produces a step function. You can set the time of occurrence of the step, and the signal magnitude before and after the step. There is a Sine Wave block for which you can set the amplitude, phase, and frequency. The Signal Generator block can be set to produce sine, square, sawtooth, or random signals. More complex signals can be generated by combining the signals from multiple source blocks using a Sum block.

Example 4-1

A signal that is very useful in determining the behavior of dynamical systems is the *unit impulse*, also known as the delta function or Dirac delta function. (For a detailed discussion, see Meirovitch [1].) The unit impulse ($\delta(t-a)$) is defined to be a signal of zero duration, having the properties:

$$\delta(t-a) = 0, \quad t \neq a$$

$$\int_{-\infty}^{\infty} \delta(t)dt = 1$$

Although the unit impulse is a theoretical signal that can't exist, it is a close approximation to real impulse signals that are very common. Physical examples are collisions, such as a wheel hitting a curb or a bat hitting a ball, or near-instantaneous velocity changes such as firing a bullet from a rifle. Another use for the unit impulse is the assessment of a system's dynamics. The motion of a system forced by a unit impulse is due purely to the dynamics inherent in the system. Thus, you can use the impulse response of a complex system to determine its natural frequencies and modes of vibration.

You can approximate a unit impulse function using two Step blocks and a Sum block as shown in Figure 4-2. The idea is to produce, at the desired time (a), a very short duration (d) pulse of a magnitude (M) such that $Md = 1$. The trick is in deciding on the proper value of d. It must be short relative to the fastest dynamics of the system. If it is too short, it can cause numerical problems such as excessive roundoff error. If it is too long, it doesn't adequately simulate a true impulse. Usually, an acceptable compromise can be found with a little experimentation.

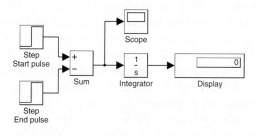

Figure 4-2   Generating a unit impulse function

The model in Figure 4-2 is set to simulate a unit impulse at 0.5 seconds with a pulse of 0.01 seconds' duration and magnitude of 100. The Step block labeled Step Start pulse is configured as follows: **Step time** is 0.5, **Initial value** is 0,

Final value is 100. The Step block Step End pulse is configured as follows: **Step time** is 0.51, **Initial value** is 0, **Final value** is 100. The simulation is configured to stop at 1 second. A plot of the output of the Sum block is shown in Figure 4-3. The Integrator block computes the time integral of the output of the Sum block, which is displayed using a Display block, and which has the desired value (1).

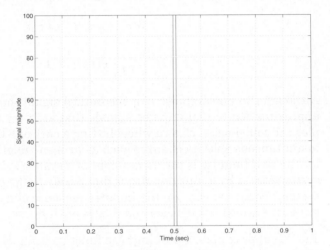

Figure 4-3   Unit impulse signal

4.6.2 From Workspace Block

The From Workspace block permits you to design a custom input signal. The block and its dialog box are illustrated in Figure 4-4. The block configuration parameter is a matrix table with the default value [T,U]. The input must be in the form of a MATLAB matrix, using variables currently defined in the MATLAB workspace. The first column of the matrix is the independent variable which corresponds to simulation time and must be monotonically increasing. The subsequent columns are values of the dependent variables corresponding to the independent variable in the first column. The block will produce as many outputs as there are dependent variables. The outputs are produced by linearly interpolating or extrapolating in the table.

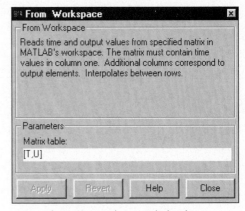

From
Workspace

(a) From Workspace block   (b) From Workspace dialog box

Figure 4-4   From Workspace block and dialog box

Example 4-2

To illustrate the use of the From Workspace block, suppose that we wish to generate a signal defined as

$$u(t) = t^2$$

Figure 4-5 illustrates an M-file that produces a suitable input table.

```
% Generate a signal for a From Workspace block
t = 0:0.1:100 ; % Independent variable
u = t.^2 ;      % Dependent variable
A = [t',u'] ;   % Form the table
```

Figure 4-5   M-file to create input table for From Workspace block

Create the M-file using a text editor, and save it as a standard M-file using the .m extension. Note that the M-file must be saved with a name different from the Simulink model file. To use this table, you must first execute the M-file from within MATLAB, creating the table A. Configure the From Workspace block by replacing [T,U] in the From Workspace dialog box with the name of the table (A).

Set **Matrix table** to A, the name of the table created in the MATLAB workspace. Click **Close**.

The block icon will display the name of the table.

From File Input Block

The From File block is very similar to the From Workspace block. The primary difference is that the matrix is stored in a file in MATLAB matrix file (.mat) format rather than coming directly from the MATLAB workspace. An additional difference is that the signals are stored in rows rather than in columns. You can produce a file (examp.mat) containing the matrix produced by the M-file in Figure 4-5 using the MATLAB commands:

```
B = A'
save examp B
```

Configure the From File block by setting the full filename (for example, examp.mat) in From File block dialog box field **File name**.

4.7 Adding Sinks

Sinks provide means to view or store model data. The Scope and XY Graph blocks produce plots of model data, and the Display block produces a digital display of the value of its input. The To Workspace block saves a signal to the MATLAB workspace, and the To File block saves a signal in MATLAB .mat file format. The Stop block causes a simulation to stop when its input is non-zero. A detailed reference for each of these blocks is available in the Block Browser. We will discuss the Scope block and XY graph block in some detail in this section.

4.7.1 Scope Block

The Scope block emulates an oscilloscope. The block shows a segment of the input signal, which may be either scalar or vector. Both the vertical range (y-axis) and horizontal range (Time, on the x-axis) can be set to any desired values. The vertical axis displays the actual value of the input signal. The horizontal axis scale always starts at zero and ends at the value specified as **time range**. So, for example, if the horizontal range is 10 and the current time is 100, the input data for the period 90 to 100 is displayed, although the x-axis labels will still be 0 to 10. The Scope block is intended primarily for use during a simulation, and therefore Scope blocks do not provide a means to save the scope image for printing or inclusion in a document. However, the Scope block will send the signals it plots to the MATLAB workspace for further analysis or plotting using, for example, the MATLAB plot command.

You can place a Scope block in a model without connecting a signal line to the input of the Scope block, and configure the block as a *floating Scope block*. A floating Scope block will use as its input any signal line that you click during the execution of a simulation.

Figure 4-6 illustrates a Scope block. Note that there is a toolbar that contains six icons along the top of the Scope block window. These buttons allow you to zoom in on a portion of the display, autoscale the display, save a configuration for future use, and open a scope properties dialog box. Table 4-1 describes the function of each button.

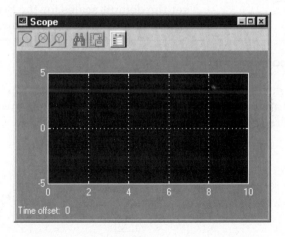

Figure 4-6   Scope block display before running simulation

Table 4-1 Scope block buttons

Button Icon	Function
	The **Zoom** button permits you to enlarge a region of the display.
	The **Zoom X** button allows you to zoom in on a portion of the display without changing the vertical scale.
	The **Zoom Y** button allows you to zoom in on a portion of the display without changing the horizontal scale.
	Autoscale changes the vertical scale such that the lower limit is the same as the minimum value in the currently displayed signal, and the upper limit is the same as the maximum value in the currently displayed signal. You can click **Autoscale** during a simulation to rescale the display.
	Save axis makes the current scale the default for this Scope block. If you change the scale and then rerun the simulation without pressing **Save axis** first, the scale will revert to the current default when the simulation starts.
	Clicking the **Open properties window** button opens the Scope properties dialog box. This dialog box allows you to set the default scales for the Scope block and to send the Scope data to the MATLAB workspace.

Zooming the Scope Display

Consider the model shown in Figure 4-7. The top Sine Wave block is configured to produce the signal $\sin(t)$ and the other Sine Wave block is configured to produce $0.4\sin(10t)$.

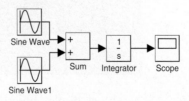

Figure 4-7   First-order system with sinusoidal input

Open the Scope block by double-clicking it. Run the simulation, resulting in the display shown here. At this point, you could rescale the display by clicking the **Autoscale** button. Instead, zoom in on the peak between 2 and 4 seconds as follows.

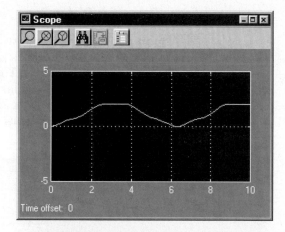

Click the **Zoom** button. Then, enclose the area you wish to zoom in on using a bounding box.

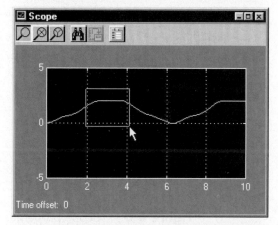

The Scope scales will change to include only the area you zoomed in on.

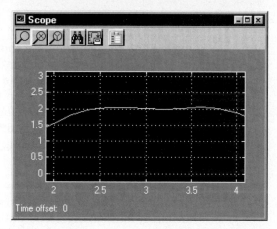

Scope Properties Dialog Box

The **Open properties window** button opens the Scope properties dialog box, which has two pages. The Axes page (Figure 4-8) has fields to enter the maximum (**Y max**) and minimum (**Y min**) values for the dependent variable. **Time range** may be set to a particular value, or may be set to auto. If **Time range** is set to auto, the range will be the same as the simulation duration specified in the **Simulation:Parameters** dialog box.

Figure 4-8   Scope properties axes page

The Settings page (Figure 4-9) has fields to control the number of points displayed and to save the data (not the display) to the MATLAB workspace. The General section of the page consists of a dropdown list containing two choices: **Decimation** and **Sample time**. If **Decimation** is selected, the corresponding data field is set to a decimation factor that must be an integer. If **Decimation** is selected and set to 1 (the default), every point in the block input is plotted. If **Decimation** is set to 2, every other point is plotted, and so on. If **Sample time** is selected, the absolute spacing between plotted points must be entered in the data field.

The Scope block stores the input points in a buffer. Check **Limit points to last** and enter a value to specify the size of the buffer (default is 5000). Autoscaling, zooming, and saving scope data to the workspace all work with this buffer. Thus, if **Limit rows to last** is set to 1000, and the simulation produces a total

Figure 4-9   Scope properties settings page

of 2000 points, only the final 1000 points are available when the simulation stops.

As stated above, there is no provision for printing the Scope display, or for embedding the Scope display in a word processing document. However, you can send the Scope data to the MATLAB workspace, and use MATLAB's extensive plotting capabilities. To send the Scope data to the MATLAB workspace, select **Save data to workspace** and enter the name of a MATLAB variable. When the simulation stops, the data displayed on the Scope will be stored in the MATLAB variable. There will be one column for the time values, and one column for each signal input to the Scope block. Thus, if the signal entering the Scope block is a vector signal with two components, the MATLAB variable will be a matrix with three columns and a number of rows equal to the number of time points displayed on the Scope.

4.7.2 XY Graph

The XY Graph block produces a graph identical to a graph produced by the MATLAB command `plot`. The XY Graph accepts two scalar inputs. You must configure the horizontal and vertical ranges using the block dialog box. The XY Graph block dialog box is illustrated in Figure 4-10. The top input port is the x-input, and the bottom input port is the y-input.

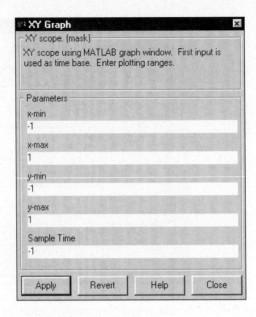

Figure 4-10 XY Graph block dialog box

4.8 Configuring the Simulation

A Simulink model is essentially a computer program that defines a set of differential and difference equations. When you choose **Simulation:Start** from the model window menu bar, Simulink solves that set of differential and difference equations numerically using one of its differential equation solvers. Before you run a simulation, you may set various simulation parameters such as the starting and ending time, simulation step size, and various tolerances. You can choose among several high-quality integration algorithms. You can also configure Simulink to acquire certain data from the MATLAB workspace, and to send simulation results to the MATLAB workspace.

To illustrate the basic idea, consider the model shown in Figure 4-11.

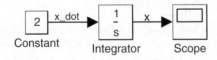

Figure 4-11 Simulink model of first-order system

This model represents the differential equation

$$\dot{x} = 2 \qquad\qquad (4\text{-}1)$$

We set the Integrator block **Initial condition** field to 1. Next, we choose **Simulation:Parameters** from the model window menu bar, and set **Start time** to 0, and Stop time to 5. Then choose **Simulation:Start** from the model window menu bar. Simulink will numerically evaluate the value of the integral to solve

$$x(\tau) = 1 + \int_0^\tau 2\,dt \qquad\qquad (4\text{-}2)$$

and plot the value of $x(\tau)$ along the interval from 0 to 5. A numerical integration algorithm that solves this kind of problem (frequently called an *initial value problem*) is referred to as an *ordinary differential equation solver*, or just *solver* for the sake of brevity.

To set simulation parameters, choose **Simulation:Parameters** from the menu bar of the model window, which opens the Simulation parameters dialog box, Figure 4-12. The Simulation parameters dialog box contains three tabbed pages: Solver, Workspace I/O, and Diagnostics. The Solver page, illustrated in Figure 4-12, selects and configures the differential equation solver. The Workspace I/O page contains optional parameters that permit you to acquire simulation initialization data from the MATLAB workspace, and to send certain simulation data to the MATLAB workspace. The Diagnostics page is used to select diagnostic modes, which are useful for troubleshooting certain simulation problems. We'll discuss each page in detail.

4.8.1 Solver Page

The Solver page consists of three sections. The first, Simulation time, contains fields to enter the start and stop times. **Start time** defaults to 0, and **Stop time** defaults to 10. The Solver options section contains fields to select the differential equation solver (numerical integration algorithm), and to set parameters that control the integration step size. The solvers are grouped in two categories: variable-step and fixed-step. Several different integration algorithms are available for each category. If a variable-step solver is chosen, there are fields to select the maximum integration step size, the initial integration step size, and absolute and relative tolerances. If a fixed-step solver is chosen, there is a single field in which to enter the step size. The Output options section controls the time spacing of points in the simulation output trajectory.

Solver Type

Simulink provides several ordinary differential equation solvers. The majority of these solvers are the result of recent numerical integration research, and are

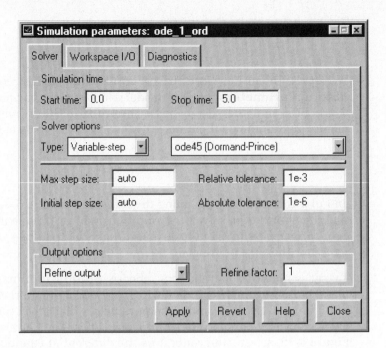

Figure 4-12 Simulation parameters dialog box

among the fastest and most accurate methods available. Detailed descriptions of the algorithms are available in the paper by Shampine [2], available from The MathWorks.

It is generally best to use the variable-step solvers, as they continuously adjust the integration step size to maximize efficiency while maintaining a specified accuracy. The Simulink variable-step solvers can completely decouple the integration step size and the interval between output points, so it is not necessary to limit the step size to get a smooth plot or to produce an output trajectory with a predetermined fixed step size. The available solvers are listed in Table 4-2. We will discuss them in more detail in Chapter 12.

Output options

The Output options section of the Solver page works in conjunction with the variable-step solvers to control the spacing between points in the output trajectory. Output options do not apply to the fixed-step solvers. The **Output options** field contains a list box with three choices: **Refine output**, **Produce additional output**, and **Produce specified output only**.

Choose **Refine output** to force the solver to add intermediate points between the solution points for successive integration steps. Simulink computes the

Table 4-2 Simulink Solvers

Solver Type	Characteristics
ODE45	Excellent general purpose single-step solver. Based on the Dormand-Prince fourth–fifth-order Runge-Kutta pair. ODE45 is the default solver, and is usually a good first choice.
ODE23	Uses the Bogacki-Shampine second–third-order Runge-Kutta pair. Sometimes works better than ODE45 in the presence of mild stiffness. Generally requires a smaller step size than ODE45 to get the same accuracy.
ODE113	Variable-order Adams-Bashforth-Moulton solver. Since ODE113 uses the solutions at several previous time points to compute the solution at the current time point, it may produce the same accuracy as ODE45 or ODE23 with fewer derivative evaluations, and thus perform much faster. Not suitable for systems with discontinuities.
ODE15S	Variable-order multistep solver for stiff systems. Based on recent research using numerical difference formulas. If a simulation runs extremely slowly using ODE45, try ODE15S.
ODE23S	Fixed-order single-step solver for stiff systems. Because ODE23S is a single-step method, it is sometimes faster than ODE15S. If a system appears to be stiff, it is a good idea to try both stiff solvers to determine which one performs better.
Discrete	Special solver for systems that contain no continuous states.
ODE5	Fixed-step version of ODE45.
ODE4	Classic fourth-order Runge-Kutta formulas using a fixed-step size.
ODE3	Fixed-step version of ODE23.
ODE2	Fixed-step second-order Runge-Kutta method, also known as Heun's method.
ODE1	Euler's method using a fixed-step size.

intermediate points using interpolation, which is much faster than using reduced integration step size. **Refine output** is a good choice if the output trajectory needs to appear smoother, but there is no need for a fixed spacing between points. If **Refine output** is chosen, there will be an additional input field labeled **Refine factor**. **Refine factor** must be an integer. Simulink divides each integration step into **Refine factor** output steps, so, for example, if **Refine factor** is set to 2, the midpoint of each integration step will be added to the output trajectory.

Produce additional output permits you to force Simulink to include certain time points in the output trajectory, in addition to the solution points at the end of each integration step. If **Produce additional output** is selected, there will be an additional field labeled **Output times**. This field must contain a vector listing the additional times for which output is requested. For example, if it is necessary to include the output at 10-second intervals, and the value of **Start time** is 0 and **Stop time** is 100, **Output times** should contain [0:10:100].

Choose **Produce specified output only** if it is necessary to produce an output trajectory containing only specified time points. For example, you may wish to compare several trajectories to evaluate the effect of changing a parameter. If **Produce specified output only** is selected, there will be an additional field labeled **Output times**, which must contain a vector of the desired output times.

4.8.2 Workspace I/O Page

The Workspace I/O page, Figure 4-13, permits you to acquire simulation input from the MATLAB workspace, and to send output directly to the MATLAB workspace. The page consists of four sections: Load from workspace, Save to workspace, States, and Save options. We'll discuss each section in detail.

Load from workspace

Selecting the **Load from workspace** check box causes Simulink to take the input time points and values of the input variables from the MATLAB workspace. **Load from workspace** works in conjunction with the Inport block found on the Connections block library. Inport blocks may be configured to accept scalar or vector data. Set the name of the time and input matrices in the **Load from workspace** field. The first matrix (default name t) is a column vector of time values, and the second matrix (default name u) consists of one column for each input variable, with a row corresponding to each row in the time matrix. If there is more than one Inport block, the columns of the input matrix are ordered corresponding to the number assigned to the Inport blocks. So, the first column corresponds to the lowest numbered Inport block, and the last column corresponds to the highest numbered Inport block. For a vector

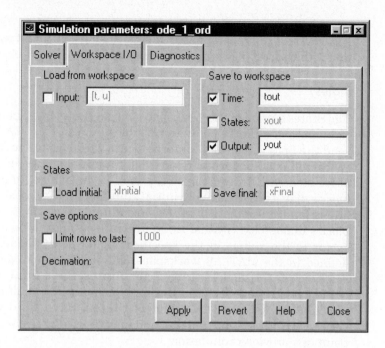

Figure 4-13 Workspace I/O page

Inport block, there must be one column in the u matrix for each element of the input vector.

Simulink Internal State Vectors

Before discussing the Save to workspace and States sections of the Workspace I/O page, we should briefly discuss Simulink's internal state variables. A Simulink model can be thought of as a set of simultaneous first-order, possibly nonlinear, differential and difference equations. In addition to the state variables associated with each integrator block, there are implicitly specified state variables associated with transfer function blocks, state-space blocks, certain nonlinear blocks, certain discrete blocks, and many of the blocks in the Extras block library. It is frequently useful to have access to a model's state variables, and Simulink provides mechanisms to facilitate this. Use of the Workspace I/O page is probably the easiest method to access a model's state variables. Accessing a model's state variables, and, in particular, identifying all of a model's state variables, is discussed further in Chapter 8.

Save to workspace

The Save to workspace section contains three fields, each activated with a check box. **Time** sends the independent variable to the specified workspace matrix (default name tout). **States** sends all of the model's state variables to the specified MATLAB workspace matrix (default name xout). **Output** works in conjunction with Outport blocks in a manner analogous to Inport blocks, discussed above.

States

The States section of the Workspace I/O page can force Simulink to load the initial values of all internal state variables from the MATLAB workspace, and to send the final values of all internal state variables to the MATLAB workspace. All Simulink state variables have default initial values, in most cases 0. States associated with Integrator blocks may be initialized to any value using the block's dialog box. Specifying initial states on the Workspace I/O page overrides any default initialization values, including initial values set in an Integrator block's dialog box. **States, Load initial** sets initial value of a model's state vector to the values in the specified input vector (default name xInitial), defined in the MATLAB workspace. The initialization vector must be of the same size as the model's state vector. **States, Save final** saves the final value of the model's state vector in the specified matrix (default name xFinal) in the MATLAB workspace. The output of **States, Save final** is a suitable initial vector for **States, Load initial**, and may be used to restart a model at the final point of a previous simulation.

Save options

The Save options section of the Workspace I/O page contains two fields, and works in conjunction with the Save to workspace section. The first field, **Limit rows to last**, sends at most the specified number of points to the MATLAB workspace. So, for example, if **Limit rows to last** is checked and set to the default value of 1000, at most the final 1000 points will be sent to the workspace. **Decimation** sets the interval between points sent to the MATLAB workspace. If **Decimation** is set to 1, every point will be sent to the workspace. If **Decimation** is set to 2, every other point will be sent to the workspace, and so on. **Decimation** must be set to an integer value.

4.8.3 Diagnostics Page

The Diagnostics page, Figure 4-14, allows you to select the action taken for five exceptional conditions, and also includes options to control automatic block output consistency checking and to disable zero crossing detection. There are three choices for the response to each of the five exception conditions. The first choice, **None**, instructs Simulink to ignore the corresponding exception. The second choice, **Warning** (the default choice), causes Simulink to issue a warning message each time the corresponding exception occurs. The final choice, **Error**, causes Simulink to abort the simulation and issue an error message whenever the corresponding exception occurs. The exceptions are detected when a model is executed. We'll briefly discuss each exceptional condition.

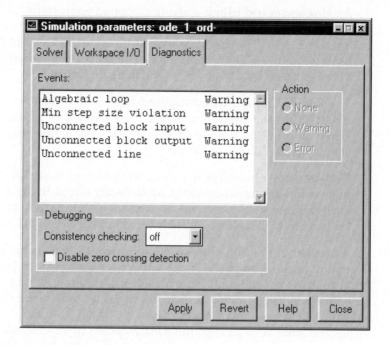

Figure 4-14 Diagnostics page

An **Algebraic loop** is an exception in which a block's input at a given instant of time is dependent on the same block's output at the same instant of time. Algebraic loops are troublesome because they can significantly reduce the speed of a simulation, and in some cases can cause the simulation to fail to execute. A detailed discussion of algebraic loops is presented in Chapter 12. It is usually best to set the algebraic loop response to **Warning**. If an algebraic loop is discovered, and if performance is acceptable, change the response to **None**.

A **Min step size violation** occurs when the solver attempts to use an integration step size smaller than the minimum. It is not possible to change the minimum step size for any of the variable step size solvers. If this exception occurs, you can change to a higher-order solver, which in general will use a larger integration step size. Your other choice is to increase the absolute and relative tolerances on the Solver page. **Min step size violation** should always be set to **Warning** or **Error**, because it indicates the simulation is not producing the expected accuracy.

An **Unconnected block input** exception occurs when a block has an input that is not used. This is generally the result of an error in building the model.

This exception should be set to **Error** or **Warning**. If the omission of a block's input is intentional, it is a good practice to connect a Ground block to the input.

An **Unconnected block output** exception occurs when a block has an output that is not connected to the input of another block. This exception is frequently harmless, but it is easy to solve. To prevent this exception, connect unused block outputs to Terminator blocks, found in the Connections block library. This exception should be set to **Warning** or **Error**.

The final exception, **Unconnected line**, is almost always due to an error in constructing the Simulink model. This exception occurs when one end of a signal line is not connected to a block. The **Unconnected line** exception should usually be set to **Error**.

Consistency checking is a debugging feature that detects certain programming errors in custom blocks. **Consistency checking** is not needed with standard Simulink blocks, and it causes a simulation to run much slower. Ordinarily, **Consistency checking** should be set to **off**.

A number of Simulink blocks exhibit discontinuous behavior. For example, the output of the Sign block, located in the Nonlinear block library, is 1 if its input is positive, 0 if its input is zero, and –1 if its input is negative. Thus, the block exhibits a discontinuity at zero. If a variable step size solver is in use, Simulink will adjust the integration step size when the input to a Sign block is approaching zero so that the switch occurs at the right time. This process is called *zero crossing detection*. You can determine whether a block invokes zero crossing detection by referring to the Characteristics table for the block in the Block Browser.

Zero crossing detection improves the accuracy of a simulation, but it can cause a simulation to run slowly. Occasionally, a system will fluctuate rapidly about a discontinuity, a phenomenon called *chatter*. When this happens, the progress of the simulation can effectively stop, as the integration step size is reduced to a very small value. If your model runs very slowly and includes one or more blocks with intrinsic zero crossing detection, selecting **Disable zero crossing detection** on the Diagnostics page can significantly increase the speed of a simulation. However, this can also adversely affect the accuracy of a simulation, so it is best used only as a tool to verify that chatter is occurring. If selecting **Disable zero crossing detection** dramatically improves the speed of a simulation, you should locate the cause of chatter and correct the problem.

4.9 Running a Simulation

You can control the execution of the model using the **Simulation** pull-down menu on the model window menu bar. To start the simulation, select **Simulation:Start**. You can stop the simulation at any time using **Simulation:Stop**.

Choose **Simulation:Pause** to temporarily halt execution. Then choose **Simulation:Continue** to resume or **Simulation:Stop** to permanently halt execution of the model. It is also possible to run a simulation from the MATLAB command line; this method will be discussed in Chapter 8.

While the simulation is executing, you can change many parameters. For example, you can change the gain of a Gain block, choose a different solver, or change integration parameters such as minimum step size. You can also select a signal line that will become the input to a floating Scope block. This permits you to check various signals as the simulation progresses.

4.10 Printing a Model

There are a variety of options for printing Simulink models. The simplest is to send the model directly to a printer. However, it is also possible to embed the model in a word processing document or other file, by either copying it to the clipboard (Microsoft Windows or Macintosh) or saving it as an Encapsulated PostScript file.

4.10.1 Printing to the Printer Using Menus

The fastest way to get a printed copy of a model is to send it directly to the printer. On Microsoft Windows or Macintosh, you can use the printing options on the **File** pull-down menu. To do this, choose **File:Printer Setup** from the model window menu bar and configure the printer as desired. Next, choose **File:Print**. On all platforms, you can print from the MATLAB command line using the print command discussed later.When you send a model directly to the printer, Simulink resizes it as necessary to fit on the page. You have no control over the size of the model.

4.10.2 Embedding the Model in a Document

Modern documentation applications such as word processors, presentation programs, desktop publishing programs, drawing programs, and even spreadsheets, allow you to insert Simulink model images in documents. Once you have embedded an image in a document, you can use the graphics capabilities of the documentation application to resize the image and to further annotate the model. Simulink model images may be embedded as bitmaps, as Windows metafiles, or as Encapsulated PostScript files. To embed an image as a bitmap or metafile using Microsoft Windows or Macintosh, select **Edit:Copy Model** from the model window menu bar. The entire model window will be copied to the clipboard. Next, make the target document active, and use the procedure for the documentation application to embed the image. For most Microsoft Windows programs, the procedure is to choose **Edit:Paste Special**, then select

Metafile (sometimes listed as Picture) or Bitmap as appropriate. Generally, it is preferable to use the Metafile format, because this format does not lose resolution when it is resized. However, as not all programs handle Metafiles correctly, the bitmap option provides a reliable alternative that will work with nearly all documentation applications.

To embed the image of a Simulink model in a document in Encapsulated PostScript form, first save the image as an Encapsulated PostScript file using the print command, which will be discussed shortly. There appears to be no standard menu convention for embedding Encapsulated PostScript images, so you'll need to refer to the application's documentation. Many programs provide an **Import** choice on the **File** menu. Others provide an **Insert** menu, or a **Graphics** menu. Note that if you use Encapsulated PostScript to embed the image, you will probably have to print the document on a PostScript printer in order for the image to be printed.

4.10.3   Using the Matlab print Command

The MATLAB print command permits you to send a model image to a printer, to the clipboard, or to a file in a variety of formats. The syntax of the print command is

```
print -smodel -ddevice filename
```

model is a MATLAB string containing the name of a currently open Simulink model. The model name is displayed in the title area of the model window. Note that filenames on your computer may be case-sensitive. If the model name contains spaces, enclose the name in single quotes:

```
print -s'Spring Mass System' -ddevice filename
```

If the model name contains a carriage return, that is, if it's shown in the window title in two lines, represent the carriage return as its ASCII code (13), enclose each line in single quotes ('), and the whole name in brackets ([ ]):

```
print -s['Damped' 13 'Spring Mass System'] -ddevice filename
```

device is a MATLAB string that specifies the type of output device. Devices include printers, files, and the Windows clipboard. Table 4-3 lists the available device types.

filename is a MATLAB string containing a valid file name, and is an optional argument. If *filename* is specified, the output will be directed to the specified file rather than to the printer. If device is an Encapsulated PostScript format, and *filename* is not specified, *filename* will default to Untitled.eps.

Table 4-3 Device codes for the `print` command

device	**Device Description**
ps	PostScript
psc	Color PostScript
ps2	Level 2 PostScript
psc2	Level 2 Color PostScript
eps	Encapsulated PostScript (must go to a file)
epsc	Color Encapsulated PostScript (must go to a file)
eps2	Encapsulated Level 2 PostScript (must go to a file)
epsc2	Color Encapsulated Level 2 PostScript (must go to a file)
win	Current printer
winc	Current printer, color
meta	Clipboard in Metafile format
bitmap	Clipboard in bitmap format
setup	Same as selecting **File:Printer Setup** from the model window's menu bar

Example 4-3

In this example, we will, from the MATLAB prompt, print a model named `xydemo.mdl` to the current default printer, then copy the model image to the clipboard in Windows Metafile format.

First, open model `xydemo.mdl`. Next, at the MATLAB prompt, enter the following command:

```
print -s'xydemo'
```

The model will be printed. Next, enter the command

```
print -s'xydemo' -d'meta'
```

The model is now copied to the clipboard. It can be pasted into a word processing document or spreadsheet.

4.11 Model Building Summary

Table 4-4 summarizes the model building procedures discussed in Chapter 3 and Chapter 4. The following terms are used:

Drag   Click and hold the left mouse button; drag object to new location

Shift-click   Holding down the Shift key, click with the left mouse button.

Shift-drag   Holding down the Shift key, drag with the left mouse button.

Control-drag   Holding down the Control key, drag with the left mouse button (Windows only).

Right-drag   Drag using the right mouse button (Windows only).

Option-drag   Holding down the Option key, drag with the mouse button (Macintosh only).

Table 4-4   Summary of Model Building Operations

Operation	Microsoft Windows and X Windows	Macintosh
Select object (block or signal line)	Click on the object with the left mouse button.	Click on the object with the mouse button.
Select another object	Shift-click the additional object (or click the center mouse button on X Windows).	Shift-click the additional object.
Select with bounding box	Click with the left mouse button at the location of one corner of the bounding box. Continuing to depress the mouse button, drag the bounding box to enclose the desired area.	Click with the mouse button at the location of one corner of the bounding box. Continuing to depress the mouse button, drag the bounding box to enclose the desired area.
Copy block from block library or another model	Select block, then drag it to the model window.	Select block, then drag it to the model window.

Table 4-4   Summary of Model Building Operations (Continued)

Operation	Microsoft Windows and X Windows	Macintosh
Flip block	Select block, then **Format:Flip Block**. Shortcut: Control-f.	Select block, then **Format:Flip Block**. Shortcut: ⌘-f.
Rotate block	Select block, then **Format:Rotate Block**. Shortcut: Control-r.	Select block, then **Format:Rotate Block**. Shortcut: ⌘-r.
Resize block	Select block, then drag handle.	Select block, then drag handle.
Add drop shadow	Select block, then **Format:Show Drop Shadow**.	Select block, then **Format:Show Drop Shadow**.
Edit block name	Click on name.	Click on name.
Hide block name	Select name, then **Format:Hide Name**.	Select name, then **Format:Hide Name**.
Flip block name	Select name, then **Format:Flip Name**. Shortcut: Drag name to new location.	Select name, then **Format:Flip Name**. Shortcut: Drag name to new location.
Delete object	Select object, then **Edit:Clear**. Shortcut: Delete key.	Select object, then **Edit:Clear**. Shortcut: Delete key.
Copy object to clipboard	Select object, then **Edit:Copy**. Shortcut: Control-c.	Select object, then **Edit:Copy**. Shortcut: ⌘-c.
Cut object to clipboard	Select object, then **Edit:Cut**. Shortcut: Control-x.	Select object, then **Edit:Cut**. Shortcut: ⌘-x.
Paste from clip-board	**Edit:Paste**. Shortcut: Control-v.	**Edit:Paste**. Shortcut: ⌘-v.
Draw signal line	Drag from output port to input port.	Drag from output port to input port.

Table 4-4 Summary of Model Building Operations (Continued)

Operation	Microsoft Windows and X Windows	Macintosh
Draw signal line in segments	Drag from output port to first bend. Release mouse button. Drag from first bend to second bend, and so on.	Drag from output port to first bend. Release mouse button. Drag from first bend to second bend, and so on.
Draw signal line at arbitrary angle	Shift-drag from output port to input port (or drag using the center mouse button on X Windows).	Shift-drag from output port to input port.
Branch from signal line	Control-drag from point of branch. Shortcut: Right-drag, starting from the point of branch.	Option-drag from the point of branch.
Split signal line	Select line. Shift-drag the new vertex.	Select line. Shift-drag the new vertex.
Move line segment	Drag segment.	Drag segment.
Move line segment vertex	Drag vertex.	Drag vertex.
Label signal line	Double-click on line, and type text.	Double-click on line, and type text.
Move signal line label	Drag the label to the desired location.	Drag the label to the desired location.
Copy signal line label	Control-drag the copy of the label to desired location. Shortcut: Right-drag to desired location.	Option-drag the copy of the label to desired location.
Delete one occurrence of signal line label that has multiple occurrences	Shift-click label, then press Delete key.	Shift-click label, then press Delete key.

Model Building   Chapter 4

Table 4-4 Summary of Model Building Operations (Continued)

Operation	Microsoft Windows and X Windows	Macintosh
Delete all occurrences of signal line label	Select label, then delete all characters in the label.	Select label, then delete all characters in the label.
Propagate signal label	Label signal line onto which you want label propagated with single character <. Then choose **Edit:Update Diagram**.	Label signal line onto which you want label propagated with single character <. Then choose **Edit:Update Diagram**.
Add annotation to model	Double-click at location of annotation, and type text.	Double-click at location of annotation, and type text.

4.12 Summary

In this chapter, we have described procedures for editing and annotating Simulink models. We have also discussed configuring and printing a Simulink model. In the next two chapters, we will discuss using these procedures to model continuous, discrete, and hybrid systems.

4.13 References and Further Reading

1. Meirovitch, Leonard, *Introduction to Dynamics and Control*, New York, John Wiley & Sons, 1985, pp. 16–17.

2. Shampine, Lawrence F., and Reichelt, Mark W., "The MATLAB ODE Suite," The MathWorks, Inc., Natick, Mass., 1996. This technical paper is available directly from The MathWorks. It provides a detailed discussion of the MATLAB differential equation solvers that are available from within Simulink.

5

Continuous Systems

In this chapter we will discuss using Simulink to model continuous systems. We'll start with scalar linear systems. Then we'll model vector linear systems. Finally, we will use blocks from the Nonlinear block library to model nonlinear continuous systems.

5.1 Introduction

After studying Chapters 3 and 4, and experimenting a little, you should be comfortable with the mechanics of building and running Simulink models. In this chapter, we will explore using Simulink to model continuous systems.

As discussed in Chapter 2, a continuous system is a dynamical system that can be described using differential equations. Thus, most physical systems and processes are continuous. We'll start this chapter by modeling simple systems using blocks from the Linear block library. Next, we'll show how to model more complex systems using vector signals. We'll also discuss using blocks from the Nonlinear block library to model nonlinear continuous systems.

5.2 Scalar Linear Systems

Scalar linear systems can be modeled using blocks in the Linear block library. These blocks are easy to use but the Integrator block has several important capabilities that merit elaboration. In this section, we will start with a detailed description of the Integrator block. Next we will illustrate modeling scalar continuous systems with two examples.

5.2.1 Integrator Block

You can configure the Integrator block as a simple integrator or as a reset integrator. A reset integrator resets its output to the initial condition value when the reset signal triggers. You can also configure an Integrator block such that its output stays within preset limits. Additionally, you can set the integrator's initial output value in the Integrator block's dialog box, or configure the integrator to receive its initial output value through an additional input port.

Double-clicking an Integrator block opens the Integrator block dialog box, shown in Figure 5-1. To use a standard integrator, the only required input is **Initial condition**, which defaults to 0.

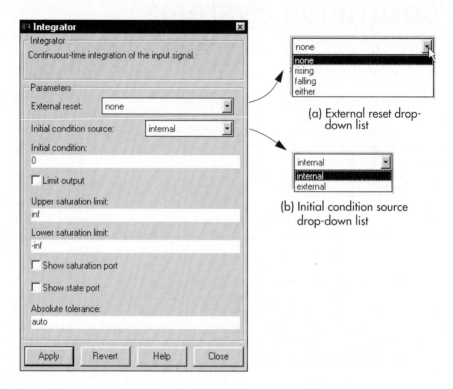

Figure 5-1 Integrator block dialog box

External reset is a drop-down list containing four choices: **none**, **rising**, **falling**, and **either**. Selecting **none** (the default) disables the external reset feature. If one of the other choices is selected, the Integrator block becomes a reset integrator block. If the reset choice is **rising**, the integrator output is reset to its initial condition value when the reset signal crosses (or departs rising, if it starts at zero) zero from below. If set to **falling**, the output is reset to the initial condition value when the reset signal crosses zero descending. If set to **either**, the output is reset to the initial condition value when the reset signal crosses zero from above or below. Figure 5-2 illustrates a simple model with the integrator External reset set to **falling**. Figure 5-3 shows the output and reset trajectories. When the reset signal crosses zero, the integrator output is reset to its initial value, and the simulation continues.

Setting **Initial condition source** to **external** adds an additional input port to the integrator. The value of this input will be used as the initial output of the

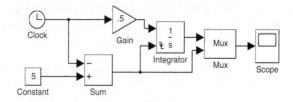

Figure 5-2   Model with reset integrator

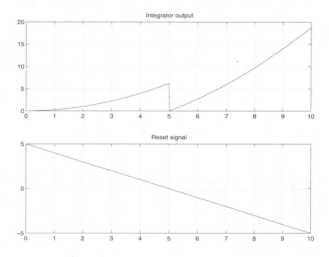

Figure 5-3   Reset integrator output and reset signals

integrator when the integration starts and when the integrator is reset if an external reset is present.

Selecting **Limit output** causes the block to function as a limited integrator. The value of the output will be no greater than **Upper saturation limit**, and no lower than **Lower saturation limit**. The default upper saturation limit is inf, which represents infinity, and the default lower saturation limit is -inf.

Selecting **Show saturation port** adds an additional output port that indicates the saturation status. The signal from this port will be –1 if the lower saturation limit is active, 1 if the upper saturation limit is active, and 0 if the output is between the saturation limits.

Selecting **Show state port** adds an additional output port to the block. This port will output the integrator state, which is the same as the integrator output. There are two situations in which the state port is needed. If the output of an Integrator block is fed back into the same block's reset or initial condition port, the state port signal must be used instead of the block output. You should also use a state port if you want to pass the output of an Integrator block in a conditionally executed subsystem (see Chapter 7 for details on conditionally executed subsystems) to another conditionally executed subsystem.

Absolute tolerance allows you to override the **Absolute tolerance** setting in the **Simulation:Parameters** dialog box for the output of a particular Integrator block. See Chapter 12 for a detailed explanation of **Absolute tolerance**. In a situation in which the absolute value of the output of an Integrator block is different by several orders of magnitude from other signals in a model, setting **Absolute tolerance** for that Integrator block appropriately can improve the accuracy of the simulation.

Figure 5-4 shows an Integrator block with all possible ports active.

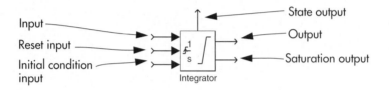

Figure 5-4   Integrator block with all options selected

Example 5-1

Consider the damped second-order system illustrated in Figure 5-5.

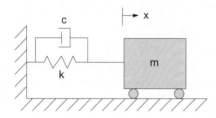

Figure 5-5   Damped second-order system

Assume that the damping coefficient $c = 1.0$ lb sec/ft, the spring constant $k = 2$ lb/ft, and the cart mass $m = 5$ slugs. There is no input to this system. We will model the motion of the cart, assuming it is initially deflected 1 ft from the equilibrium position.

In order to model the system, it is necessary to write the equation of motion. Using the Newtonian approach, we note that there are two forces acting on the cart: the spring force and the damping force. The spring force is kx, and the damping force is $c\dot{x}$. The force due to the acceleration of the cart is $m\ddot{x}$. Since

Continuous Systems   Chapter 5

there are no externally applied forces, the sum of these three forces must be zero. Thus, we can write the equation of motion

$$m\ddot{x} + c\dot{x} + kx = 0$$

Since this is a second-order system, we will need two integrators to model its behavior. Open a new model window, then start building the model by dragging two integrators from the Linear block library. Label them as shown and connect the output of the Velocity integrator to the input of the Displacement integrator.

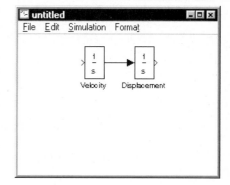

The output of the Velocity integrator is $\dot{x}$, so its input must be $\ddot{x}$. Rewrite the equation of motion to compute $\ddot{x}$ as a function of x and $\dot{x}$:

$$\ddot{x} = -\frac{c}{m}\dot{x} - \frac{k}{m}x$$

Substituting the values of the parameters,

$$\ddot{x} = -0.2\dot{x} - 0.4\,x$$

with $x(0) = 1$, $\dot{x}(0) = 0$.

Add a Sum block to compute $\ddot{x}$. The Sum block is configured with two minus signs ($--$).

Add Gain blocks to compute the ratio of damping force to mass and the ratio of the spring force to mass. Draw signal lines as shown and label the Gain blocks to show their function more clearly.

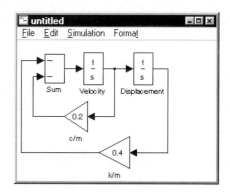

Set the **Initial condition** field in the Velocity integrator's dialog box to 0, and the **Initial condition** field in the Displacement integrator's dialog box to 1.

Add a Scope block to display the block position.

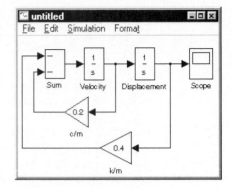

Choose **Simulation:Parameters** from the model window menu bar, and set **Stop time** to 50. Choose **Simulation:Start** from the model window menu bar. The Scope display should be as shown in Figure 5-6 after it is autoscaled.

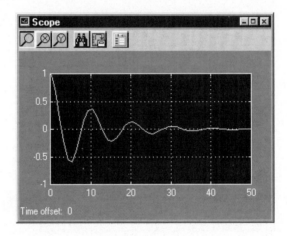

Figure 5-6   Damped second-order system response

5.2.2 Transfer Function Blocks

Simulink provides two blocks that implement transfer functions: the Transfer Fcn block and the Zero-Pole block. These blocks are equivalent, differing in the notation used to represent the transfer function. The Transfer Fcn block dialog box has two fields: **Numerator** and **Denominator**. **Numerator** contains the coefficients of the numerator of the transfer function in decreasing powers of s, and **Denominator** contains the coefficients of the denominator polynomial in decreasing powers of s. The Zero-Pole block dialog box has three fields: **Zeros**,

Poles, and **Gain**. **Zeros** contains the zeros of the numerator of the transfer function, **Poles** contains the zeros of the denominator of the transfer function, and **Gain** scales the transfer function. Refer to the Block Browser for detailed explanations of these blocks.

Example 5-2

Consider the spring, mass, damper system depicted in Figure 5-7. This system is the same as that in Example 5-1, with the addition of a forcing function F. Assume that the system is initially at its static equilibrium point ($x = 0$, $\dot{x} = 0$), and that the forcing function is a step input of 1 lb. Ignoring friction, the equation of motion of this system is

$$m\ddot{x} + c\dot{x} + kx = F \tag{5-1}$$

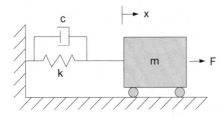

Figure 5-7   Forced second-order system

Taking the Laplace transform and ignoring initial conditions yields

$$m s^2 X(s) + c s X(s) + k X(s) = F(s) \tag{5-2}$$

The ratio of the Laplace transform of the output ($X(s)$) to the Laplace transform of the input ($F(s)$) is the transfer function ($G(s)$),

$$G(s) = \frac{X(s)}{F(s)} = \frac{(1/m)}{s^2 + \dfrac{c}{m}s + \dfrac{k}{m}} \tag{5-3}$$

Figure 5-8 shows a Simulink model of this system using the primitive linear blocks.

Figure 5-9 shows a Simulink model of the same system built using a single Transfer Fcn block. The Transfer Fcn block dialog box field **Numerator** contains [0.2], and **Denominator** contains [1 0.2 0.4].

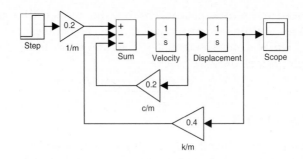

Figure 5-8   Forced second-order system with primitive blocks

Figure 5-9   Forced second-order system using a Transfer Fcn block

5.3   Vector Linear Systems

In the examples we have examined so far, the signal lines carried scalar signals. It is often convenient to use vector signals, as they provide a more compact, easier-to-understand model. In this section we will discuss the mechanics of using vector signals, and then use them with the State-Space block.

5.3.1   Vector Signal Lines

You can combine several scalar signals to form a vector signal using the Mux (multiplexer) block from the Connections block library. In Figure 5-10 we have combined three scalar signals to form a vector signal. Before you use a Mux block, you must configure it by setting the number of inputs. To make it easier to identify vector signal lines, choose **Format:Wide Vector Lines** from the model window menu bar. The components of the vector signal are referred to as u(1), u(2),..., u(n), where n is the number of components. The top input to the Mux block is u(1); the bottom input is u(n).

The Demux block permits you to split a vector signal into a set of scalar signals. The Demux block must be configured for the correct number of outputs. Figure 5-11 illustrates splitting a vector signal into three scalar signals.

Figure 5-10   Forming a vector signal using a Mux block

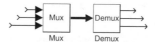

Figure 5-11   Splitting a vector signal into scalar signals

Most Simulink blocks will take vector inputs. The behavior of a block with a vector input will depend on both the type of block and the block configuration parameters. Linear blocks with vector inputs produce vector outputs of the same dimension as the input. The configuration parameters for linear blocks with vector inputs must be either of the same dimension as the input or scalar. In the case of scalar block parameters, Simulink automatically performs *scalar expansion*, which produces an implicit parameter vector of the same dimension as the input, and which has all elements set to the value of the block's scalar parameter. Consider the Simulink model fragment illustrated in Figure 5-12.

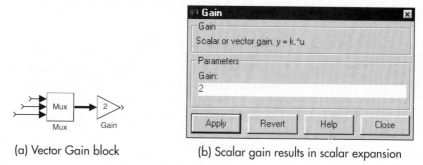

(a) Vector Gain block   (b) Scalar gain results in scalar expansion

Figure 5-12   Gain block with vector input signal

The output of the Gain block is a three-element vector in which each element is the corresponding element of the input vector multiplied by 2. Now consider Figure 5-13. Notice that the gain is the vector [2,3,4]. In this case, the first element of the output is the first element of the input multiplied by 2, the second element of the output is the second element of the input multiplied by 3, and the third element of the output is the third element of the input multi-

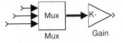

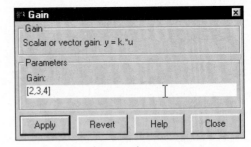

(a) Gain block with vector gain   (b) Configuring the vector gain

Figure 5-13   Gain block with vector gain

plied by 4. The initial value of the output of an Integrator block behaves the same as the value of gain of a Gain block with respect to vector signals.

Scalar expansion also applies to blocks with scalar inputs. For example, if the input to the Gain block in Figure 5-13 were a scalar signal, the output would be a three-component vector. The first component would be the input multiplied by 2, the second component would be the input multiplied by 3, and the third component would be the input multiplied by 4.

Other blocks, such as the Fcn block (Nonlinear block library), produce only scalar outputs, regardless of the input. The Block Browser describes the behavior of each block with respect to vector signals.

5.3.2 State-Space Block

The State-Space block implements a linear state-space model of a system or a portion of a system. The block dialog box has fields for each of the four linear state-space matrices (A, B, C, D as defined in Section 2.3.2), and a fifth field **Initial conditions**. Each field contains a MATLAB matrix.

Example 5-3

Consider again the spring-mass system shown in Figure 2-11. In this example we will model the impulse response of the system. Substituting in the model parameters, the equations of motion in state-space form are

$$\dot{x}_1 = x_2$$
$$\dot{x}_2 = -0.4x_1 - 0.2x_2 + 0.2\delta(t)$$

where $\delta(t)$ is the unit impulse function. The system matrix is

$$A = \begin{bmatrix} 0 & 1 \\ -0.4 & -0.2 \end{bmatrix}$$

and the input matrix is

$$B = \begin{bmatrix} 0 \\ 0.2 \end{bmatrix}$$

Define the output to be the block position,

$$C = \begin{bmatrix} 1 & 0 \end{bmatrix}$$

There is no direct transmittance, so we can also set

$$D = 0$$

We can approximate the unit impulse as a positive step function followed by a negative step:

$$\delta(t) \cong 100u(t) - 100u(t - 0.01)$$

as was illustrated in Example 4-1.

Figure 5-14 shows a Simulink model of this formulation of the equations of motion and Figure 5-15 shows the State-Space block dialog box. Note that the State-Space block includes initial conditions for each state variable.

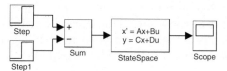

Figure 5-14   State-space model of spring-mass system

5.4   Modeling Nonlinear Systems

Simulink provides a variety of blocks for modeling nonlinear systems. These blocks are in the Nonlinear block library. The behavior of nonlinear blocks with respect to vector inputs varies. Some blocks, such as the Relay, produce vector

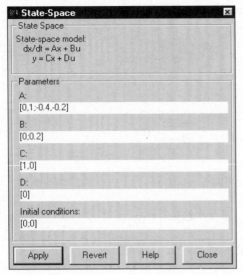

Figure 5-15   State-Space dialog box

outputs of the same dimension as the input. Other blocks produce only scalar outputs, or scalar or vector outputs depending on the dimensionality of the inputs. Consult the Block Browser for details on a particular block.

Example 5-4

To illustrate the use of several blocks from the Nonlinear block library, we will model the motion of the rocket-powered cart shown in Figure 5-16. The cart is powered by two opposing rocket motors. The controller fires the left motor if the sum of cart velocity and displacement is negative, and fires the right motor if the sum of cart velocity and displacement is positive. The objective of the controller is to bring to cart to rest at the origin. This type of control is sometimes called *bang-bang control*. (This is actually a simple example of a very powerful technique called *sliding mode control*, explained by Khalil [4].)

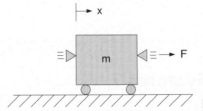

Figure 5-16   Rocket-powered cart

Assume that the cart mass is 5 slugs, and that the motor force F is 1 lb.

Continuous Systems   Chapter 5

We begin by writing the equation of motion of the cart:

$$m\ddot{x} = F$$

This is a second-order system, so two Integrator blocks are needed to solve for the cart position.

Open a new model window and copy two Integrator blocks from the Linear block library. Label the blocks as shown.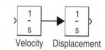

The input to the first integrator block is acceleration. Solving the equation of motion for acceleration,

$$\ddot{x} = \frac{F}{m}$$

Add a Gain block to multiply the rocket motor force by $1/m$. The input to this Gain block will be the motor force F.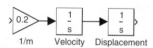

The motor force F is 1.0 if the sum of velocity and displacement is negative, and –1.0 if the sum is positive. We can build a suitable bang-bang controller using a Sum block from the Linear block library and a Sign block from the Nonlinear block library. The output of a Sign block is 1.0 if its input is positive, –1.0 if its input is negative, and 0.0 if its input is exactly 0.

Add the Sum block and Sign block and connect them as shown. The Sum block is configured with two minus signs (– –) because the motor force is to be opposite in sign to the sum of velocity and displacement.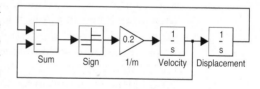

To display the results of the simulation of the model, we will use an XY Graph block to draw a *phase plot* as the simulation progresses. A phase plot is a plot of velocity versus displacement.

Drag an XY Graph block from the Sinks block library. Connect the output of the displacement Integrator to the X input (the upper input port) and the output of the velocity Integrator to the Y (lower) input port.

To display simulation time as the simulation progresses, add a Clock block from the Sources block library, and connect it to a Display block from the Sinks block library.

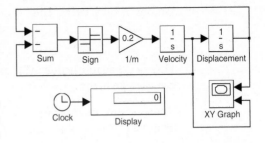

We don't know how long it will take the solution to reach the origin, so for convenience, let's add logic to the model to cause the simulation to automatically stop when the objective is reached. Specifically, we will add logic that causes the simulation to stop when the sum of the absolute values of velocity and displacement falls below a threshold value of 0.01. We can accomplish this task with a Stop Simulation block from the Sinks block library. This block forces Simulink to stop the simulation when the block's input is nonzero. We wish for the input to the Stop Simulation block to be zero until

$$|x| + |\dot{x}| \leq 0.01$$

Copy two Abs blocks from the Nonlinear block library and a Sum block from the Linear block library. Next, copy a Relational Operator block from the Nonlinear block library. Double-click on the Relational Operator block and choose <= from the **Operator** drop-down list. Add a Constant block from the Sources block library and set its value to 0.01. Finally, drag a Stop Simulation block from the Sinks block library, and connect the signal lines as shown.

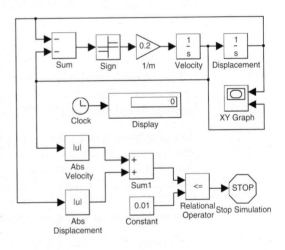

We will assume that the cart is initially at rest, displaced 1 ft to the right. So, set the **Initial condition** for the velocity Integrator block to 0, and that for the displacement Integrator block to 1.

The Sign block switches instantaneously when its input changes sign. However, any physically realizable switch takes a finite amount of time to change state. To model that behavior, we can use a fixed step size solver. Let's assume that the switch time is 0.05 sec. Choose **Simulation:Parameters** from the model window menu bar. Set the Solver options **Type** fields to Fixed-step and ODE5 (Dormand-Prince). Then, set the **Fixed step size** to 0.05. Set **Stop time** to 200.

Continuous Systems   Chapter 5

Now, we are ready to run the simulation. Choose **Simulation:Start** from the model window menu bar. The simulation will execute, and will stop when the cart is at rest at the origin. The XY Graph should appear as shown in Figure 5-17.

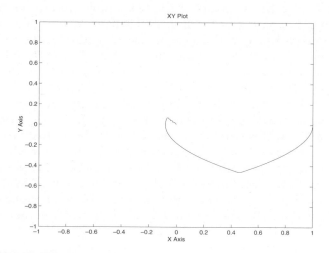

Figure 5-17   Cart phase plot

If you look closely at the phase plot, you will see that as the phase trajectory approaches the origin, it oscillates about the line $\dot{x} = -x$. This phenomenon is called *chatter* (discussed in detail by Khalil [4]). Try replacing the Sign block with a Saturation block with **Upper limit** set to 0.05 and **Lower limit** set to -0.05. Also try replacing the Sign block with a Dead Zone block, with **Start of dead zone** set to -0.05 and **End of dead zone** set to 0.05. When you use the Saturation block or Dead Zone block instead of the Sign block, you can use a variable-step solver since neither block changes instantaneously from -1.0 to $+1$.

5.4.1 Function Blocks

Two particularly useful nonlinear blocks are the Fcn (C function) block and the MATLAB Fcn block. Both blocks perform specified mathematical operations on the input, but the blocks have some important differences. Simulink evaluates the Fcn block much faster than the MATLAB Fcn block. However, the Fcn block can't perform matrix computations, use MATLAB functions, or produce a vector output. Because of the speed advantage, it is always better to use the Fcn block unless the special capabilities of the MATLAB Fcn block are needed.

Fcn Block

The Fcn block is shown in Figure 5-18. The dialog box contains a single field which contains an expression in the C language syntax. The expression operates on the elements of the block input vector, referring to the elements as u[n], where n is the desired element. If the input is a scalar, the input is referred to as u[1]. Note the use of square brackets ([and]) as in the C language, rather than parentheses, as in the MATLAB language. The block may also use as a parameter any variable currently (at the time of execution of the simulation) defined in the MATLAB workspace. If the workspace variable is a scalar, it may be referred to by its name. For example, if there is a scalar workspace variable a and two inputs to the Fcn block, a valid expression would be: a*(sin(u[1])+u[2]). If the workspace variable is a vector or matrix, it is referred to using the appropriate MATLAB (not C) syntax: A(1), or A(2,3) (Note the parentheses here.) The Fcn block can perform all the standard scalar mathematical functions such as sin, abs, atan, C syntax relational operations (==, !=, >, <, >=, <=), and C syntax logical operations (&& (logical AND), || (logical OR)). The Fcn block produces a scalar output.

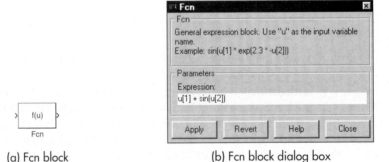

(a) Fcn block   (b) Fcn block dialog box

Figure 5-18   Fcn block

MATLAB Fcn Block

The MATLAB Fcn block is more powerful than the Fcn block in that it can perform matrix computations and produce vector outputs. However, it is also much slower than the Fcn block, and thus should be used only in situations in which the Fcn block can't be used. The MATLAB Fcn block is illustrated in Figure 5-19. The dialog box has two fields. The first may contain any valid MATLAB expression, in standard MATLAB syntax. The value of the expression is the block output. The nth element of the block input vector is referred to as u(n), similar to the Fcn block. If the function field contains a MATLAB function with no arguments (as in Figure 5-19(b)), the operation is performed on all elements of the input. The second input field specifies the dimension of the output vector.

Enter −1 if the output is to be the same width as the input. No matter whether **Output width** is specified explicitly or allowed to default to the input width, the vector dimension of the result of the expression in the **MATLAB function** field must be the same as the value specified in **Output width**.

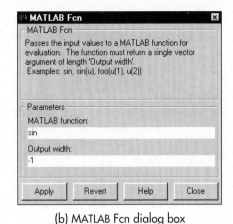

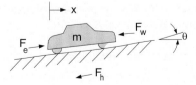

(a) MATLAB Fcn block (b) MATLAB Fcn dialog box

Figure 5-19   MATLAB Fcn block

The final continuous example will illustrate the use of nonlinear blocks to build a simple model of a car and proportional gain cruise control. The model will include aerodynamic drag, the gravity force due to climbing hills, and wind.

Example 5-5

Consider the automobile traveling on a straight, hilly road shown in Figure 5-20.

There are three forces acting on the automobile: the forward thrust produced by the engine and transmitted through the tires (or the braking force if negative) (F_e), the aerodynamic force (including wind) (F_w), and the tangential component of gravity as the automobile climbs and descends hills (F_h). Applying Newton's second law, the equation of motion of the automobile can be written

$$m\ddot{x} = F_e - F_w - F_h$$

Figure 5-20   Automobile on a hilly road

where m represents the mass of the automobile and x the distance traveled. F_e must have upper and lower bounds. The upper bound is the maximum force that the engine can transmit through the wheels to the road, and the lower bound is the maximum braking force. We will assume that $-2000 \le F_e \le 1000$, with units of lb, and that the mass is 100 slugs.

The aerodynamic force is the product of the drag coefficient (C_D), the automobile's frontal area (A), and the dynamic pressure (P), where

$$P = \frac{\rho V^2}{2}$$

and ρ represents the air density and V the sum of the automobile speed and wind speed (V_w). Assume that

$$\frac{C_D A \rho}{2} = 0.001$$

and that the wind speed varies sinusoidally with time according to the rule

$$V_w = 20\sin(0.01t)$$

so that the aerodynamic force can be approximated by

$$F_w = 0.001(\dot{x} + 20\sin(0.01t))^2$$

Next, assume that the road angle varies sinusoidally with distance according to the rule

$$\theta = 0.0093\sin(0.0001x)$$

Then the hill force is

$$F_h = 30\sin(0.0001x)$$

We will control the automobile speed using the simple proportional control law

$$F_c = K_e(\dot{x}_{desired} - \dot{x})$$

Here, F_c is the commanded engine (or braking) force, $\dot{x}_{desired}$ is the commanded speed (ft/sec), and K_e is the feedback gain. Thus, the command engine force is proportional to the speed error. The actual engine force (F_e) is, as stated earlier, bounded from above by the maximum engine thrust from below by the maximum braking force. We choose $K_e = 50$.

A Simulink model of this system is shown in Figure 5-21. We will simulate the motion of the car for 1000 sec.

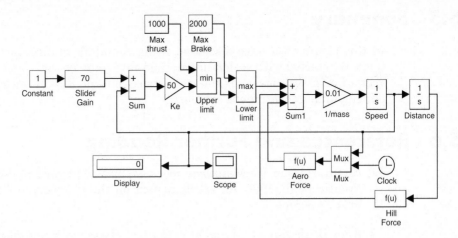

Figure 5-21 Automobile model with proportional speed control

The input to the proportional controller is the desired automobile speed in ft/sec. This is implemented with a Slider Gain block (from the Linear block library) with a constant input. Double-click the Slider Gain block to open a slider window, which allows you to vary the desired speed while the simulation runs.

The proportional controller consists of a Sum block that computes the speed error (the difference between the commanded speed and the actual speed) and a Gain block.

The upper and lower limits on engine force are imposed using MinMax blocks. The constant blocks labeled Max thrust and Max Brake together with the Min and Max blocks are used here to illustrate the use of those blocks. This part of the model could be replaced with a Saturation block from the Nonlinear block library. (Why not try that?)

The nonlinear hill and aerodynamic forces are computed by Fcn blocks. The **Expression** field of the block dialog box for the Fcn block labeled Aero Force contains 0.001*(u[1]+20*sin(0.01*u[2]))^2. The **Expression** field for the Fcn block labeled Hill Force contains 30*sin(0.0001*u[1]).

A Display block serves as a speedometer (which indicates ft/sec), and the speed is plotted using a Scope block.

This model is a good example of a slightly stiff system. To observe the effect of this stiffness, run the model using solver ODE45, then repeat the simulation using ODE15S. See Chapter 12 for a discussion of stiff systems.

5.5 Summary

In this chapter we have discussed using Simulink to model continuous systems. We started with scalar, linear, time-invariant systems, and progressed to vector linear systems using the state-space concept. Finally, we discussed modeling nonlinear continuous systems.

5.6 References and Further Reading

1. Khalil, Hassan K., *Nonlinear Systems*, 2nd ed., Upper Saddle River, N.J., Prentice Hall, 1996. An excellent text on the analysis and design of nonlinear systems.

2. Kuo, Benjamin C., *Automatic Control Systems*, Englewood Cliffs, N.J., Prentice Hall, 1995, pp. 226–230. This is a comprehensive text covering all the basics of control system analysis and design.

3. Lewis, Paul H., and Yang, Charles, *Basic Control Systems Engineering*, Upper Saddle River, N.J., Prentice Hall, 1997. This text provides an introduction to control systems analysis and design, and includes a brief introduction to Simulink. Simulink is used in many of the examples.

4. Ogata, Katsuhiko, *Modern Control Engineering*, Englewood Cliffs, N.J., Prentice Hall, 1990. This book presents a thorough coverage of the standard techniques for the analysis and design of controls for continuous systems.

5. Scheinerman, Edward C., *Invitation to Dynamical Systems*, Upper Saddle River, N.J., Prentice Hall, 1996. This text provides a good introduction to nonlinear systems.

6. Shahian, Bahram, and Hassul, Michael, *Control System Design Using MATLAB*, Englewood Cliffs, N.J., Prentice Hall, 1993. This book provides an introduction to MATLAB programming, and uses MATLAB to solve many of the standard problems in classical control and modern control theory.

7. Strum, Robert D., and Kirk, Donald E., *Contemporary Linear Systems Using MATLAB*, Boston, Mass., PWS Publishing Co., 1994. Chapter 2 provides a nice introduction to continuous systems and the state-space concept.

8. Vidyasagar, M., *Nonlinear Systems Analysis*, 2nd ed., Englewood Cliffs, N.J., Prentice Hall, 1993. This book presents a detailed coverage of the analysis of nonlinear systems.

6

Discrete-Time Systems

In this chapter we will discuss using Simulink to model discrete-time systems. First, we'll model discrete-time systems using blocks from the Linear, Discrete, and Nonlinear block libraries. Then, we'll discuss modeling hybrid systems, which include both continuous and discrete components.

6.1 Introduction

Simulink provides extensive capabilities for modeling discrete-time systems. The Discrete block library contains simple discrete blocks such as Zero- and First-Order Holds, Discrete integrators, and the Unit Delay. The Nonlinear block library contains additional blocks that are useful in discrete-time systems, such as logical operators and a Combinatorial Logic (truth table) block. Additionally, there are a number of blocks in the Linear (such as Sum and Gain) and Nonlinear (for example, Product, Sign, Fcn) block libraries that have the same purpose when used with continuous or discrete-time models. Discrete-time models may be single-rate, or they may be multirate, including offset sample times. Simulink will optionally color-code the signal lines in multirate models such that the signal line color indicates the sample period.

6.2 Scalar Linear Discrete-Time Systems

Modeling scalar linear discrete-time systems is very similar to modeling continuous systems. Discrete-time models can use the Gain and Sum blocks from the Linear block library. These blocks behave the same in discrete systems as they do in continuous systems. The Discrete block library contains the discrete analogs to the continuous Integrator and Transfer Fcn blocks. We will discuss these blocks next and show how they may be used.

Each discrete block is assumed to have a sampler at its input and a zero-order hold at its output. Discrete blocks have the additional configuration parameter **Sample time**. **Sample time** is either a scalar interval between samples, or a two-element vector consisting of the interval between samples and an offset or time skew. For example, if the block is to have a sample interval of 1.5 sec, and no offset, **Sample time** would be set to 1.5. If the sample time is to be 0.75 sec, with a 0.25 sec offset, the **Sample time** would be set to [0.75, 0.25].

All of the differential equation solvers listed in the **Simulation:Parameters Solver options** are compatible with discrete systems. A special solver, named "discrete (no continuous states)," is the best choice for purely discrete systems, because this solver is optimized for these systems.

6.2.1 Unit Delay

As discussed in Chapter 2, the Unit Delay is the fundamental discrete-time block. The output of the unit delay block is the input at the previous sample time. The unit delay represents the difference equation

$$y(k) = x(k-1) \tag{6-1}$$

where y is the output sequence and x is the input sequence. The Unit Delay block dialog box has two fields. The first field is **Initial condition**. This field contains the value of the block output at the start of the simulation. The second field is **Sample time**.

Example 6-1

In this example we will build a Simulink model for the amortization of an automobile loan, as discussed earlier in Example 2-6. At the end of each month, the loan balance $b(k)$ is the sum of the balance at the beginning of the month $(b(k-1))$ and the interest for the month $(i\,b(k))$, less the end-of-month payment $p(k)$. Thus, the balance at the end of month k is

$$b(k) = rb(k-1) - p(k)$$

where $r = 1 + i$, and i is the monthly interest rate.

Assume that the initial loan balance is \$15,000, the interest rate is 1% per month (12% annual interest), and that the monthly payment is \$200. Compute the loan balance after 100 payments.

Figure 6-1 shows a Simulink model of this system. The Unit Delay block computes $b(k$ - $1)$. The Unit Delay block **Initial condition** is the initial loan balance (15,000). The Unit Delay block **Sample time** is set to 1. Set solver type to **Fixed-step, discrete (no continuous states)**, and let **Start time** be 0, and **Stop time** be 100. After running the simulation, the Display block shows the ending balance.

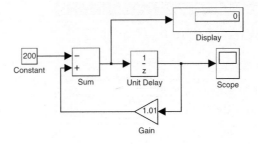

Figure 6-1   Block diagram of loan amortization

6.2.2 Discrete-Time Integrator

The Simulink Discrete-Time Integrator block can be configured to model each of the three varieties of discrete-time integrators discussed in Section 2.4.4. The Discrete-Time Integrator block dialog box is shown in Figure 6-2. The fields in this dialog box are the same as the fields for the Integrator dialog box, with two additions. For a detailed discussion of the Integrator block dialog box fields, refer to Section 5.2.1. The two additional fields are **Integrator method** and **Sample time**.

Integrator method is one of three choices: **Forward Euler, Backward Euler**, and **Trapezoidal**. Because the Discrete Integrator is a discrete block, it has a sample and zero-order hold at its input. Thus, at each time step, a Discrete integrator block has access to only two values of $u(t)$: $u(Tk)$ at its input, and $u(T(k-1))$ via a built-in unit delay.

Example 6-2

Consider the automobile loan problem of Example 2-6. The loan balance at the end of the month can be computed as

$$b(k) = b(k-1) + \int_{T(k-1)}^{Tk} (ib(k-1) - p)dt$$

Examining the integrand, we can see that this problem can be solved using forward Euler integration. Figure 6-3 shows the Simulink model revised to use a Discrete-Time Integrator block with **Integrator method** set to **Forward Euler.** The Discrete-Time Integrator block **Initial condition** is set to 15000, and **Sample time** to 1. Note that, in this case, the feedback gain is set to 0.01.

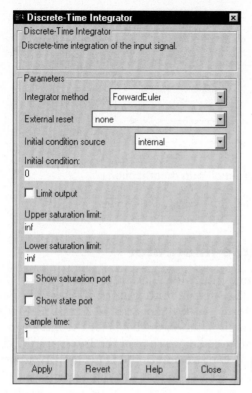

Figure 6-2 Discrete-Time Integrator
block dialog box

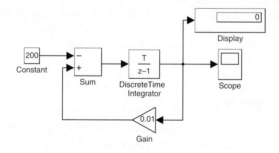

Figure 6-3 Loan amortization using a Discrete-Time Integrator block

6.2.3 Discrete Transfer Function Blocks

The Discrete block library provides three blocks that implement discrete transfer functions: Discrete Filter, Discrete Transfer Fcn, and Discrete Zero-Pole. These blocks are equivalent, differing only in the definitions of the coefficients for the numerator and denominator polynomials. The Discrete Filter block requires vectors of coefficients of polynomials of ascending powers of z^{-1}, whereas the Discrete Transfer Fcn block requires vectors of coefficients of polynomials of descending powers of z. Thus, these blocks are identical, differing only in the way the transfer function is displayed on the block icon. The Discrete Zero-Pole block requires vectors of zeros (numerator) and poles (denominator) of the transfer function and a gain that scales the transfer function.

Example 6-3

Control systems frequently contain filters to remove high-frequency noise from input signals. The MATLAB Signal Processing Toolbox provides a variety of filter design algorithms. You can include a filter designed using MATLAB in a Simulink model using a Discrete Transfer Fcn block.

Suppose we are designing a control system with a noisy sinusoidal input, and we need to filter out the noise. The sampling period is 0.1 sec, and we wish to remove signals with a frequency higher than 1.0 Hz. Design a fourth-order Butterworth filter using the MATLAB command butter as shown in Figure 6-4. The first argument to butter is the filter order and the second argument is the cutoff frequency ω_m, where $0 < \omega_m < 1$ (and where 1 corresponds to one-half the sample rate). So here, ω_m = 1 Hz / 5 Hz = 0.2 (See Orfanidis [4] to learn about digital filters.)

```
» [B,A]=butter(4,0.2)
B =
     0.0048     0.0193     0.0289     0.0193     0.0048
A =
     1.0000    -2.3695     2.3140    -1.0547     0.1874
```

Figure 6-4   Designing a Butterworth filter

We can test the filter with the Simulink model shown in Figure 6-5. The top Sine Wave block is configured to a frequency of 0.5 rad/sec and an amplitude of 1. The lower Sine Wave block is configured to a frequency of 10 rad/sec and an amplitude of 0.4, and represents the unwanted high-frequency noise. The Discrete Transfer Fcn block field **Numerator** contains the vector [0.0048 0.0193 0.0289 0.0193 0.0048] and **Denominator** contains [1.0000 −2.3695

2.3140 −1.0547 0.1874]. **Sample time** contains 0.1. The model is configured to use the discrete solver since there are no continuous states. **Stop time** is set to 20. The Mux block creates a vector signal containing the unfiltered input and the filtered output of the Discrete Transfer Fcn block. Scope block field **Save data to workspace** is checked. After running the simulation, the MATLAB commands shown in Figure 6-6 are used to plot the filtered and unfiltered output signal, resulting in the plots shown in Figure 6-7.

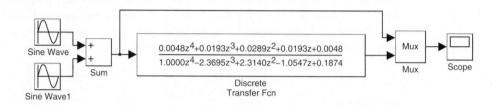

Figure 6-5   Simulink model to test filter

```
» t = ScopeData(:,1) ;
» y_raw = ScopeData(:,2) ;
» y_filt = ScopeData(:,3) ;
» subplot(2,1,1)
» plot(t,y_raw);
» title('Unfiltered Signal')
» grid
» subplot(2,1,2)
» plot(t,y_filt);
» title('Filtered Signal')
» xlabel('Time (sec)')
» grid
```

Figure 6-6   MATLAB commands to plot filtered signal

6.3 Logical Blocks

The Logical Operator and Combinatorial Logic blocks found in the Nonlinear Block library are also useful in modeling discrete-time systems. These are discrete rather than discrete-time blocks since they have neither samplers at their inputs nor zero-order holds at their outputs. In fact, these blocks can be used in continuous models, although they are more commonly used in discrete-

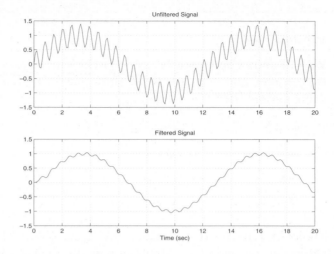

Figure 6-7   Filtering a noisy signal

time models. The Logical Operator block can be configured to perform any of the following logical operations: AND, OR, NAND, NOR, XOR, NOT. The Logical Operator block can be configured to accept any number of inputs. If the input signals are vectors, each must be of the same size, and the output will also be a vector.

The Combinatorial Logic block implements a truth table. The input to the Combinatorial Logic block is a vector of n elements. The truth table must have 2^n rows, arranged such that the values of a row's inputs provide an index into the table. The first element in the input vector is the leftmost column in this binary index. Thus, if there is a single input, there will be two rows, the first corresponding to an input of 0, the second corresponding to an input of 1 (or any non-zero number). If there are two inputs, there must be four rows in the table. The block parameter, **Truth table**, consists of one or more column vectors, in which each row represents the block output corresponding to the row's index. Each column in **Truth table** produces a different output, and thus a single Combinatorial Logic block can implement multiple logical operations. The block outputs do not have to be 0 or 1; any number is acceptable.

Example 6-4

We will build Combinatorial Logic blocks that implement the three following expressions, and compare these three blocks with equivalent models built using Logical Operator blocks

Expression	Equivalent
$\bar{a}$	NOT a
ab	a AND b
$ab + bc$	(a AND b) OR (b AND c)

The truth table for the $\bar{a}$ is shown in Figure 6-8(a). The corresponding **Truth table** parameter is the output column, entered as [1;0]. A Simulink model that implements this expression using both Logical Operator blocks and a Combinatorial Logic block is shown in Figure 6-8(b).

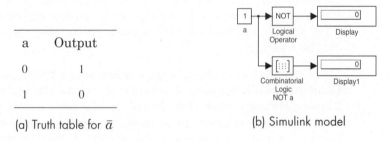

a	Output
0	1
1	0

(a) Truth table for $\bar{a}$

(b) Simulink model

Figure 6-8   NOT expression

The truth table for ab is shown in Figure 6-9(a). Note that we have chosen a to be the leftmost column, thus the input vector to the block must be [a,b]. The block **Truth table** parameter is the same as the output column, [0;0;0;1]. Figure 6-9(b) shows a Simulink model that implements ab using both Logical Operator blocks and a Combinatorial Logic block. The input vector is composed using a Mux block such that the components are in the order [a,b].

The final combinatorial logic expression, $ab + bc$, has the truth table shown in Figure 6-10(a). Examining the output column, the **Truth table** parameter is [0;0;0;1;0;0;1;1]. Figure 6-10(b) implements the expression $ab + bc$ using both Logical Operator blocks and a Combinatorial Logic block.

a	b	Output
0	0	0
0	1	0
1	0	0
1	1	1

(a) Truth table for ab

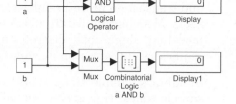

(b) Simulink model

Figure 6-9   AND expression

a	b	c	Output
0	0	0	0
0	0	1	0
0	1	0	0
0	1	1	1
1	0	0	0
1	0	1	0
1	1	0	1
1	1	1	1

(a) Truth table of $ab + bc$

(b) Simulink model

Figure 6-10   Model of the expression $ab + bc$

6.4   Vector Discrete-Time Systems

The Discrete block library provides a Discrete State-Space block as defined in Section 2.5. The use of this block is completely analogous to the State-Space block discussed in 5.3.2.

6.5   Multirate Discrete-Time Systems

Many discrete-time systems involve subsystems that operate at different rates, and with phase differences as well. For example, a typical computer has numerous discrete subsystems including the central processing unit, serial and parallel interface controllers, disk drive and video controllers, and input devices such as the keyboard and mouse. Models of communications systems and transaction processes also consist of subsystems that operate at different rates. Modeling multirate discrete-time systems with Simulink is similar to modeling single-rate discrete-time systems. However, multirate systems require careful attention to sample times and offsets.

Simulink's sample time colors capability provides help in keeping track of sample times. This capability will automatically color-code blocks and signal lines corresponding to up to five different values of sample time. To activate this feature, choose **Format:Sample Time Colors**. If you change the model after activating sample time colors, choose **Edit:Update Diagram** to update the colors. Table 6-1 lists the sample time colors and their meanings.

Table 6-1 Sample time colors

Color	Meaning
Black	Continuous blocks
Magenta	Constant blocks (used with Real-Time Workshop)
Yellow	Hybrid (groups of blocks with varying sample times or mixed continuous and discrete elements)
Red	Fastest discrete sample time
Green	Second fastest discrete sample time
Blue	Third fastest discrete sample time
Light blue	Fourth fastest discrete sample time
Dark green	Fifth fastest discrete sample time
Cyan	Triggered sample time (Used with triggered subsystems. See Chapter 6.)

Inherently continuous blocks (such as integrators) and inherently discrete blocks (such as unit delays) are assigned colors using the definitions in Table 6-1. Signal lines and blocks that are neither inherently continuous nor discrete (such as Gain blocks) are assigned colors based on the sample times of their inputs. Thus, if a signal line is carrying the output of an Integrator, it will be black, and if it is carrying the output of a Unit Delay, it will be colored according to the sample time of the Unit Delay. If the input to a block (such as a Sum block) consists of several signals such that the sample times of all signals are integer multiples of the sample time of the fastest signal, the block is colored corresponding to the fastest signal. If the sample times are not integer multiples of the fastest signal, the block is colored black.

Only the five fastest discrete sample times are assigned unique colors. If there are more than five sample times, all blocks sampled slower than the fifth fastest sample time are colored yellow.

Note that Simulink does not provide a mechanism to help identify phase relationships among blocks. If there are portions of a model with the same sample time, but different values for sample offset (phase), you must keep track of the phase manually.

Example 6-5

Control systems for discrete processes frequently operate at a lower frequency than the update frequency of the process, usually due to limitations of computer speed. Additionally, display systems usually are updated at a frequency sufficiently low such that the display is readable. As a simple example of a multirate system, suppose that some process to be controlled behaves according to the following discrete state-space equations:

$$x_1(k+1) = x_1(k) + 0.1x_2(k)$$
$$x_2(k+1) = -0.05\sin x_1(k) + 0.094x_2(k) + u(k)$$

where $u(k)$ is the input. The process is assumed to have a sample time of 0.1 sec. We will control the process using proportional control with a sample time of 0.25 sec, and update the display every 0.5 sec. A Simulink model of this system appears in Figure 6-11. The model is annotated to indicate the colors of the signal lines and blocks.

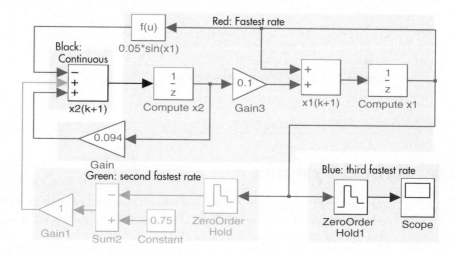

Figure 6-11   Multirate system

The blocks in the section of the model with the red signal lines are configured with a sample time of 0.1 sec. This section represents the process dynamics.

The section with green signal lines models the controller. This is a proportional controller. The Zero-Order Hold block causes the controller to update at its sample interval of 0.25 sec. The controller produces an output signal that is proportional to the difference between the setpoint (here 0.75) and the value of the input to the Zero-Order Hold (x_1)at the most recent sample time.

The section with the blue signal lines models the display device, here a Scope block. The Zero-Order Hold in this section is configured with a sample time of 0.5 sec.

Running the simulation results in the trajectory shown in Figure 6-12.

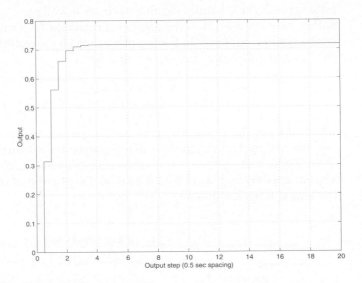

Figure 6-12   Multirate system output

6.6 Hybrid Systems

As discussed in Section 2.7, *hybrid systems* consist of both discrete and continuous components. Modeling hybrid systems in Simulink is straightforward, as illustrated in the following example.

Discrete-Time Systems   Chapter 6

Example 6-6

To illustrate the construction of a hybrid model, let's replace the continuous controller in Example 5-5 with a discrete proportional-integral-derivative (PID) controller with a sample time of 0.5 sec.

Figure 6-13 illustrates a continuous PID controller. The controller consists of three sections, each of which operates on the difference (v) between the plant output and the commanded value of the plant output. The proportional section produces a signal proportional to the difference between the commanded value of the system output and the actual value. Thus, the output of the proportional section is

$$u_p = K_p v$$

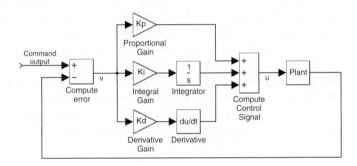

Figure 6-13   Continuous PID controller

The integral section of a PID controller is intended to remove the steady-state error. This component produces an output that is proportional to the time integral of the error signal:

$$u_i = K_i \int_0^t v \, dt$$

One problem with the integral section is that if the plant's response to changes in the input signal (u) is relatively slow, u_i can grow rapidly. This phenomenon is called *wind-up*. Wind-up can be avoided by placing upper and lower bounds on the value of u_i.

The derivative section of a PID controller provides damping. Its output is proportional to the rate of change of v:

$$u_d = K_d \dot{v}$$

A discrete PID controller replaces the integral section with a discrete integrator and the derivative section with a discrete approximation to a derivative block. For a detailed discussion of discrete PID controllers, refer to Ogata [3]. A first-order numerical derivative approximation is

$$u_d(k) \approx \frac{v(k) - v(k-1)}{T}$$

The transfer function of this derivative approximation is

$$\frac{U_d(z)}{V(z)} = \frac{K_d}{T}\left(\frac{z-1}{z}\right)$$

Figure 6-14 shows a Simulink model of an automobile using a discrete PID controller with $K_p = 50$, $K_i = 0.75$, and $K_d = 75$. The model is identical to the model in Example 5-5, except for the controller. The proportional part of the controller consists of a Zero-Order hold and a proportional Gain block. The proportional gain (50) in this controller is the same as the proportional gain in the continuous proportional controller in Example 5-5. The integral part of the PID controller consists of a Discrete-Time Integrator block and a Gain block (set to 0.75). In the Discrete-Time Integrator block, we selected **Limit output**, and set the saturation limits to ± 100 to control wind-up. The derivative part of the controller is constructed using a Discrete Transfer Fcn block and a Gain block (set to 75). In this example, the simulation was configured to run for 1000 sec, and the Slider Gain was set to command a speed of 80 ft/sec. The Scope display is shown in Figure 6-15.

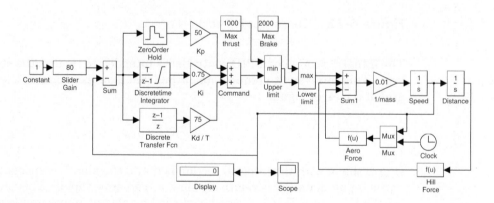

Figure 6-14   Car model with discrete controller

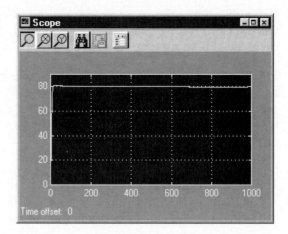

Figure 6-15   Car speed controller performance

6.7   Summary

In this chapter we have discussed using Simulink to model discrete-time systems. We started with scalar linear discrete-time systems, discussing the Unit Delay, Discrete-Time Integrator, and Discrete Transfer Fcn blocks in particular. We briefly discussed vector discrete systems. We concluded with discussions of multirate discrete-time systems and hybrid systems.

6.8   References and Further Reading

1. Kuo, Benjamin C., *Automatic Control Systems,* 7th ed., Englewood Cliffs, N.J., Prentice Hall, 1995, pp. 839–840. This text covers both continuous and discrete control systems design and includes lots of practical examples, including MATLAB scripts. Although Simulink is not used, the block diagrams are easily converted to Simulink models.

2. Ogata, Katsuhiko, *Designing Linear Control Systems with MATLAB*, Englewood Cliffs, N.J., Prentice Hall, 1993, pp. 50–67. This book presents brief tutorials and MATLAB implementations of several important linear systems design techniques, including pole placement, state observers, and linear quadratic regulators.

3. Ogata, Katsuhiko, *Discrete-Time Control Systems*, 2nd ed., Englewood Cliffs, N.J., Prentice Hall, 1994, pp. 114–118.

4. Orfanidis, Sophocles J., *Introduction to Signal Processing*, Englewood Cliffs, N.J., Prentice Hall, 1996, pp 605-614. This book provides detailed coverage of Z-transforms, transfer functions, and digital filter design.

5. Phillips, Charles L., and Nagle, H. Troy, *Digital Control System Analysis and Design*, 3rd ed., Englewood Cliffs, N.J., Prentice Hall, 1995. This book provides a comprehensive coverage of discrete-time control systems analysis and design. It presents many practical examples, and makes good use of MATLAB.

6. Shahian, Bahram, and Hassul, Michael, *Control System Design Using MATLAB*, Englewood Cliffs, N.J., Prentice Hall, 1993. This book provides an introduction to MATLAB programming, and uses MATLAB to solve many of the standard problems in classical control and modern control theory.

7. Strum, Robert D., and Kirk, Donald E., *Contemporary Linear Systems Using MATLAB*, Boston, Mass., PWS Publishing Co., 1994.

Subsystems and Masking

In this chapter, we will explore some of the ways we can use Simulink to model more complex systems. We will build hierarchical models and develop custom Simulink blocks called masked blocks. We will also discuss conditionally executed subsystems, which can make Simulink models much more efficient.

7.1 Introduction

In the preceding chapters, we discussed the basics of building Simulink models for continuous, discrete, and hybrid systems. Using the procedures we covered in the proceeding chapters, it is possible to model any physical system. However, as your Simulink models become more complex, additional Simulink capabilities and programming techniques can make the models easier to develop, to understand, and to maintain. In this chapter, we'll start with a discussion of Simulink subsystems, which provide a capability within Simulink similar to subprograms in traditional programming languages. Next, you'll learn to use masking to make subsystems easier to use and understand. Last, we will discuss conditionally executed subsystems, which facilitate the development of models with multiple modes or phases of operation.

7.2 Simulink Subsystems

Most engineering programming languages include the capability to employ *subprograms*. In FORTRAN, there are subroutine subprograms and function subprograms. C subprograms are called functions; MATLAB subprograms are called function M-files. Simulink provides an analogous capability called *subsystems*. There are two important reasons for using subprograms: abstraction and software reuse.

As models grow larger and more complex, they can easily become difficult to understand and maintain. Subsystems solve this problem by breaking a large model into a hierarchical set of smaller models. As a simple example, consider the automobile model of Example 5-5. The Simulink model is repeated in Figure 7-1. The model consists of two main parts: the automobile dynamics and the controller. Examining the model, it is not clear which blocks represent the automobile dynamics, and which blocks constitute the controller. In Figure 7-2,

7-2, we have converted the automobile and controller portions of the model into subsystems. In this version, the conceptual structure is clear in the top level of the model Figure 7-2, but the details of the controller and automobile dynamics are hidden in the subsystems (Figure 7-3). This hierarchical structure is an example of software abstraction.

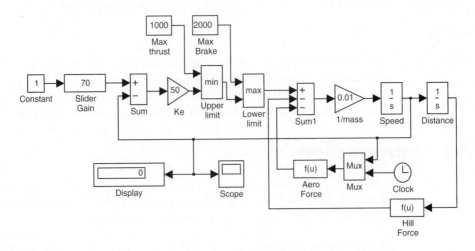

Figure 7-1 Automobile model with proportional speed control

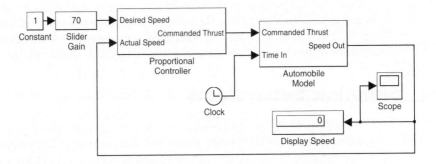

Figure 7-2 Hierarchical automobile model

Subsystems can also be viewed as reusable model components. Suppose that we wish to compare several different controller designs using the same automobile dynamics model. Rather than building a complete new block diagram each time, it is more convenient to build only the part of the model that is new each time—the controller. Not only does this save time building the model, but it also ensures that we are using exactly the same automobile dynamics. An important advantage of software reuse is that once we have verified that a subsystem is correct, we don't have to repeat the testing and debugging process

Subsystems and Masking   Chapter 7

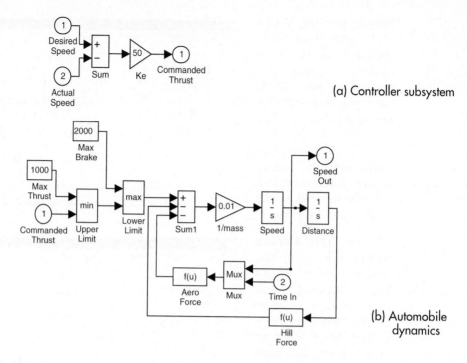

(a) Controller subsystem

(b) Automobile dynamics

Figure 7-3   Hierarchical automobile model subsystems

each time we use the subsystem in a new model. Subsystems greatly simplify the task of modeling physical systems that contain several instances of a particular component, such as, for example, the four tire models that would be required to model the ride characteristics of an automobile.

There are two methods to build Simulink subsystems. The first method is to encapsulate a portion of an existing model in a subsystem using **Edit:Create Subsystem**. The second method is to use a Subsystem block from the Connections block library. We'll discuss both methods.

7.2.1   Encapsulating a Subsystem

To encapsulate a portion of an existing Simulink model into a subsystem, proceed as follows:

Select all the blocks and signal lines to be included in the subsystem using a bounding box. *Note that you must use a bounding box in this instance.* It is frequently necessary to rearrange some blocks so that you can enclose only the desired blocks in the bounding box.

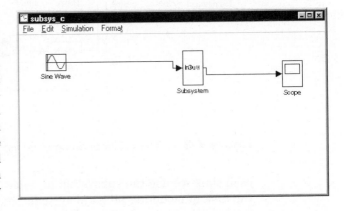

Choose **Edit:Create Subsystem** from the model window menu bar. Simulink will replace the selected blocks with a Subsystem block with an input port for each signal entering the new subsystem, and an output port for each signal leaving the new subsystem.

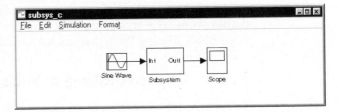

Simulink will assign default names to the input and output ports.

Resize the Subsystem block so that the port labels are readable, and rearrange the model as desired.

To view or edit the subsystem, double-click the block. A new window will appear, containing the subsystem. In addition to the original blocks, an Inport block is added for the signal entering the subsystem, and an Outport block is added for the signal exiting the subsystem. Changing the labels on these ports changes the labels on the new block's icon. Click the control to close the subsystem window when you've finished editing the subsystem.

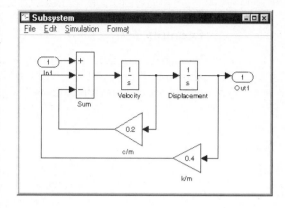

Edit:Create Subsystem does not have an inverse operation. Once you encapsulate a group of blocks into a subsystem, there is no menu choice to reverse the process. Therefore, it is a good idea to save the model before creating the subsystem. If you decide you don't want to accept the newly created subsystem, close the model window without saving, then reopen the model. To manually reverse the encapsulation of a subsystem, copy the subsystem to a new model window, open the subsystem, then copy the blocks from the subsystem window to the original model window.

7.2.2 Subsystem Blocks

If, when building a model, you know that you will need a subsystem, you may find it convenient to build the subsystem in a subsystem window directly. This eliminates the need to rearrange the blocks that will compose the subsystem to fit in a bounding box. It also avoids having to tidy up the model window after the subsystem is encapsulated.

To create a new subsystem using a Subsystem block, drag a Subsystem block from the Connections block library to the model window. Double-click the Subsystem block. The subsystem window will appear. Build the subsystem using the standard procedures for constructing a model. Use Inport blocks for all signals entering the subsystem, and Outport blocks for all signals leaving the subsystem. If desired, change the labels on the Inport and Outport blocks to identify the purpose of each input and output. Close the subsystem window when you've finished building the subsystem. Note that you do not need to choose **File:Save** before closing the subsystem window; the subsystem is part of the model in which the subsystem is created, and is saved when that model is saved.

Example 7-1

We wish to model the spring-mass system composed of carts connected as shown in Figure 7-4. We will build the model from subsystem blocks that model each cart as shown in Figure 7-5.

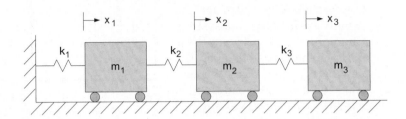

Figure 7-4   Spring-mass system

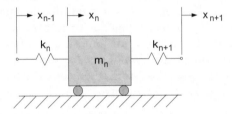

Figure 7-5   Single-cart model

The equation of motion for a single cart is

$$\ddot{x}_n = \frac{1}{m_n}[k_n(x_{n-1} - x_n) + k_{n+1}(x_n - x_{n+1})]$$

Using the procedure discussed in Section 7.2.2, construct the subsystem as shown in Figure 7-6. This subsystem will model cart 1. The inputs to the single cart subsystem are x_{n-1} (position of the cart to the left) and x_{n+1} (position of the cart to the right). The subsystem output is x_n (position of cart). Notice that each spring is referenced in two subsystem blocks, one for the cart to the right of the spring, and one for the cart to the left.

Once the subsystem is complete, close the subsystem window. Make two copies of the subsystem block, and connect the blocks as shown in Figure 7-7.

It is convenient in this case to enter the spring constants (k1, k2, k3) and cart masses (m1, m2, m3) as MATLAB variables, and assign values to the variables using a MATLAB script M-file (which we named set_x4a.m), as shown in

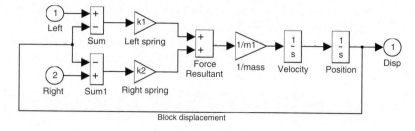

Figure 7-6   Cart model subsystem for cart 1

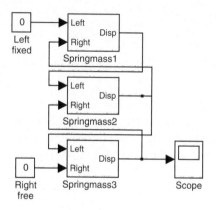

Figure 7-7   Three-cart model using subsystems

Figure 7-8. Execute this script M-file from the MATLAB prompt before running the simulation. (Note that the script M-file (extension .m) must have a name that is different from the name of the Simulink model. For example, if the Simulink model is named examp_1.mdl, and you name the script M-file examp_1.m, MATLAB will open the Simulink model when you enter the command examp_1 at the MATLAB prompt.)

The block parameters for each block in each copy of the subsystem must now be set. For cart 1 set the value of **Gain** for the Gain block labeled Left Spring to k1, and for Gain block Right Spring to k2. Next, set **Gain** for the Gain block labeled 1/mass to 1/m1. Initialize the Velocity Integrator block to 0, and the Position Integrator block to 1.

For cart 2, set the value of **Gain** for the Gain block labeled Left Spring to k2, and for Gain block Right Spring to k3. Next, set **Gain** for the Gain block labeled 1/mass to 1/m2. Initialize the Velocity Integrator block to 0, and the Position Integrator block to 0.

For cart 3, set the value of **Gain** for the Gain block labeled Left Spring to k3, and for Gain block Right Spring to 0 since there is no right spring for this cart. Next, set **Gain** for the Gain block labeled 1/mass to 1/m3. Initialize the Velocity Integrator block to 0, and the Position Integrator block to 0.

```
% Set the spring constants and block mass values
k1 = 1 ;
k2 = 2 ;
k3 = 4 ;
m1 = 1 ;
m2 = 3 ;
m3 = 2 ;
```

Figure 7-8   MATLAB script set_x4a.m to initialize spring constants

We configured the Scope block to save the scope data to the workspace, and set the simulation **Start time** to 0 and **Stop time** to 100. After running the simulation, the scope data was plotted from within MATLAB, resulting in the trajectory plot for cart 3 shown in Figure 7-9.

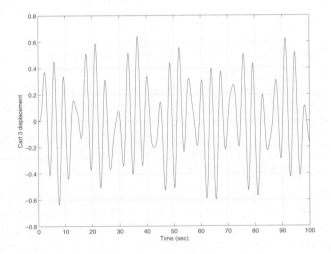

Figure 7-9   Trajectory of cart 3

7.3 Masked Blocks

Masking is a Simulink capability that extends the concept of abstraction. Masking permits us to treat a subsystem as if it were a simple block. A masked block may have a custom icon, and it may also have a dialog box in which configuration parameters are entered in the same way parameters are entered for blocks in the Simulink block libraries. The configuration parameters may be used directly to initialize the blocks in the underlying subsystem, or they may be used to compute data to initialize the blocks.

To understand the concept of masking, consider the model shown in Figure 7-10(a). This model is equivalent to the model in Example 7-1, but it is easier to use. Double-clicking the block labeled Spring-mass 1 opens the dialog box shown in Figure 7-10(b). Instead of opening the dialog box for each Gain block and each Integrator to set the block parameters, you can enter all the parameters for each subsystem in the subsystem's dialog box. The dialog box in Figure 7-10(b) "masks" a subsystem that is nearly identical to the subsystem in Figure 7-6.

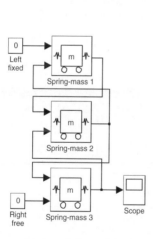

(a) Simulink model

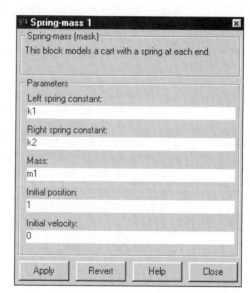

(b) Dialog box for Spring-mass 1

Figure 7-10 3-cart model using masked subsystems

In this section, we will explain the steps in creating a masked subsystem. The examples will show how to create the spring-mass masked subsystem. Additional examples will illustrate other masking features.

The process of producing a masked block can be summarized as follows:

1. Build a subsystem using the procedures discussed in Section 7.2.

2. Select the subsystem block, then choose **Edit:Mask Subsystem** from the model window menu bar.

3. Using the Mask Editor, set up the mask documentation and dialog box and, optionally, build a custom icon.

7.3.1 Converting a Subsystem into a Masked Subsystem

The first step in creating a masked subsystem is to create a subsystem using the procedures described in Section 7.2. To illustrate the process, let's build a spring-mass masked block starting with one of the subsystems in the model in Figure 7-7.

Open the model shown in Figure 7-7. Next, open a new model window. Drag a copy of the block labeled Spring-mass 1 to the new model window.

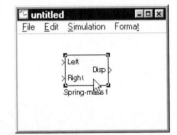

Select the block, then choose **Edit:Mask Subsystem** from the new model window menu bar.

The Mask Editor dialog box will appear. Note that the Mask Editor has three tabbed pages. We will discuss each page in the following subsections.

Before proceeding, save the new model window using the name spm_msk.

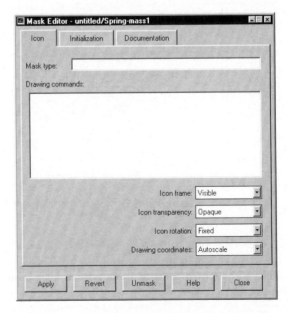

7.3.2 Mask Editor Documentation Page

The Documentation page is illustrated in Figure 7-11(a). The page consists of three fields, which in Figure 7-11(a) have been filled in for the Spring-mass block. All fields in the Documentation page are optional.

After filling in the fields as shown, select **Close**. Then, double-click the Spring-mass block, opening the dialog box shown in Figure 7-11(b). You can return to the Mask Editor by selecting the block, then choosing **Edit:Edit Mask** from the model window menu bar.

We will discuss each field in the Documentation page next.

Mask type field

The contents of the first field, **Mask type**, will be displayed as the block type in the masked block's dialog box. Notice that there are two labels in the upper left corner of the block dialog box (Figure 7-11(b)). The label in the window title bar (here Spring-mass1) is the label of the currently selected block. The label inside the dialog box (here Spring-mass) is the block type. Every instance of this new block will have the same block type, but each instance in a particular model must have a different label. Also, note the word mask in parentheses appended to block type, indicating that this is a masked block. (Compare the masked block dialog box to the dialog box for a block from a block library.)

Block description field

The second field, **Block description**, is displayed in a bordered area at the top of the masked block's dialog box. This area should contain a brief description of the block's purpose, and any needed reminders concerning the use of the block.

Block help

The third field, **Block help**, will be displayed by the MATLAB Help system when the masked block's dialog box Help button is pressed. This field should contain detailed information concerning the use, configuration, and limitations of the masked block and the underlying subsystem.

7.3.3 Mask Editor Initialization Page

The Initialization page (Figure 7-12) is used to set parameters of blocks in the subsystem underlying the masked block. The Initialization page can be divided into three sections. The top section contains the **Mask type** field. The center section contains a set of fields that define the fields in the masked block's dialog box, and which define a local variable corresponding to each field in the masked block's dialog box. The bottom section contains the **Initialization**

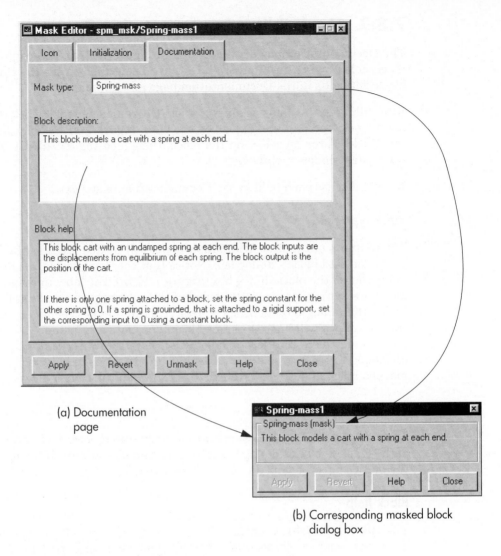

(a) Documentation page

(b) Corresponding masked block dialog box

Figure 7-11   Mask Editor Documentation page

commands field, which can be used to define additional variables to set parameters in the block dialog box or to be used on the Icon page (to be discussed later). We will describe each section.

Mask type field

The top section of the page contains the **Mask type** field, which is identical to the **Mask type** field on the Documentation page. **Mask type** may be entered

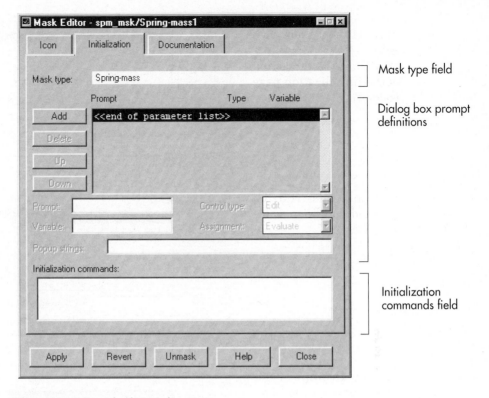

Figure 7-12 Blank Initialization page

or edited on this page, or on the other Mask Editor pages. Changing **Mask type** on one page changes it on the other pages as well.

Block Dialog Box Prompt Section

The center section of the Mask Editor Initialization page is used to create, edit, and delete dialog box fields. This section consists of a scrolling list of dialog box fields, buttons to add, delete, and move fields, and five fields used to configure the block dialog box. To add the first prompt field in the Spring-mass block dialog box, proceed as follows:

Select the block, then open the Mask Editor by choosing **Edit:Edit Mask** from the model window menu bar. Select the Initialization page.

Click <<end of parameter list>>, then click **Add**. (Note that here only the Prompt section of the Initialization page is shown.)

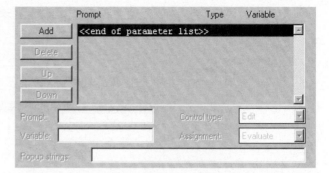

A blank line will be inserted in the parameter list.

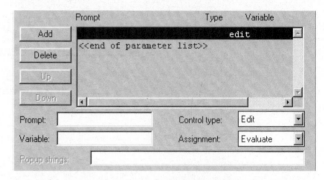

In the **Prompt** field, enter Left spring constant.

In the **Variable field**, enter k_left.

Notice that the prompt and the variable name are displayed in the parameter list. You'll have to scroll the parameter list to the right to see all of k_left.

Choose **Close**.

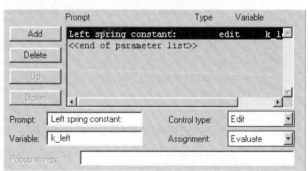

Double-click the Spring-mass sub-system. The block dialog box now has a prompt. The value entered in the field corresponding to the prompt will be assigned to MATLAB variable k_left.

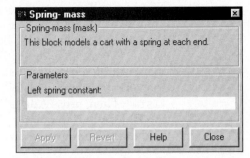

Add prompt Right spring constant with variable k_right, prompt Mass with variable mass, prompt Initial position with variable x0, and prompt Initial velocity with variable x_dot0.

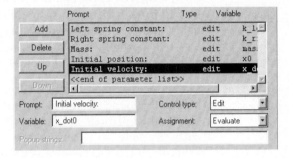

That completes the process of creating the dialog box fields. To see the results, press **Close** to save the changes and exit the Mask Editor.

Double-click the Spring-mass block, opening the block dialog box, which should look like this.

Now, we will discuss in more detail the buttons and fields in the dialog box prompt section of the Mask Editor. First, notice that there are four buttons on the left side of the dialog box prompt section. These buttons are used to add, delete, and arrange dialog box prompts. To create a new field, click the line in the scrolling parameter list of the item you wish to follow the new field. If you wish for the new field to be the bottom field, click on <<end of parameter list>>. Then, press **Add**. A blank line will appear in the scrolling list. Pressing the **Delete** button deletes the selected field. **Up** and **Down** move the selected field in the appropriate direction in the list of fields.

Field **Control type** is a drop-down list with three options: **Edit**, **Checkbox**, and **Popup**. **Edit** produces a field in which data is entered (a fill-in-the-blank field), and is the most common type of field. **Check box** generates a field that has two possible values, depending on whether or not the box is checked. **Popup** produces a list of choices set in **Popup strings**.

The value assigned to the internal variable associated with a block dialog box field will depend upon the contents of the **Assignment** field. **Assignment** may be set to **Evaluate** or **Literal**. If **Evaluate** is chosen, the variable associated with the field will contain the value of the expression in the field. So, for example, if the field contains k1, and in the MATLAB workspace k1 is assigned the value 2.0, the variable associated with the dialog field will be assigned the value 2.0. If **Literal** is chosen, the variable associated with the dialog field will contain the character string 'k1'.

Setting **Control type** to **Checkbox** produces a checkbox field. The variable associated with a checkbox field will be assigned a value depending on the setting of **Assignment**. If **Assignment** is **Evaluate**, the variable associated with the field will be set to 0 if not checked, or 1 if checked. If **Assignment** is **Literal**, the variable associated with the field will be set to 'no' if not checked, and 'yes' if checked.

Example 7-2

Suppose we wish to configure a masked subsystem such that its block dialog box has a checkbox allowing the user to specify that angular inputs are to be in degrees rather than radians. The value of the variable associated with the checkbox (c_stat) is to be 0 if the box is not checked, and 1 if the box is checked. Figure 7-13(a) shows the Mask Editor prompt section configured to accomplish this task, and Figure 7-13(b) shows the corresponding masked block dialog box. In this example, set **Mask type** to Check box example, and **Block description** (on the Documentation page) to This block illustrates a check box.

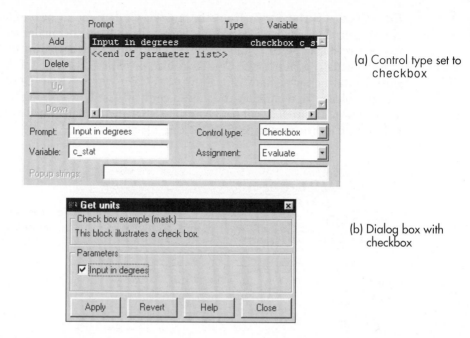

(a) Control type set to checkbox

(b) Dialog box with checkbox

Figure 7-13   Check box field

If **Control type** is set to **Popup**, the field **Popup strings** is used to define a list of choices, as will be shown in Example 7-3. The variable associated with a popup field will be assigned a value depending upon the setting of **Assignment**. If **Assignment** is set to **Evaluate**, the variable associated with the field will be set to the ordinal number of the selected popup choice. So, for example, if the first choice is selected, the value of the variable will be set to 1. If the second choice is selected, the value of the variable will be set to 2, and so on. If **Assignment** is set to **Literal**, the variable will contain the character string corresponding to the selected choice. The list of choices for a popup field is set in **Popup strings**. The choices are entered in sequence, separated with the pipe symbol (|). For example, if the choices are to be Very hot, Hot, Warm, Cool, and Cold, **Popup strings** should contain Very hot|Hot|Warm|Cool|Cold.

Example 7-3

Suppose we wish to create a masked block that produces an output signal defined by a popup list containing choices Very hot, Hot, Warm, Cool, and Cold. To do this, open a new model, then drag a Constant block into the model window. Select the Constant block using a bounding box, then choose

Edit:Create Subsystem from the model window menu bar. Select the new subsystem, then choose **Edit:Mask Subsystem** from the model window menu bar. Set **Mask type** to Popup example, and **Block description** to This block illustrates a popup list. Configure the prompt section of the Mask Editor Initialization page as shown in Figure 7-14(a). Choose **Close**. Double-click the masked block, then click on the popup control. The block dialog box should be as shown in Figure 7-14(b). In Example 7-6 we will show how to configure the **Initialization commands** field for this block.

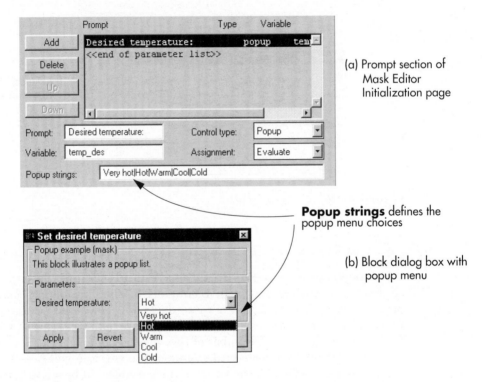

(a) Prompt section of Mask Editor Initialization page

Popup strings defines the popup menu choices

(b) Block dialog box with popup menu

Figure 7-14   Popup menu

Initialization commands

The bottom section of the Initialization page is the field **Initialization commands**. This field can contain one or more MATLAB statements that assign values to MATLAB variables used to configure blocks in the masked subsystem. The MATLAB statements may use any of MATLAB's operators, built-in or user written functions, and control flow statements such as if, while, and end. The scope of variables in the **Initialization commands** field is local; variables defined in the MATLAB workspace are not accessible.

The **Initialization commands** field displays only four lines, but may contain many lines. You can move up and down in the field using the cursor keys.

Each command in the **Initialization commands** field should normally be terminated with a semicolon (;). If you omit the semicolon for a command, the results of the command will be displayed in the MATLAB window whenever the command is executed. This provides a convenient means to debug the commands.

Example 7-4

The Spring-mass block icon will need two wheels. To prepare to draw the wheels, create two vectors, one con-

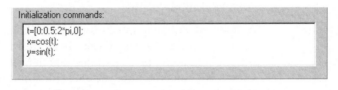

Initialization commands:

```
t=[0:0.5:2*pi,0];
x=cos(t);
y=sin(t);
```

taining the *x* coordinates of a small circle, and the other the *y* coordinates. These variables will be used in the Icon page to draw the wheels.

Configuring Subsystem Blocks

The blocks in the masked subsystem must be configured to use the variables defined on the Initialization page. To configure the blocks in the Spring-mass subsystem, select the subsystem, then choose **Edit:Look Under Mask** from the model window menu bar. Double-click the Gain block labeled Left spring, and set **Gain** to k_left. Likewise, set the value of **Gain** for Gain block Right spring to k_right and for Gain block 1/mass to 1/mass. Set **Initial condition** for Integrator Velocity to x_dot0, and Integrator Position to x0. The subsystem should now appear as shown in Figure 7-15. Close the subsystem and save the model.

Local Variables

An important difference between masked subsystems and non-masked subsystems is the scope of variables in the dialog boxes for the blocks in a subsystem. Blocks in non-masked subsystems may use any MATLAB variable currently defined in the MATLAB workspace. This feature was used to initialize the subsystems in Example 7-1. The blocks in a masked subsystem can't access variables in the MATLAB workspace; a masked subsystem has its own

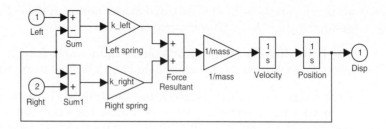

Figure 7-15 Spring-mass subsystem configured to use masked block variables

internal name space that is independent of the MATLAB workspace and all other masked subsystems in a Simulink model. This is an extremely valuable feature of masked subsystems, as it eliminates the possibility of unintentional variable name conflicts.

A masked subsystem's internal variables are created and assigned values using the Mask Editor dialog fields and initialization commands. Each dialog field in a masked block's dialog box defines an internal variable accessible only within the masked subsystem. Additional internal variables may be defined in the **Initialization commands** field of the Initialization page.

The connections between the MATLAB workspace and a masked subsystem are the contents of the masked block's dialog box fields. An input field in a masked block's dialog box may contain constants or expressions using variables defined in the MATLAB workspace. The value of the contents of the input field is assigned to the masked subsystem internal variable associated with the input field. This internal variable may be used to initialize a block in the masked subsystem, or it may be used to define another internal variable defined in the **Initialization commands** field.

Consider the model shown in Figure 7-10, with the masked subsystem configured as shown in Figure 7-15. The spring constant for the left spring in each instance of the masked subsystem is k_left. However, the contents of k_left in each instance is different. k_left for the first Spring-mass block should be set (using the Spring-mass block dialog box) to k1. k_left for the second block should be set to k2, and for the third Spring-mass block to k3.

Example 7-5

To illustrate the use of internal variables in a masked subsystem, consider the assignment of a value to the spring constant of the right spring in the cart subsystem of Figure 7-10. In Figure 7-12, the contents of the cart subsystem dialog field **Right spring constant** are associated with internal variable k_right. In Figure 7-16, we see that the Gain block labeled Right spring is set to k_right.

Thus, when the M-file script in Figure 7-8 is executed, the value of the gain for the Gain block `Right spring` in this particular instance of the cart subsystem is set to 2.

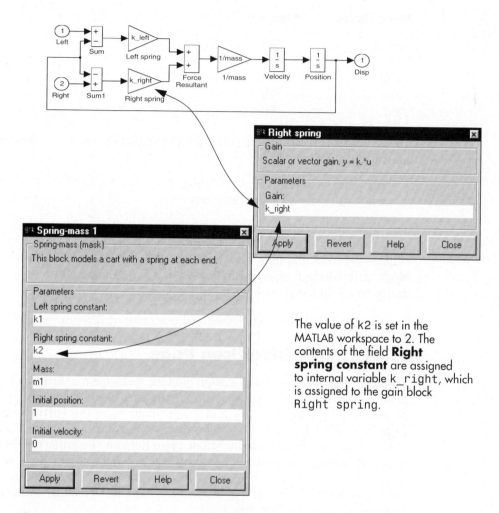

The value of k2 is set in the MATLAB workspace to 2. The contents of the field **Right spring constant** are assigned to internal variable k_right, which is assigned to the gain block `Right spring`.

Figure 7-16 Right spring constant Gain block initialization

Example 7-6

For the masked subsystem in Example 7-3, set a variable `temp_val` as follows:

Menu choice	`temp_val`
Very hot	120
Hot	100
Warm	85
Cool	70
Cold	50

To accomplish this task, place the following statements in the **Initialization commands** field:

```
temp_list = [120,100,85,70,50] ;
temp_val = temp_list(temp_des) ;
```

The first statement creates a vector of temperatures. The second statement uses `temp_des` (the variable associated with the popup list in Example 7-3 (Figure 7-14)) as an index into the vector. Choose **Close**, then, with the masked block still selected, choose **Edit:Look Under Mask** and set Constant block dialog box field **Constant value** to `temp_val`.

7.3.4 Mask Editor Icon Page

The Icon page allows you to design custom icons for masked blocks. The Icon page used to create the custom icon for the cart block in Figure 7-10 is shown in Figure 7-17. (Recall that x and y were defined in the **Initialization commands** field in Example 7-4.) The page consists of six fields. The top field, **Mask type**, is identical to the **Mask type** field on the other two Mask Editor pages. **Drawing commands** is a multiple line field in which we enter one or more MATLAB statements to draw and label the icon. The remaining four fields configure the block icon. It will be easier to explain **Drawing commands** if we first discuss the configuration fields.

Icon frame field

The first icon configuration field, **Icon frame**, is a drop-down list containing two choices: **Visible** and **Invisible.** The icon frame is the border of the block icon. Figure 7-18 illustrates the Spring-mass block with and without the icon frame.

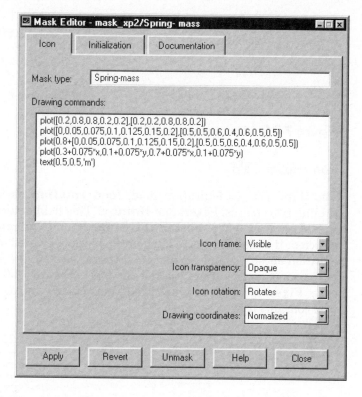

Figure 7-17 Mask Editor Icon page for the cart subsystem

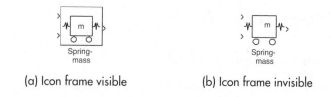

(a) Icon frame visible   (b) Icon frame invisible

Figure 7-18 Icon frame visibility

Icon transparency field

The second icon configuration field, **Icon transparency**, is a drop-down list containing two choices: **Transparent** and **Opaque**. Figure 7-19 shows the Spring-mass block with **Icon transparency** set to both options. Note that when **Transparent** is selected, the labels on the Inport and Outport blocks in the subsystem underlying the mask are visible. Selecting **Opaque** hides the labels.

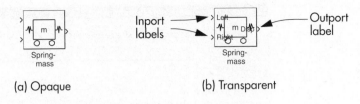

(a) Opaque   (b) Transparent

Figure 7-19   Icon transparency

Icon rotation field

The third icon configuration field, **Icon rotation**, is a drop-down list containing two choices: **Fixed** and **Rotates**. This field determines the behavior of the block icon when **Format:Flip block** and **Format:Rotate block** are selected. If **Fixed** is selected, when the block is rotated or flipped, the icon orientation doesn't change. When **Rotates** is selected, the orientation of the icon is the same as the orientation of the block. Figure 7-20 illustrates the difference. **Fixed** is frequently desirable, particularly in cases in which the block icon contains text.

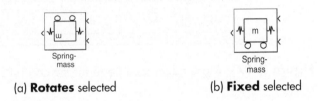

(a) **Rotates** selected   (b) **Fixed** selected

Figure 7-20   Icon rotation

Drawing coordinates field

The final icon configuration field, **Drawing coordinates**, determines the scale used in plotting icon graphics and locating text on the icon. The field is a drop-down list consisting of three choices: **Pixel**, **Autoscale**, and **Normalized.**

Pixel is an absolute scale, and will result in an icon that isn't resized when the block is resized. The coordinates of the lower left corner of the icon are (0,0). The units are pixels, and therefore the size of the icon will depend on the display resolution. Figure 7-21 shows a masked block with **Drawing coordinates** set to **Pixel**.

Autoscale adjusts the size of the icon to exactly fit in the block's frame (even if the frame is invisible). Figure 7-22 shows the masked block in Figure 7-21

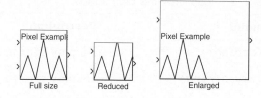

Figure 7-21 Drawing coordinates set to **Pixel**

reset to **Autoscale.** Note that the text on the icon does not change size when the block is resized.

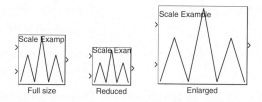

Figure 7-22 Drawing coordinates set to **Autoscale**

Normalized specifies that the drawing scale is 0.0 to 1.0 in both the horizontal and vertical axes. The coordinates of the lower left corner of the icon (in its default orientation, not rotated or flipped) are defined to be (0,0), and the coordinates of the upper right corner of the icon are (1,1). When the block is resized, the coordinates are also resized. Text does not change size when the block is resized. Figure 7-23 illustrates a masked block with **Drawing coordinates** set to **Normalized.**

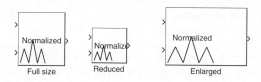

Figure 7-23 Drawing coordinates set to **Normalized**

Drawing commands

Several different MATLAB statements may be entered in **Drawing commands** to customize a block's icon. Table 7-1 lists these commands.

Table 7-1   Icon drawing commands

Command	Description
disp(*string*)	Display *string* in the center of the icon.
text(x,y,*string*)	Display *string* starting at (*x,y*).
fprintf(*string,list*)	Display the results of the fprintf statement at the center of the icon.
plot(*x_vector,y_vector*)	Draw a plot on the icon.
dpoly(*num,denom*)	Display a transfer function centered on the icon.
dpoly(*num,denom*,'z')	Display a discrete transfer function in ascending powers of z.
dpoly(*num,denom*,'z-')	Display a discrete transfer function in descending powers of z.
droots(zeros,poles,gain)	Display a transfer function in zero-pole-gain format.

Three of the commands display text on the icon. The simplest, disp(*string*), displays *string* centered on the icon. This command is useful for placing a simple descriptive title in the center of the icon. The text(x,y,*string*) command permits you to locate a string anywhere on the icon, using the icon coordinate system as specified in the **Drawing coordinates** field. The third text command, fprintf(*string,list*) is identical to the MATLAB fprintf statement. (Enter help fprintf at the MATLAB prompt for details on fprintf.) Using fprintf, you can build labels that use variables defined by the block's dialog fields and the statements in the field **Initialization commands** on the Initialization page. Embed a newline character (\n) in the string to produce a label with multiple lines. Like the disp command, fprintf places the label at the center of the icon.

A character string used to display text on the icon may be a literal string, or it may be a MATLAB string variable. A literal string is a sequence of printable characters enclosed in single quotes. For example, to place the label "Special Block" in the center of a block's icon, use the command:

```
disp('Special Block')
```

A string variable is a MATLAB variable that represents a character string instead of a number. MATLAB provides several functions for building and manipulating string variables. These functions can be used in the field **Initialization commands** on the Initialization page to create strings for use in the text display commands. A particularly useful string function is `sprintf`. `sprintf` is similar to `fprintf`, but it writes to a character string instead of the screen or a file. An excellent reference for a detailed discussion of MATLAB string variables and functions is the text by Hanselman and Littlefield [1].

Example 7-7

Suppose we wish to change the icon shown in Figure 7-10 such that the cart mass is displayed on the icon just above the wheels, and the units of mass are kilograms. Add the following command to the **Initialization commands** field on the Initialization page of the Mask Editor:

```
b_label =sprintf('%1.1f kg',m);
```

Then, enter the following command in the **Drawing commands** field of the Icon page:

```
text(0.3,0.35,b_label);
```

The block icon will be as shown in Figure 7-24.

Spring-
mass

Figure 7-24   Displaying the cart mass on its icon

The `plot(x_vector,y_vector)` command displays graphics on the block icon. This command is similar to the MATLAB `plot` command, but has fewer options. In particular, the Mask Editor `plot` command does not support options to set line styles or colors, and will not plot two-dimensional arrays. The command expects pairs of vectors specifying sequences of x- and y-coordinates. There may be more than one pair of vectors in a single `plot` command, and there may be more than one `plot` command for an icon. Figure 7-17 shows the commands used to create the cart icon.

Example 7-8

Suppose we wish to display sine and cosine functions on an icon. Placing the following commands in the **Initialization commands** field will produce the necessary vectors:

```
x_vector = [0:0.05:1] ;
y_sin = 0.5 + 0.5*sin(2*pi*x_vector) ;
y_cos = 0.5 + 0.5*cos(2*pi*x_vector) ;
```

Next, place the following command in **Drawing commands**:

```
plot(x_vector,y_sin,x_vector,y_cos)
```

The block will appear as shown in Figure 7-25.

Sin/Cos
Example

Figure 7-25   Drawing curves on a block icon

Example 7-9

The Simulink Logical Operator block can be configured to implement AND and OR gates, but the block icon is a rectangle with the logical operator it implements displayed on the icon. By placing copies of the Logical Operator block into masked subsystems, we can produce AND and OR blocks that more closely resemble the conventional icons for these gates.

To produce the AND gate block, start with a Logical Operator block configured to implement AND. Select the block using a bounding box, then choose **Edit:Create subsystem** from the model window menu bar. Select the subsystem, then choose **Edit:Mask Subsystem** from the model window menu bar. Open the Mask Editor, and place the following command in the **Initialization commands** field on the Initialization page:

```
t=-pi/2:0.1:pi/2;
```

Change to the Icon page, and set **Icon frame** to **Invisible**, and **Drawing coordinates** to **Normalized**. Place the following commands in **Drawing commands**:

```
plot([0.5,0,0,0.5],[0,0,1,1],0.5+0.5*cos(t),0.5+0.5*sin(t))
text(0.05,0.65,'a');
text(0.05,0.2,'b');
text(0.75,0.45,'ab');
```

To produce the OR gate block, the process is the similar, using the following in **Drawing commands**:

```
plot([0,0],[0,1],t,0.5*t.^2,t,1-0.5*t.^2);
text(0.05,0.65,'a');
text(0.05,0.2,'b');
text(0.6,0.45,'a+b');
```

The logic gate blocks that result are shown in Figure 7-26.

Figure 7-26   Logic gate masked blocks

The final drawing commands dpoly(*num,denom*) and droots(*zeros,poles, gain*), display a transfer function on the block's icon.

dpoly displays the transfer function in polynomial form. The arguments *num* and *denom* are vectors containing the coefficients of the transfer function numerator and denominator in descending powers of s. dpoly will also display discrete transfer functions in either descending powers of z or ascending powers of $1/z$. To display the transfer function in descending powers of z, use the command dpoly(*num,denom*,'z'). To display the transfer function in ascending powers of $1/z$, use dpoly(*num,denom*,'z-').

droots displays a transfer function in factored pole-zero form. *zeros* is a vector containing the zeros of the transfer function (roots of the numerator), and *poles* is a vector containing the poles of the transfer function (roots or the denominator). *gain* is a scalar.

7.3.5   Looking Under and Removing Masks

There are two additional masking commands that permit you to view a subsystem underlying a mask and to delete the mask.

To examine the subsystem underlying a masked block, select the masked block, then choose **Edit:Look under mask**.

To convert a masked block into an unmasked block or subsystem, select the block, then open the Mask Editor. Press the **Unmask** button at the bottom of the Mask Editor. If you change your mind about removing the mask, select the block and choose **Edit:Mask Subsystem**. The masking information will be preserved until you close the model. Once you close the model after removing the mask, it is not possible to restore the mask.

7.3.6 Using Masked Blocks

Once you have created a masked block, it can be copied to a model window in a manner identical to that used to copy a block from a Simulink block library. For example, to build the model shown in Figure 7-10(a), open a new model window, then drag three copies of the Spring-mass block to the new model window. Add the Constant and Scope blocks and connect the blocks with signal lines as shown. Configure the blocks as shown in Table 7-2.

Table 7-2 Cart model configuration parameters

Field	Spring-mass 1	Spring-mass 2	Spring-mass 3
Left spring constant	k1	k2	k3
Right spring constant	k2	k3	0
Mass	m1	m2	m3
Initial position	1	0	0
Initial velocity	0	0	0

Now the model is complete. Configure the Scope block and simulation parameters as in Example 7-1, then save the model. In the MATLAB workspace, run the script M-file (set_x4a.m) to assign values to the spring constants and masses. This model will produce results identical to the model in Example 7-1.

7.3.7 Creating a Block Library

A *block library* is a special Simulink model that serves the same purpose as a subroutine library in a conventional programming language. When a block is copied from a block library to a model, the copy remains linked to the version of the block in the block library. If the version of the block in the block library is changed, the change is effective each place the block is used. A block in a block library is called a *library block*. A copy of library block in a model is called a *reference block*. Each reference block has its own data (the dialog box fields), but the functionality is defined by the library block.

A reference block can't be changed. So, for example, if you select a reference block for which the library block is a masked subsystem, then choose **Edit** from the model window menu bar, the **Edit:Edit Mask** menu choice will not be present. **Edit:Look Under Mask** will be present. But if you look under the mask, and then try to edit the underlying subsystem, Simulink will display an error message.

Creating a Block Library

Create a block library by selecting **File:New Library** from the Simulink block library menu bar. Copy the desired blocks to the new library, and then save the block library. Once the library has been saved, the blocks in the library are library blocks, and blocks copied from the library are reference blocks.

You can create nested block libraries by adding subsystems to a block library window. For example, each of the block libraries (Sources, Sinks, etc.) in the Simulink block library is a subsystem that contains a set of unconnected blocks. To create a subsystem block library, drag an empty Subsystem block to the block library window. Open the Subsystem block, and add the desired blocks to the subsystem window. A subsystem library can be masked, as are the block libraries in the Simulink block library. The masked subsystem can have a custom icon, but it must not have any dialog box fields (the prompt section of the Initialization page should be empty), and the **Block description field** on the Documentation page must be blank. Otherwise, double-clicking the block library icon would open a block dialog box, instead of opening a subsystem window from which to copy blocks.

The final step in creating a block library is to add the directory in which the library is stored to the MATLAB path. Reference blocks can find only library blocks that are in the MATLAB path or the current directory (the current MATLAB directory).

Modifying a block library

Once a block library has been saved, it is locked and cannot be changed. If it is necessary to change a block library, either to add more blocks or to edit a block, the block library must be unlocked. To unlock a block library, choose **Edit:Unlock Library** from the block library window menu bar. The library will be unlocked as long as it remains open. To relock a block library, close the library, then reopen it.

When a block in a library is changed, the change will be applied to each corresponding reference block when the model containing the reference block is opened or run, or when **File:Update Diagram** is selected from the model window menu bar.

To quickly find the library block corresponding to a reference block, select the reference block and then choose **Edit:Go to Library Link** from the model window menu bar.

Unlinking a block

A reference block can be converted into a normal block by breaking the link to the library block. To remove the link, select the block and then choose **Edit:Break Library Link** from the model window menu bar. Breaking a link affects only the instance of the reference block that was selected. The library block and all other corresponding reference blocks are unaffected.

Troubleshooting links

If Simulink is not able to find a library block corresponding to a reference block, the reference block is displayed with a red dashed border and an error message is displayed. To correct the problem, delete the reference block from the model and then reinstall the reference block. An alternative is to double-click the reference block. A dialog box will appear, prompting you for the path to the library block.

Example 7-10

In this example, we will create a custom block library. The library will contain a Gain block and a block library containing the Spring-mass block.

Open a new library window by choosing **File:New Library**.

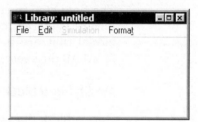

Copy a Gain block from the Linear block library and a Subsystem block from the Connections block library.

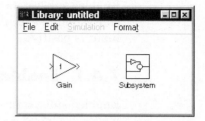

Label the subsystem My Library.

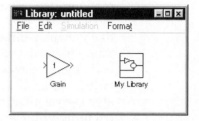

Double-click subsystem My Library, opening the subsystem window. Drag a copy of the Spring-mass block to the subsystem window, and rename the block Spring-mass. Then, close the subsystem window. Select the subsystem and choose **Edit:Mask Subsystem** from the model window menu bar.

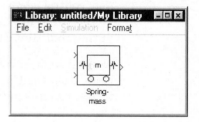

In the **Drawing commands** field on the Icon page, enter disp('Personal\nMasked\nBlocks') ;. Leave all other fields in the Mask Editor blank.

Choose **Apply** and **Close**. Resize My Library to fit the block icon. Save the model using the name pers_lib.

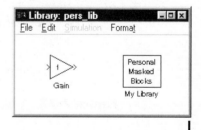

7.4 Conditionally Executed Subsystems

The Connections block library provides two blocks that cause subsystems to execute conditionally. The Enabled subsystem block causes a subsystem to execute only if a control input is positive. The Triggered subsystem block causes a subsystem to execute once when a trigger signal is received. Placing both the

Enabled subsystem and Triggered subsystem blocks in a subsystem causes the subsystem to execute once when a trigger signal is received only if an enable input is positive.

7.4.1 Enabled Subsystems

Enabled subsystems permit us to model systems that have multiple operating modes or phases. For example, the aerodynamics of a jet fighter in the landing configuration are quite different from the aerodynamics of the same airplane in supersonic flight. The digital flight control system for such an airplane will likely employ different control algorithms in the different flight regimes. A Simulink model of the airplane and its control system might need to include both flight regimes. It is possible to model such a system using logic blocks or switch blocks. If we use this approach, every block in the model will be evaluated each simulation time step, including the blocks that are not currently contributing to the system's behavior. If we convert the various flight dynamics and control algorithm subsystems into enabled subsystems, only the subsystems that are active during a particular simulation step will be evaluated during that step. This can provide a significant computational savings.

A subsystem is converted into an enabled subsystem by adding an Enable block from the Connections block library to the subsystem. Figure 7-27 illustrates a simple proportional controller converted into an enabled subsystem.

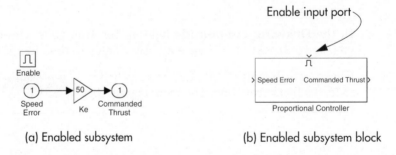

(a) Enabled subsystem   (b) Enabled subsystem block

Figure 7-27   Creating an enabled subsystem

The Enable block's dialog box is shown in Figure 7-28. The dialog box has two fields. The first field, **States when enabling**, is a drop-down menu with two options: **reset** and **held**. Choose **reset** to cause any internal states in the subsystem to be reset to the specified initial conditions each time the block is enabled. If you choose **held,** when the block is re-enabled, it will resume with all internal states at the values they held when the block was last executed. The second field, **Show output port**, is a checkbox. When selected, the Enable block will have an output port. This output port passes through the signal received at the Enable input port when the block is enabled.

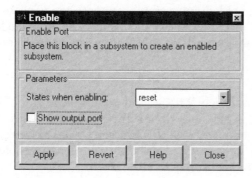

Figure 7-28 Enable block dialog box

It is also important to configure the Outport blocks of an enabled subsystem. The dialog box for the Outport block (Figure 7-29) has three fields. The first field, **Port number**, determines the order in which the ports are displayed on the subsystem block icon. The second field, **Output when disabled**, is a drop-down menu with two options: **reset** and **held**. Choose **reset** to cause the output to reset to the value in the third field, **Initial output**. Choose **held** to cause the output to remain at the last value output before the subsystem was disabled.

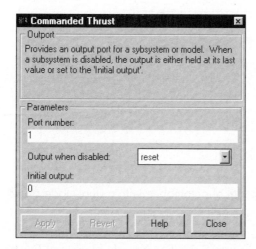

Figure 7-29 Enabled subsystem Outport block dialog box.

An enabled subsystem is enabled when the signal at the Enable input port is positive. The input signal may be either a scalar or vector. If the signal is a vector, the subsystem is enabled if any element of the vector is positive.

Example 7-11

To illustrate the use of enabled subsystems, suppose we wish to modify the automobile speed control of Example 6-5 such that it has two modes of operation depending on the speed error. If the absolute value of speed error

$$v_{err} = \left| \dot{x}_{desired} - \dot{x} \right|$$

is less than a threshold value, say 2 ft/sec, and the absolute value of the rate of change speed error, $\dot{v}_{err}$, is also less than a threshold value, say 1 ft/sec^2, we wish to switch to proportional-integral (PI) control. Once PI control is enabled, it is to remain enabled as long as v_{err} is less than a larger threshold value, 5 ft/sec. Otherwise, proportional control is to be enabled.

The Simulink model is shown in Figure 7-30. The mode selector subsystem, shown in Figure 7-31, produces two outputs. Choose PI is set to 1.0 if the conditions for PI control are satisfied, and 0.0 otherwise. Choose P is always the logical inverse of Choose PI.

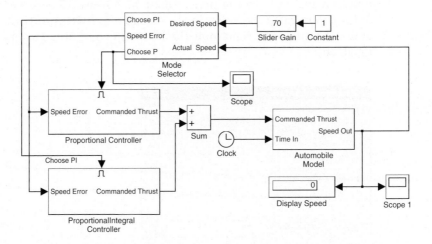

Figure 7-30 Simulink model of automobile with a dual-mode speed control

The proportional controller subsystem is illustrated in Figure 7-27. The PI subsystem block is shown in Figure 7-32. The Enable block and Outport block for both controller subsystems are configured to **reset**.

Executing the simulation results in the speed trajectory shown in Figure 7-33(a). The Choose P signal for this simulation is plotted in Figure 7-33(b). Initially, proportional control is enabled. Since the rate of change of speed error is

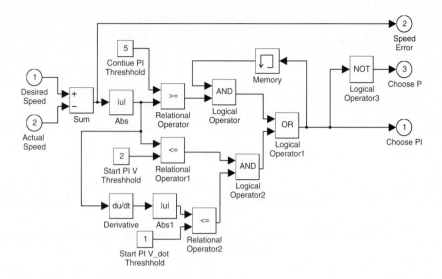

Figure 7-31   Mode selector subsystem

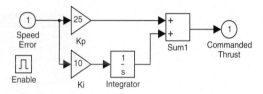

Figure 7-32   Proportional-integral enabled subsystem

less that the threshold value, as soon as the speed error decreases below 2 ft/sec, PI control is enabled.

7.4.2   Triggered Subsystems

A triggered subsystem is executed once each time a trigger signal is received. A triggered subsystem and the trigger dialog box are shown in Figure 7-34. The first field, **Trigger type**, is a drop-down menu with three choices: **rising**, **falling**, and **either**. If **rising** is selected, a trigger signal is defined as the trigger input crossing zero while increasing. If **falling** is selected, the trigger signal is defined as the trigger input crossing zero decreasing. If **either** is selected, the trigger signal is defined as the trigger input crossing zero increasing or decreasing. The second field in the Trigger block dialog box,

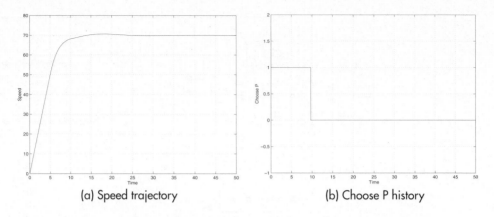

(a) Speed trajectory (b) Choose P history

Figure 7-33 Speed trajectory and Choose P signal history for dual mode
controller model

Show output port, is a checkbox. If the box is checked, the Trigger block will
have an output port that passes through the trigger signal.

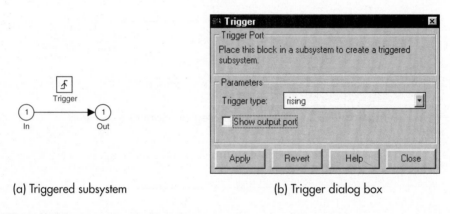

(a) Triggered subsystem (b) Trigger dialog box

Figure 7-34 Triggered subsystem

A triggered subsystem holds its output value after the trigger signal is
received. The initial output value of a triggered subsystem is set using the subsystem's Outport blocks.

The trigger signal may be either a scalar or a vector. If the signal is a vector,
the subsystem is triggered when any element of the vector satisfies the
Trigger type selection.

Example 7-12

The triggered subsystem illustrated in Figure 7-34 passes its input to its output when a trigger signal is received, and holds its output at that value until another trigger signal is received. The Outport block is initialized to 0. In Figure 7-35, we have added this subsystem to the automobile speed control model, and routed the subsystem output to a Display block from the Sinks block library. The trigger input is connected to the enable signal for the PI controller. The Display block displays 0 until the PI controller is activated, and afterwards it displays the most recent activation time.

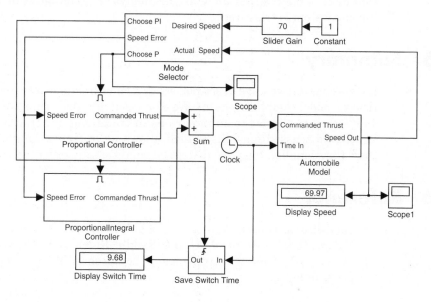

Figure 7-35 Automobile model with triggered subsystem

7.4.3 Trigger when Enabled Subsystems

Placing both an Enable block and a Trigger block in a subsystem produces a triggered when enabled subsystem. This subsystem will have both a trigger input and an enable input. The subsystem behaves the same as a triggered subsystem, but the trigger signal is ignored unless the enable signal is positive.

7.4.4 Discrete Conditionally Executed Subsystems

All three types of conditionally executed subsystems may contain continuous blocks, discrete blocks, or both continuous and discrete blocks. Discrete blocks in an enabled subsystem execute based on their sample time. They use the same time reference as the rest of the Simulink model; time in the subsystem is referenced to the start of the simulation, and not the activation of the subsystem. Consequently, an output dependent upon a discrete block won't necessarily change at the instant the subsystem is enabled.

Discrete blocks in triggered subsystems must have their sample times set to −1, indicating that they inherit their sample time from the driving signal. Note that discrete blocks that include time delays (z^{-1}) change state once each time the subsystem is triggered.

7.5 Summary

In this chapter, we have described several Simulink features that make it practical to model complex systems. We discussed Simulink subsystems, which provide a facility similar to subprograms in traditional programming languages. We then discussed masking, which allows us to create subsystems that hide their functionality. Last, we discussed conditionally executed subsystems.

7.6 Reference

1. Hanselman, Duane C., and Littlefield, Bruce R., *Mastering MATLAB 5: A Comprehensive Tutorial*, Upper Saddle River, N.J., Prentice Hall, 1998, pp. 97–112. This text provides a comprehensive tutorial on MATLAB programming.

Simulink Analysis Tools

In this chapter you'll learn to use Simulink analysis tools to gain understanding of Simulink models and to aid in the design process. Using the linearization tools we'll extract linear state-space models from block diagrams. We'll then use the trim tools to find equilibrium points. Finally, we'll use the Optimization Toolbox to optimize model parameters.

8.1 Introduction

In the previous chapters we described the process of modeling dynamical systems using Simulink. In this chapter, we will show how you can use Simulink to gain insight into the behavior of those systems.

All of the analysis and design capabilities we will discuss in this chapter are used from within the MATLAB workspace. From the MATLAB prompt, you can determine the structure of a model's state vector, the number of inputs and outputs, and other important parameters. You can run the simulation from within the MATLAB workspace using the MATLAB function `sim`, and can change certain model parameters and inputs. The linearization commands (`linmod`, `linmod2`, and `dlinmod`) allow you to linearize a Simulink model about any point in its state-space. The trim command (`trim`) locates equilibrium points. These tools can be used both to analyze the behavior of a system, and to facilitate the design of certain system parameters.

8.2 Determining Model Characteristics

In order to use many of the capabilities of the analysis tools to be discussed in this chapter, you must know the structure of the Simulink state vector for the model. In this section, we will start with a brief discussion of Simulink state vectors. Then, we will show how to determine the structure of a model's state vector from the MATLAB command line.

8.2.1 Simulink State Vector Definition

A Simulink model is a graphical description of a set of differential and difference equations. Simulink converts this graphical representation into a state-space representation consisting of a set of simultaneous first-order differential and difference equations. For example, the second-order continuous system shown in Figure 8-1 is represented by Simulink as two first-order differential equations as follows:

$$\dot{x}_1 = x_2$$
$$\dot{x}_2 = -0.5x_1 - 2x_2 \tag{8-1}$$

Here, x_1 is a state variable corresponding to the output of the Integrator block labeled Displacement, and x_2 is a state variable corresponding to the output of the Integrator block labeled Velocity. Recall that the state variable representation of a system is not unique. An equally valid choice of state variables in this example would be to associate x_1 with Velocity, and x_2 with Displacement. (Of course, if we change the state variable definition, we also must write the differential equations in terms of the new state variables.)

Since the analysis tools we will discuss in this chapter work in terms of the Simulink state vector, we must know how Simulink structures the state vector for a particular model. For example, the sim command includes the option to set the initial conditions for the model's state vector. If you wish to set the initial value of velocity to 1.0, and the initial value of displacement to 0.0, you must know which state variable corresponds to each quantity.

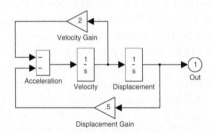

Figure 8-1 Simulink model of second-order continuous system

Simulink divides a model's state vector into continuous and discrete components. There is one continuous state vector component for each continuous integrator, including integrators present implicitly, due, for example, to Transfer Fcn blocks and State-Space blocks. Similarly, there is a discrete state vector component for each time delay, including delays present implicitly.

8.2.2 Using the *model* Command

The *model* command permits us to determine the structure of a Simulink model's state vector. There are three versions of the *model* command as follows:

```
sizes = model([ ],[ ],[ ],0)
[sizes, x0] = model([ ],[ ],[ ],0)
[sizes,x0,states] = model([ ],[ ],[ ],0)
```

where *model* is the name of the Simulink model. Note that the input arguments are the same for each version. The first three arguments are empty matrices, and the fourth argument is 0.

The first output argument, sizes, is a six-element vector defined in Table 8-1. The first two elements of sizes contain the number of continuous and discrete states. So, for example, if sizes(1) is 2 and sizes(2) is 3, the state vector will have a total of five elements. The first two elements will be the continuous states, and the last three elements will be the discrete states.

Table 8-1   Contents of the sizes vector

Component	Meaning
sizes(1)	Number of continuous states. This will include explicit states associated with Integrator blocks, and implicit states, such as those associated with Transfer Fcn blocks and State-Space blocks.
sizes(2)	Number of discrete states. This will include explicit states associated with Unit delays and implicit states, such as those associated with Discrete Transfer Fcn blocks.
sizes(3)	Number of outputs. An output is counted for each component of each Outport block. Thus, if the signal entering an Outport block is a scalar, there will be one output associated with that block. If the signal entering an Outport block is a three-component vector, there will be three outputs associated with that block. Note that To Workspace blocks and To File blocks do not count as outputs.
sizes(4)	Number of inputs. An input is counted for each component of each Inport block. Note that From Workspace blocks and From File blocks do not count as inputs.
sizes(5)	Number of discontinuous roots in the system. This information does not pertain to the analysis tools discussed in this chapter.
sizes(6)	Flag that is set to 1 if a subsystem has direct feedthrough of an input. This information does not pertain to the analysis tools discussed in this chapter.

The second output argument (x0) is optional. If present, it is the initial value of the Simulink model's state vector. Recall that the integrator states may be initialized using the dialog box for each integrator, and that this initialization may be overridden using the Workspace I/O page of the **Simulation:Parameters** dialog box.

The third output argument (`states`) is a cell array that identifies the block associated with each component of the Simulink state vector using the convention

```
model file name/top level subsystem/2nd level subsystem/.../block.
```

So, for example, the state associated with an integrator block labeled `Velocity` at the top level of a model named `sysmdl_a` would be `sysmdl_a/Velocity`. If this same block were located in a subsystem named `subsys_1` in model `sysmdl_a`, the state would be named `sysmdl_a/subsys_1/Velocity`.

Example 8-1

Consider the Simulink model shown in Figure 8-2. Suppose we have saved this model in a file named `sysmdl_a.mdl`.

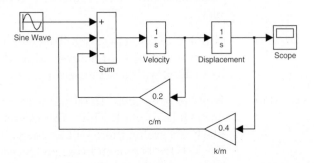

Figure 8-2   Second-order system with no inputs or outputs, stored in `sysmdl_a.mdl`

From the MATLAB prompt, we enter the following command:

```
[sizes, x0, states]=sysmdl_a([ ],[ ],[ ],0)
```

resulting in the output shown in Figure 8-3.

From this output we can determine the structure of the model state vector. `sizes(1)` is 2, so there are two continuous states as we would expect since the model has two Integrator blocks. `sizes(2)` is 0, so there are no discrete states. Using `sizes` and `states`, the state vector can be described as follows:

Component	Type	Associated with block
1	Continuous	Displacement
2	Continuous	Velocity

```
sizes =
     2
     0
     0
     0
     0
     0
     1
x0 =
     0
     0
     0
     0
states =
     'sysmdl_a/Displacement'
     'sysmdl_a/Velocity'
```

Figure 8-3   Model characteristics of `sysmdl_a`

Example 8-2

We can also identify the model characteristics for a Simulink model containing subsystems. Suppose we saved the model shown in Figure 8-4 in file `sysmdl_b.mdl`. From the MATLAB prompt, we enter the command.

```
[sizes, x0, states]=sysmdl_b([ ],[ ],[ ],0)
```

resulting in the output shown in Figure 8-5.

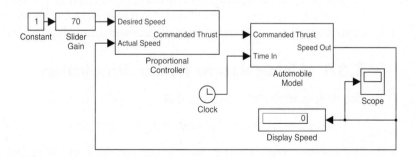

Figure 8-4   Automobile model using subsystems

```
sizes =
       2
       0
       0
       0
       0
       0
       1
x0 =
       0
       0
       0
       0
states =
     'sysmdl_b/Automobile Model/Speed'
     'sysmdl_b/Automobile Model/Distance'
```

Figure 8-5   Model characteristics of `sysmdl_b`

Note that the block names in `states` consist of the full path to the block, including the name of the subsystem.

8.3   Executing Models from MATLAB

The MATLAB `sim` command permits us to run Simulink models from the MATLAB prompt or from within M-files. This capability makes it easy to access model states for analysis, or to run a simulation repeatedly using different values for parameters, different inputs, or different initial conditions. `sim` may be used in conjunction with MATLAB command `simset`, which creates and edits a simulation options data structure, and `simget`, which gets the simulation options structure from a model. After discussing these commands, we will show how they can be used to facilitate the analysis of model behavior.

8.3.1   Using `sim` to Run a Simulation

The syntax of the `sim` command is

```
[t,x,y] = sim(model,TimeSpan,Options,ut)
```

The return variable list is optional. It can be omitted or can contain only one return variable, two return variables, or all three return variables. The first returned variable (t) contains the value of simulation time at each output point. Recall that the default behavior is to produce an output point at the end of each integration step, but that the Output options section of the **Simulation:Parameters** dialog box allows you to override this default by either adding output points or explicitly specifying the time of each output point. The second returned variable (x) is the state variable trajectory, with one column for each state variable, and one row corresponding to each time point in the first returned variable (t). The final returned variable (y) contains the output variable trajectory, one column for each output vector element, and one row corresponding to each time point. If there are no Outport blocks, but an output variable (y) is present, it will contain the empty vector [ ].

The first argument to the sim command (*model*) is a MATLAB string containing the name of the Simulink model, without the filename extension (.mdl). This argument is mandatory. The remaining arguments are optional, and allow us to override various model configuration parameters.

TimeSpan specifies the output time points. If TimeSpan is specified, it overrides the output times specified in the **Simulation:Parameters** dialog box. TimeSpan may have four different forms, as listed in Table 8-2.

Table 8-2 Specifying the simulation output times in the sim command

Value of TimeSpan	Output time point values
[ ]	Default to values specified in the **Simulation:Parameters** dialog box.
[T_Final]	Time points default to values specified in the **Simulation:Parameters** dialog box. The simulation will stop when the simulation time reaches T_Final.
[T_Start T_Final]	The simulation will start at time T_Start, and stop at T_Final. The value of time at intermediate points will be as specified in the **Simulation:Parameters** dialog box. Note that this is a two-element vector.
[OutputTimes]	If OutputTimes is a vector of three or more components, there will be one output time point corresponding to each element of OutputTimes. The contents of the first return variable (t) will be identical to OutputTimes. Probably the most common form of OutputTimes is [T_Start:TimeSpacing:T_final], producing a vector of equally spaced points.

Options is a MATLAB data structure that allows you to override many of the parameters in the **Simulation:Parameters** dialog box. The options structure is created, updated, and displayed using the MATLAB command simset, which we will discuss shortly.

ut overrides the Load from workspace section of the Workspace I/O page of the **Simulation:Parameters** dialog box. ut may be either an input table or a string containing the name of a MATLAB function. If ut is an input table, it must be of the form [t,u1,u2,...], where t is a column vector of time points, and u1, u2, etc., are column vectors of the values of the inputs corresponding to the time points in t. The inputs are associated with Inport blocks, ordered according to the Inport block numbers. Simulink treats ut as a lookup table, linearly interpolating between time points. If ut is a string, it must name a function that returns an input vector, given a single argument of time.

When input arguments are supplied to the sim command to override simulation parameters, the Simulink model is not changed. The sim command arguments affect the Simulink model only during the execution of the simulation. When the simulation stops, the model parameters are the same as they were before the sim command was executed.

Example 8-3

Suppose we wish to set ut for a model with a single input according to the rule

$$u = \frac{1}{2}t \qquad t \le 1$$

$$u = t - \frac{1}{2} \qquad t > 1$$

The following MATLAB statement will create an input table compatible with the sim command. Simulink will interpolate in this table, producing values that correspond to the rule.

$$ut=[[0,1,100]',[0,1/2,99.5]']$$

Example 8-4

Suppose we wish to set ut for a model with two inputs to the vector function

$$\boldsymbol{u}(t) = \begin{bmatrix} \sin t & \cos t \end{bmatrix}$$

Figure 8-6 illustrates a function M-file that returns this vector.

```
function u = ut_fun(t)
u = [sin(t),cos(t)] ;
```

Figure 8-6   M-file to return the vector `[sin(t),cos(t)]`

We set ut using the MATLAB statement

$$ut='ut\_fun'$$

Example 8-5

In this example, we run the model illustrated in Figure 8-2 using the model's default configuration. This is equivalent to selecting **Simulation:Start** from the model's menu bar. At the MATLAB prompt, enter the command:

```
sim('sysmdl_a')
```

Simulink will run the model, and if the Scope is open, will display the plot of the output when the simulation is complete.

8.3.2 Setting Simulation Parameters with `simset`

The `simset` command is used to create and edit the options structure. There are three forms of the `simset` command. The first form is

```
options = simset('name_1',value_1,'name_2',value_2,...)
```

where *name_1*, value_1, etc., are property name, property value pairs as defined in Table 8-3. Refer to Section 4.8 for a detailed description of the simulation parameters. Notice that the property names are MATLAB strings. The property values may be either numbers or strings. So, for example, to assign the value of 0.0001 to the relative error tolerance, and to select the fourth-order fixed-step size Runge-Kutta solver you could use the following MATLAB command:

```
opts = simset('RelTol',1.0E-4,'Solver','ode4')
```

The second form of `simset` is

```
options = simset(oldopts,'name_1',value_1,...)
```

which allows you to change an existing options structure, either by changing previously set options, or by adding more options.

The third form of `simset` is

```
options = simset(oldopts,newopts)
```

where both `oldopts` and `newopts` are options structures previously created using `simset`. This form of `simset` merges the contents of `oldopts` and `newopts`, with the contents of `newopts` having priority.

Table 8-3 describes the properties which may be set using `simset`.

Table 8-3 Simulation property names and values

Property name	Property value and associated Simulation:Parameters fields
Solver	Selects the Simulink differential equation solver. Permissible values are: 'ode45', 'ode23', 'ode113', 'ode15s', 'ode23s', 'ode5', 'ode4', 'ode3', 'ode2', 'ode1', 'FixedStepDiscrete', 'VariableStepDiscrete'
RelTol	Overrides the contents of the **Relative tolerance** field.
AbsTol	Overrides the contents of the **Absolute tolerance** field.
Refine	Equivalent to setting **Output options** to **Refine output**. The property value must be set to a positive integer. If the output time points are specified explicitly, this property is ignored.
MaxStep	Upper bound on integration step size. Overrides **Max step size**.
Initial-Step	Initial integration step size. Overrides the contents of **Initial step size**.
MaxOrder	Maximum order if solver ODE15S is used. Otherwise ignored.
FixedStep	Integration step size if a fixed step solver is used. Overrides **Fixed step size**.
Output-Points	Set to either the string 'specified' or the string 'all'. Select 'specified' (the default) to produce output points only at the time points specified in TimeSpan. Select 'all' produce output points at the time points specified in TimeSpan and at each integration step. This property is equivalent to selecting **Produce specified output only** or **Produce additional output** in **Output options**.

Simulink Analysis Tools   Chapter 8

Table 8-3   Simulation property names and values (Continued)

Property name	Property value and associated Simulation:Parameters fields
Output-Variables	Overrides the three checkboxes in the Save to workspace section of the Workspace I/O page. The property value is a string of up to 3 characters. If the string contains 't', simulation time is output to the MATLAB workspace, equivalent to selecting the **Time** checkbox. Including 'x' is equivalent to selecting the **States** checkbox, and including 'y' is equivalent to selecting the **Output** checkbox. Thus, this property value could be set to 'txy', 'ty', 'yx', etc.
MaxRows	Places an upper bound on the number of rows in the output matrices. Equivalent to selecting the **Limit to last** checkbox, and entering a value in the **Limit to last** input field.
Decimation	Overrides the **Decimation** field. Setting this property value to 1 causes every point to be output, setting it to 2 causes every other point to be output, and so on. Must be a positive integer.
Initial-State	Set to a vector containing the initial values of all of the model's state variables. Overrides the **Load initial** checkbox and field in the States section of the Workspace I/O page.
Final-StateName	Character string containing the name of the MATLAB workspace variable in which to save the final value of the state vector. Overrides the **Save final** checkbox and field in the States section of the Workspace I/O page.
Trace	Set to contain a comma-separated list of strings which may include 'minstep', 'siminfo', 'compile', or ' '. For example, to include all three options, the string could be 'siminfo,compile,minstep'. 'minstep' is equivalent to setting the **Minimum step size violation** event to **warning**. 'siminfo' causes Simulink to produce a brief report listing key parameters in effect at the start of a simulation. 'compile' causes Simulink to produce a model compilation listing in the MATLAB workspace as the model is compiled, before it runs. The compilation listing is intended primarily for use by The MathWorks in troubleshooting Simulink problems.

Table 8-3 Simulation property names and values (Continued)

Property name	Property value and associated Simulation:Parameters fields
`SrcWork-space`	Select the MATLAB workspace in which to evaluate MATLAB expressions defined in the model. May be set to 'base' (the default), 'current', or 'parent'. This option is extremely important if you are running a Simulink model from within a function M-file. `'base'` indicates that all variables used to initialize block parameters are to be taken from the base MATLAB workspace. `'current'` indicates that the variables are to be taken from the private workspace from which `sim` is called. `'parent'` indicates that the variables are to be taken from the workspace from which the current function (the one that called `sim`) was called (the next higher function). No corresponding field in **Simulation:Parameters**.
`DstWork-space`	Select the MATLAB workspace in which to assign MATLAB variables defined in the model. May be set to `'base'`, `'current'`, or `'parent'`. `DstWorkspace` determines where To Workspace blocks send their results. No corresponding field in **Simulation:Parameters.**
`ZeroCross`	Overrides the **Disable zero crossing detection** checkbox. May be either 'on' or 'off'.

It is particularly important to ensure that the properties `SrcWorkspace` and `DstWorkspace` are set properly. There are three options for each: `'base'`, `'current'`, and `'parent'`. The base workspace is the MATLAB prompt. Thus, variables defined in the base workspace are those variables listed when the command `who` is entered at the MATLAB prompt. Each function M-file has a private workspace; variables defined in a function M-file are not visible outside the M-file. `'current'` indicates that variables are to be taken from or returned to the workspace from which the `sim` command is run. `'parent'` indicates that variables are to be taken from or returned to the workspace from which the currently executing function was called. It is permissible for `SrcWorkspace` and `DstWorkspace` to be set to different values. It is not possible for some model parameters to be defined in the base workspace, and others in a function M-file.

8.3.3 Getting Simulation Parameters with `simget`

The command `simget` gets either the options structure or the value of a single property. To get the options structure from a model, the syntax is

```
opts = simget(model)
```

To get the value of a single property, the syntax is

```
value = simget(model,property_name)
```

where *model* is a MATLAB string containing the name of the Simulink model without the filename extension (.mdl), and property_name is a string containing one of the names listed in Table 8-3. property_name can also be a cell array in which each cell is a string containing one of the names listed in Table 8-3.

Example 8-6

A useful tool in the analysis of nonlinear second-order systems is the *state portrait*. Consider the following system, discussed in detail by Scheinerman [6]:

$$\dot{x}_1 = -x_2$$
$$\dot{x}_2 = x_1 + x_2^3 - 3x_2$$

A state portrait graphically depicts the behavior of the system in the state plane (the (x_1, x_2) plane) in the vicinity of an *equilibrium*. An equilibrium is a point in the state plane at which both state derivatives are zero. If, in some sufficiently small region in the vicinity of an equilibrium, every trajectory converges to the equilibrium, the equilibrium is said to be stable. This system has one equilibrium, located at the origin. A Simulink model of this system is shown in Figure 8-7.

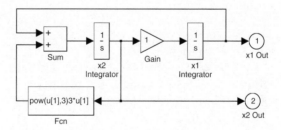

Figure 8-7   Simulink model of nonlinear second-order system

We start the analysis process by identifying the elements of the model's state vector. In Figure 8-8, we execute the model, stored in file sysmdl_e.mdl, with the fourth argument (flag) set to 0. We note that there are two states, the first associated with x_1, the second with x_2.

We can produce a simple state portrait by repeatedly running the model, starting each simulation at a different point in the state-space. An M-file that

```
»[states,x0,sizes]=sysmdl_e([ ],[ ],[ ],0)
states =
     2
     0
     2
     0
     0
     0
     1
x0 =
     0
     0
sizes =
     'sysmdl_e/x1 Integrator'
     'sysmdl_e/x2 Integrator'
```

Figure 8-8   Identifying the states from the MATLAB prompt

produces a state portrait in this manner is shown in Figure 8-9. The state portrait is shown in Figure 8-10. Notice that each state trajectory goes to the origin and stops there. Thus, from the state portrait it appears that the origin is a stable equilibrium.

```
% Produce a state portrait for the Simulink model sysmdl_e
%
for x1 = -1:0.5:1
  for x2 = -1:0.5:1
    opts = simset('InitialState',[x1,x2]) ;
    [t,x,y] = sim('sysmdl_e',15,opts) ;
    hold on ;
    plot(x(:,1),x(:,2)) ;
  end
end
axis([-1,1,-1,1]);
xlabel('x1') ;
ylabel('x2') ;
grid ;
```

Figure 8-9   M-file to produce simple state portrait

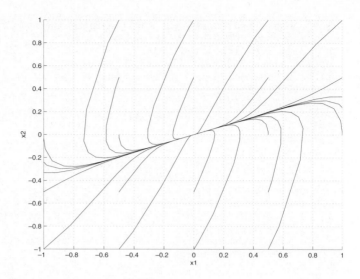

Figure 8-10 Simple state portrait

Example 8-7

The simple state portrait in the previous example shows the system behavior close to the origin and is easy to produce, but there are some problems with this approach. First, there is no easy method to determine the proper TimeSpan. Some of the trajectories approach the origin rapidly, others slowly. A more serious problem is that if the simulation is started at a point in the state-space where the system is unstable, one or more of the state variables will rapidly diverge, causing floating-point overflow and the failure of the Simulink simulation. This is not a weakness of Simulink; it is the natural consequence of modeling the behavior of an unstable system.

The M-file illustrated in Figure 8-11 overcomes these problems. As before, we run the simulation repeatedly, starting each simulation at a different point in the state-space. However, each simulation performs only one integration step. Using the final point of each state trajectory and the corresponding initial point, we form an approximation of the slope of the state portrait at each initial point. Using these slopes, we produce the quiver plot shown in Figure 8-12. In addition to being easier to read, this state portrait shows the behavior of the system in the unstable region of the state plane.

```
% Produce a state portrait for the Simulink model sysmdl_e
% using a quiver plot
h = 0.01 ; % Fixed step size
opts = simset('Solver','ode5','FixedStep',h) ;
x1 = -2.5:0.25:2.5 ;    % Set up the x1 and x2 grid
x2 = -2.5:0.25:2.5 ;
[nr,nc] = size(x1) ;
x1m = zeros(nc,nc) ;   % Allocate space for the output vectors
x2m = x1m ;
for nx1 = 1:nc
  for nx2 = 1:nc
    opts = simset(opts,'InitialState',[x1(nx1),x2(nx2)]) ;
    [t,x,y] = sim('sysmdl_e',h,opts) ;
    dx1 = x(2,1)-x1(nx1) ;
    dx2 = x(2,2)-x2(nx2) ;
    l = sqrt(dx1^2 + dx2^2)*7.5 ;  % Scale the arrows
    if l > 1.e-10
      x1m(nx2,nx1)=dx1/l ;            % Notice the reversed indexes
      x2m(nx2,nx1)=dx2/l ;
    end
  end
end
quiver(x1,x2,x1m,x2m,0) ;
axis([-2.5,2.5,-2.5,2.5]) ;
xlabel('x1') ;
ylabel('x2') ;
grid ;
```

Figure 8-11   M-file to produce quiver plot state portrait

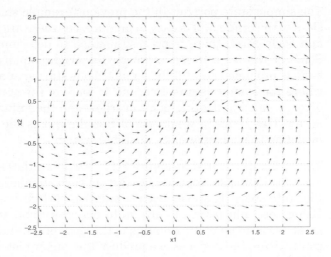

Figure 8-12   Quiver plot state portrait

8.4 Linearization Tools

While the dynamics of most physical systems are nonlinear, many useful techniques for analysis and control system design rely on linear models. For example, frequency domain analysis tools such as Bode plots and root locus plots are based on linear systems theory. Modern control techniques such as pole placement via state variable feedback and the linear quadratic regulator also rely on linear systems theory. Thus, it is frequently convenient to form linear approximations to nonlinear systems. We will begin this section with a short discussion of linearization. Then, we will show how the Simulink linearization tools may be used to facilitate analysis of nonlinear systems and control system design.

8.4.1 Linearization

A linear model of a nonlinear system is formed by computing matrices of the partial derivatives of the system state vector time rate of change and the output vector with respect to the state vector and input vector. As discussed in Chapter 2, the general form of the state-space model of a dynamical system is

$$\dot{\boldsymbol{x}} = \boldsymbol{f}(\boldsymbol{x}, \boldsymbol{u}, t) \tag{8-2}$$

$$\boldsymbol{y} = \boldsymbol{g}(\boldsymbol{x}, \boldsymbol{u}, t) \tag{8-3}$$

where $\dot{\boldsymbol{x}}, \boldsymbol{f}$, and $\boldsymbol{x}$ are vectors of order n, $\boldsymbol{u}$ is an input vector of order m, and $\boldsymbol{y}$ and $\boldsymbol{g}$ are vectors of order p. Given a nominal point $\boldsymbol{x}$ and a nominal input $\boldsymbol{u}$, at some time t, we can approximate to first-order the change in the jth component of the state vector time rate of change $(\dot{x}_j)$ due to a small variation in the ith component of the state vector (x_i) as

$$\delta \dot{x}_{ji} = \frac{\partial}{\partial x_i} f_j(\boldsymbol{x}, \boldsymbol{u}, t) \delta x_i \tag{8-4}$$

and the change due to a small variation in the kth component of the input vector as

$$\delta \dot{x}_{jk} = \frac{\partial}{\partial u_k} f_j(\boldsymbol{x}, \boldsymbol{u}, t) \delta u_k \tag{8-5}$$

The total change in $\dot{\boldsymbol{x}}$ due to a small variation in each element of the state vector and input vector can be approximated by the matrix equation

$$\delta \dot{\boldsymbol{x}} = \boldsymbol{A} \delta \boldsymbol{x} + \boldsymbol{B} \delta \boldsymbol{u} \tag{8-6}$$

where each element of A is

$$A_{ji} = \frac{\partial}{\partial x_i} f_j(\boldsymbol{x}, \boldsymbol{u}, t) \tag{8-7}$$

and each element of B is

$$B_{jk} = \frac{\partial}{\partial u_k} f_j(\boldsymbol{x}, \boldsymbol{u}, t) \tag{8-8}$$

Note that A is composed of n rows and n columns, and B of n rows and m columns.

Using similar reasoning, we can approximate the change in the output vector due to small variations in the state and input as

$$\delta \boldsymbol{y} = \boldsymbol{C} \delta \boldsymbol{x} + \boldsymbol{D} \delta \boldsymbol{u} \tag{8-9}$$

where

$$C_{ji} = \frac{\partial}{\partial x_i} g_j(\boldsymbol{x}, \boldsymbol{u}, t) \tag{8-10}$$

and

$$D_{jk} = \frac{\partial}{\partial u_k} g_j(\boldsymbol{x}, \boldsymbol{u}, t) \tag{8-11}$$

Here, C is composed of p rows and n columns, and D is composed of p rows and m columns.

Together, matrices A, B, C, and D may be used to form the linear state-space approximation

$$\dot{\boldsymbol{x}} = \boldsymbol{A}\boldsymbol{x} + \boldsymbol{B}\boldsymbol{u} \tag{8-12}$$

$$\boldsymbol{y} = \boldsymbol{C}\boldsymbol{x} + \boldsymbol{D}\boldsymbol{u} \tag{8-13}$$

This approximation may be valid only in some small region in the vicinity of the nominal point and nominal input. If the system is time-varying, the approximation may be valid for a short period of time. Furthermore, some nonlinear systems can't be effectively linearized because important features of the dynamics are lost in the linearization. However, for a large number of physical systems, the linear approximation is quite useful, providing insight into the system's behavior, and providing access to a variety of control system design techniques.

8.4.2 Simulink Linearization Commands

Simulink provides three commands to extract linear state-space approximations from Simulink models. `linmod` forms state-space models of continuous systems. `linmod2` is an alternative to `linmod` that uses different techniques to obtain the linearization, striving to reduce truncation error. `dlinmod` forms linear approximations of systems containing both continuous and discrete components.

The syntax of the linearization commands is as follows:

```
[A,B,C,D]=LINMOD(model,X,U,PARA,XPERT,UPERT)
[A,B,C,D]=LINMOD2(model,X,U,PARA,APERT,BPERT,CPERT,DPERT)
[A,B,C,D]=DLINMOD(model,TS,X,U,PARA,XPERT,UPERT)
```

All of the output arguments and all of the input arguments except *model* are optional. If no output arguments are specified, the system matrix (A) for the linear model is returned. The input arguments are defined in Table 8-4. The output arguments are the four state-space matrices, as discussed in Section 8.4.1.

The steps for using the linearization tools are as follows:

1. Prepare a Simulink model configured with Inport blocks for the inputs, and Outport blocks for the outputs. Note that blocks from the Sources block library do not count as inputs, and blocks from the Sinks block library do not count as outputs. It is not necessary to have an Inport block, but there should be at least one Outport block.

2. Use the procedures discussed in Section 8.2 to determine the number and ordering of the model's states.

3. Execute the appropriate linearization command from the MATLAB command line or from within an M-file. If you are interested only in the system matrix, use a single output argument, such as

   ```
   A = linmod('sysmdl_a')
   ```

   If you need the entire linear state-space model, use all of the output arguments.

The Derivative block and Transport Delay block should not be used in models to be linearized, as they can cause numerical trouble for the linearization functions. Replace Derivative blocks with Switched Derivative blocks. The Switched Derivative block is the Linearization block library, which is, in turn, found in the Simulink Extras library located in the Blocksets and Toolboxes block library.

Table 8-4   Linearization command input arguments

Argument	Definition
model	MATLAB string containing the name of the Simulink model. For example, if the Simulink model is stored in file ex1.mdl, the first argument would be 'ex1'. This argument is required.
X	Value of the model nominal state vector. Simulink will linearize the model about any point in the model's state-space. Identify the components of the model's state vector using the procedure described in Section 8.2. X defaults to a zero vector of appropriate dimension, if either the argument X is not present, or if it is the empty matrix [ ].
U	Value of the nominal input vector. Simulink will linearize input matrix and direct transmittance matrix about the specified input vector and state vector. The components of U correspond to the numbering of Inport blocks.
PARA	Vector containing two elements. The first is a perturbation value to be used in computing the numerical partial derivatives, and defaults to 10^{-5} for linmod and dlinmod. For linmod2, PARA(1) is the minimum perturbation value, and defaults to 10^{-8}. The second element is the time at which to perform the linearization, and defaults to 0 sec.
XPERT	Vector of perturbation values for each component of the system state vector. This vector of perturbations overrides the default, computed according to the rule XPERT=PARA(1)+1e-3*PARA(1)*abs(X).
UPERT	Vector of perturbation values for each component of the input vector. This vector overrides the default, according to the rule UPERT=PARA(1)+1e-3*PARA(1)*abs(U).
APERT	Matrix of maximum perturbation values for the system matrix. APERT must be either empty ([ ]), or the same size as A. linmod2 uses a fairly complex algorithm to compute the optimal perturbation value for each element of each matrix. The perturbation value for each element of the system matrix (A(i,j)) will be bounded from above by APERT(i,j) and from below by PARA(1).

Table 8-4   Linearization command input arguments (Continued)

Argument	Definition
BPERT	Matrix of maximum perturbation values for the input matrix (B). The perturbation value for each element of B will be bounded from above by the corresponding element of BPERT and from below by PARA(1).
CPERT	Matrix of maximum perturbation values for the output matrix (C). The perturbation value for each element of C will be bounded from above by the corresponding element of CPERT, and from below by PARA(1).
DPERT	Matrix of maximum perturbation values for the direct transmittance matrix (D). The perturbation value for each element of D will be bounded from above by the corresponding element of DPERT, and from below by PARA(1).
TS	Sample time for dlinmod. Defaults to the maximum sample time for the model.

Once you have obtained the linear model, you can use a variety of MATLAB commands to analyze the system dynamics or to design linear controllers.

Example 8-8

Consider the nonlinear system discussed in Example 8-6:

$$\dot{x}_1 = -x_2$$
$$\dot{x}_2 = x_1 + x_2^3 - 3x_2$$

We wish to linearize this system about the origin. Applying Equation (8-7), we compute

$$A = \begin{bmatrix} 0 & -1 \\ 1 & -3 \end{bmatrix}$$

A Simulink model of this system is shown in Figure 8-7. From the state portrait (Figure 8-12), it appears that this system exhibits stable behavior without oscillation. Thus, we would expect both eigenvalues of A to be real and negative. Figure 8-13 shows how to verify this using MATLAB. First, the system matrix is determined using linmod, then eig is used to compute the eigenvalues of the system matrix, which are indeed real and negative.

```
» A = linmod('sysmdl_e')
A =
          0   -1.0000
     1.0000   -3.0000
» eig(A)
ans =
    -0.3820
    -2.6180
```

Figure 8-13   Using `linmod` to compute the system (**A**) matrix of a nonlinear second-order system

Example 8-9

In this example we will discuss the design of a linear controller for a nonlinear system. Consider the cart with an inverted pendulum illustrated in Figure 8-14. This system approximates the dynamics of a rocket immediately after lift-off. The objective of the rocket control problem is to maintain the rocket in a vertical attitude while it accelerates. The objective in the control of this model is to move the cart to a specified position (x) while maintaining the pendulum vertical. Ogata [4] presents a detailed explanation of the design of a linear controller for this system using the technique of pole placement and MATLAB.

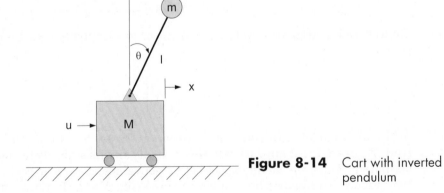

Figure 8-14   Cart with inverted pendulum

Referring to Figure 8-14, the input to the system is a horizontal force (u) applied to the cart of mass M. The pendulum is free to rotate without friction in the plane of the page. The pendulum is of length l, and the pendulum mass (m) is assumed to be concentrated at the end. The equations of motion of this system in terms of the cart displacement and pendulum angle can be written

$$(M+m)\ddot{x} - ml\dot{\theta}^2\sin\theta + ml\ddot{\theta}\cos\theta = u$$

$$m\ddot{x}\cos\theta + ml\ddot{\theta} = mg\sin\theta$$

where g is the acceleration due to gravity. Examining these equations, we notice that $\ddot{x}$ and $\ddot{\theta}$ appear in both equations. If we build a Simulink model using these equations, the model will contain an algebraic loop (see Chapter 12 for a detailed discussion of algebraic loops). Employing a little algebra, the equations of motion can be rewritten to eliminate the algebraic loop:

$$\ddot{x} = \frac{ml\dot{\theta}^2\sin\theta - mg\cos\theta\sin\theta + u}{M + m\sin\theta^2}$$

$$\ddot{\theta} = \frac{-(ml\dot{\theta}^2\cos\theta\sin\theta - mg\sin\theta + u\cos\theta - Mg\sin\theta)}{l(M + m\sin\theta^2)}$$

In order to follow the procedure of Ogata [4], our next task is to build a Simulink model of the system, with u as the input, and x as the output. We choose as state variables x, $\dot{x}$, θ, $\dot{\theta}$, and will need all four state variables in our controller. The model is enclosed in a subsystem with a scalar Inport block and a vector Outport block, as shown in Figure 8-15. Note that the equations of motion are computed using Function blocks, and the system parameters are variables defined in the MATLAB workspace. The subsystem is placed in a Simulink model that has a single input (u), and a single output (x), as shown in Figure 8-16. A Demultiplexer block decomposes the state vector into its components. x is routed to an Outport block, and the remaining components of the state vector are routed to Terminator blocks.

The system parameters are:

$$M = 2 \text{ kg}$$
$$m = 0.1 \text{ kg}$$
$$l = 0.5 \text{ m}$$
$$g = 9.8 \text{ m/sec}^2$$

The M-file shown in Figure 8-17 determines the model characteristics, producing the output shown in Figure 8-18.

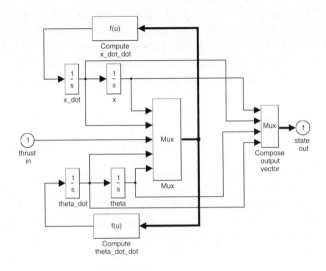

Figure 8-15 Inverted pendulum subsystem

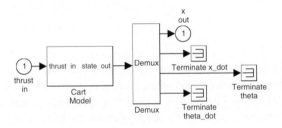

Figure 8-16 Simulink model to be linearized

```
% Initialize the system parameters and obtain the
% model characteristics
%
% System parameters
l = 0.5 ;   % Pendulum length
g = 9.8 ;   % Gravity
m = 0.1 ;   % Pendulum bob mass
M = 2 ;     % Cart mass
% Get the model characteristics
[sizes,x0,states] = sysmdl_h([ ],[ ],[ ],0)
```

Figure 8-17 M-file to determine the characteristics of the inverted pendulum model

```
»crt_init
sizes =
     4
     0
     1
     1
     0
     1
     1
x0 =
     0
     0
     0
     0
states =
     'sysmdl_h/Cart   Model/x'
     'sysmdl_h/Cart   Model/x_dot'
     'sysmdl_h/Cart   Model/theta_dot'
     'sysmdl_h/Cart   Model/theta'
```

Figure 8-18   Inverted pendulum model characteristics

Note that the Simulink state vector is

$$\begin{bmatrix} x \\ \dot{x} \\ \dot{\theta} \\ \theta \end{bmatrix}$$

which is ordered differently from the state vector at the outport block of the subsystem.

Next, we incorporate the subsystem in a Simulink model that includes a state feedback controller with an integrator in the forward path, shown in Figure 8-19. The input to the control system is the desired cart position. The Step function block is configured to produce a unit step at 1.0 sec. The output is the current cart position, displayed using a Scope block.

Figure 8-20 shows an M-file that computes the controller gains according to the procedure of Ogata [4]. The M-file uses linmod to obtain the state-space matrices. Then, Ackermann's method is used to compute the gains. The results of executing this M-file are shown in Figure 8-21. Finally, we test the controller using the M-file shown in Figure 8-22. This M-file runs the simulation, then plots the x and θ trajectories. The plots are shown in Figure 8-23.

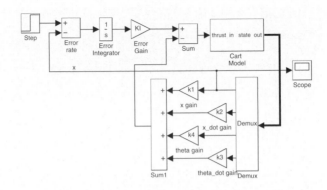

Figure 8-19 Inverted pendulum control Simulink model

```
% Design the feedback gain matrix for the cart with inverted
% pendulum example. This example follows the procedure
% outlined in Example 2-3 of "Designing Linear Control
% Systems with MATLAB", by K. Ogata
%
% Note that for this model, the state vector is
% [x ; x_dot ; theta_dot ; theta]', so the arrangement of the system
% matrices will be different than in the Ogata example.
%
% System parameters
l = 0.5 ;    % Pendulum length
g = 9.8 ;    % Gravity
m = 0.1 ;    % Pendulum bob mass
M = 2 ;      % Cart mass
% Get the system matrices
[A,B,C,D] = linmod('sysmdl_h',[0,0,0,0],[0])
A1 = [A zeros(4,1) ; -C 0] ;
B1 = [B ; 0] ;
% Define the controllability matrix M
MM = [B1 A1*B1 A1^2*B1 A1^3*B1 A1^4*B1] ;
% Check rank of MM, must be 5 if system is completely controllable
rank(MM)
% Obtain the characteristic polynomial
J = [-1+sqrt(3)*i,0,0,0,0;0,-1-sqrt(3)*i,0,0,0;...
     0,0,-5,0,0;0,0,0,-5,0;0,0,0,0,-5] ;
Phi = polyvalm(poly(J),A1) ;
% Get the feedback matrix using Ackermann's formula
KK = [0,0,0,0,1]*(inv(MM))*Phi
k1 = KK(1)  ; % x gain
k2 = KK(2)  ; % x_dot gain
k3 = KK(3)  ; % theta_dot gain
k4 = KK(4)  ; % theta gain
KI = -KK(5) ; % error integrator gain
```

Figure 8-20 Controller design M-file

Simulink Analysis Tools   Chapter 8

```
A =
         0    1.0000         0         0
         0         0         0   -0.4900
         0         0         0   20.5800
         0         0    1.0000         0
B =
         0
    0.5000
   -1.0000
         0
C =
    1    0    0    0
D =
    0
ans =
    5
KK =
   -56.1224   -36.7868   -35.3934  -157.6412      51.0204
```

Figure 8-21   Inverted pendulum linear model and controller gains

```
% Run the inverted pendulum simulation
opts = simset('InitialState',[0,0,0,0,0],'Solver','ode45') ;
[t,x] = sim('sysmdl_i',[0:0.1:10],opts) ;
% Plot the position and pendulum angle
subplot(2,1,1);
plot(t,x(:,1));
grid;
ylabel('x');
subplot(2,1,2);
plot(t,x(:,4));
grid;
xlabel('Time (sec)') ;
ylabel('theta');
```

Figure 8-22   M-file to test the inverted pendulum controller

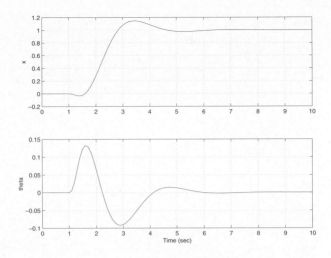

Figure 8-23 Inverted pendulum simulation results

8.5 Trim Tools

It is frequently useful to find equilibrium points of systems. As discussed in Example 8-6, an equilibrium point is a point at which all state derivatives are zero. For example, a valuable technique in nonlinear systems analysis is to linearize a system about an equilibrium point in order to assess the system stability in the vicinity of the equilibrium point using linear systems approximations. Another situation in which equilibrium point location is useful is the assessment of the accuracy of a control system, as the steady-state behavior of the system can be thought of as an equilibrium.

The Simulink `trim` command locates equilibrium points, and also locates partial equilibrium points, where we define a partial equilibrium point to be a point at which selected state derivatives are zero, but other state derivatives are allowed to be nonzero. `trim` locates an equilibrium point by numerically searching for a point (values of x, u, y) such that the maximum absolute value of the state derivative is minimized. If elements of the state (x), input (u), or output (y) are fixed, the fixed elements are treated as constraints which the algorithm will attempt to satisfy. In this case, the algorithm minimizes both the state derivative and the constraint error. The syntax of the `trim` command is

```
[x,u,y,dx] = trim(model,x0,u0,y0,ix,iu,iy,dx0,idx,options,t)
```

All of the output arguments and all of the input arguments except *model* are optional. The arguments are defined in Table 8-5.

It is generally best not to over-constrain the problem. Thus, if an output is the same as an element of the state vector, and that element is to be fixed, specify (using x0, ix or y0, iy) either the state vector element or the output vector element, but not both.

Input arguments x0, u0, and y0 define the starting point for the search. There is no guarantee, however, that trim will locate the equilibrium closest to the starting point. Additionally, trim may not converge, even if an equilibrium point exists. If trim fails to converge, it frequently helps to try a different starting point.

Table 8-5   trim command arguments

Argument	Meaning
x	Value of the state vector at the equilibrium point. If no output arguments are specified, trim will return x.
u	Value of the input vector at the equilibrium point. u will be the empty vector if the system has no inport blocks. Source blocks are not considered inputs to the system.
y	Value of the output vector at the equilibrium point. If there are no Outport blocks, y will be the empty vector.
dx	Value of the state derivative vector at the equilibrium point.
'model'	Name of the Simulink model, enclosed in single quotes ('), and without the file extension. For example, if the model is stored in the file s_examp.mdl, the first input argument is 's_examp'. This input argument is required.
x0	Initial guess for the state vector. The algorithm will begin the search for the equilibrium at this point. Some elements of the state vector may be fixed at the value specified in x0, using argument ix. x0 must be a column matrix, for example, [0;1;0;0]. If x0 is specified, all elements must be present.
u0	Initial guess for the input vector. Some elements of the input vector may be fixed at the value specified in u0, using argument iu.
y0	Initial guess for the output vector. Some elements of the output vector may be fixed at the value specified in y0, using argument iy.

Table 8-5   trim command arguments (Continued)

Argument	Meaning
ix	Vector indicating which elements of the state vector are to be fixed, that is, treated as constraints. For example, if the second and fourth elements of the state vector are to be fixed at the value specified in x0, ix would be [2,4].
iu	Vector indicating which elements of the input vector are to be fixed, that is, treated as constraints. For example, if the second and fourth elements of u0 are to be treated as constraints, iu would be [2,4].
iy	Vector indicating which elements of the output vector are to be fixed, that is, treated as constraints. For example, if the second and fourth elements of y0 are to be treated as constraints, iy would be [2,4].
dx0	State derivative vector at a partial equilibrium point. dx0 is used in conjunction with idx to fix certain elements of the state derivative.
idx	Vector indicating which elements of the state derivative vector are to be fixed at the value specified in dx0. For example, if the third element of the state derivative is to be fixed at dx0(3), idx will be [3]. The remaining elements of the state derivative vector will be free.
options	Vector of optimization options that will be passed to the constrained optimization function. For details on options, refer to the MATLAB help screen for FOPTIONS. This argument is usually omitted or left empty ([ ]). If trim fails to converge, changing optimization parameters may help.
t	Value of time at which to locate the equilibrium. This input argument needs to be specified only if the state derivative is time-dependent.

Example 8-10

Consider the differential system

$$\dot{x}_1 = x_1^2 + x_2^2 - 4$$
$$\dot{x}_2 = 2x_1 - x_2$$

We wish to locate the equilibrium points of this system and assess the system stability at each equilibrium point. A Simulink model of this system is shown in Figure 8-24. Figure 8-25 shows a state portrait for this system, produced using a suitably modified version of the M-file shown in Figure 8-11. We note that there appear to be two equilibrium points, located near (−1,−2) and (1,2). Furthermore, from the state portrait, it appears that the equilibrium near (−1,−2) is stable, and the equilibrium near (1,2) is unstable.

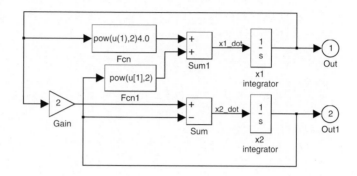

Figure 8-24 Simulink model of nonlinear system.

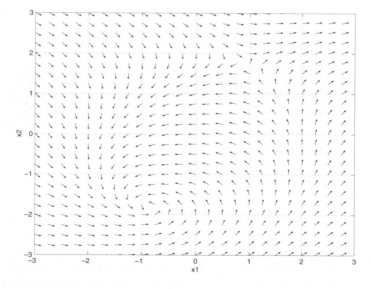

Figure 8-25 State portrait

To assess the stability of the equilibrium point, we first locate the equilibrium points using trim. Next, using linmod, we linearize the system about each equilibrium point. Finally, we use MATLAB function `eig` to compute the eigenvalues of the linearized system at each equilibrium point. An M-file that performs these operations is shown in Figure 8-26, and the results of executing this M-file are shown in Figure 8-27.

```
% Locate the two equilibrium points for the system
% Linearize the system about each equilibrium,
% then compute the eigenvalues at each equilibrium.
xa = trim('sysmdl_1',[-1;-2]) ;   % Locate the equilibrium
A = linmod('sysmdl_1',xa) ;
eigv_a = eig(A) ;
fprintf('Eigenvalues at (%f,%f):\n',xa) ;
eigv_a
xb = trim('sysmdl_1',[1;2]) ;  % Locate the other equilibrium
A = linmod('sysmdl_1',xb) ;
eigv_b = eig(A) ;
fprintf('Eigenvalues at (%f,%f):\n',xb) ;
eigv_b
```

Figure 8-26 M-file to assess system stability using linearization at the equilibrium points

```
Eigenvalues at (-0.894427,-1.788854):
eigv_a =
  -1.3944+ 2.6457i
  -1.3944- 2.6457i
Eigenvalues at (0.894427,1.788854):
eigv_b =
    3.4110
   -2.6222
```

Figure 8-27 Equilibrium assessment results

Examining the results in Figure 8-27, we can see that the equilibrium point near $(-1,-2)$ is actually located at $(-0.89,-1.79)$. Since the real parts of both eigenvalues at this point are negative, we can conclude that the system is stable in the vicinity of this equilibrium point (this equilibrium point is called a *stable focus*). One of the eigenvalues at the equilibrium point at $(0.89,1.79)$ is negative, and the other is positive. Thus, the system behavior in the vicinity of this point should be unstable (this type of equilibrium is called a *saddle point*).

Example 8-11

Consider the rotating pendulum shown in Figure 8-28. The system consists of a motor driving a pendulum of length l, hinged at O. The mass (m) of the pendulum is assumed to be concentrated at the end. The rotating parts of the motor are modeled as a flywheel with moment of inertia I_m. The input to the system is the motor torque (τ). Friction and aerodynamic drag may be ignored. Our task is to determine the motor angular velocity $(\dot{\phi})$ that is consistent with a constant pendulum deflection (θ) of 0.5 rad.

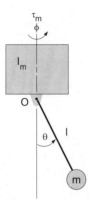

Figure 8-28   Rotating pendulum

We start by writing the equations of motion in terms of the shaft angle (ϕ) and the pendulum deflection (θ):

$$\ddot{\theta} = \frac{(l\dot{\phi}^2 \cos\theta - g)\sin\theta}{l}$$

$$\ddot{\phi} = \frac{\tau - 2ml^2\dot{\phi}\dot{\theta}\sin\theta\cos\theta}{I_m + ml^2\sin^2\theta}$$

where g represents the acceleration due to gravity. Figure 8-29 shows a Simulink model of this system. The equations of motion are in the two function blocks.

The MATLAB code in Figure 8-30 sets the model parameters and verifies that the ordering of the states is the same as the order of the model Outport blocks.

The pendulum deflection at the desired equilibrium is 0.5 rad, and the motor angular velocity is not zero, so we choose the initial state vector

```
x0=[0.5;0;0;5]
```

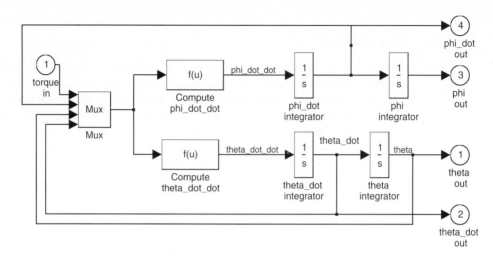

Figure 8-29 Simulink model of rotating pendulum

```
% Set the parameters for the rotating pendulum.
% Verify the ordering of the states.
% System parameters
l = 0.3 ;              % Pendulum length (meters)
I_m = 0.75 ;           % Motor moment of inertia
(kilograms*meters^2)
g = 9.8 ;              % Gravity (meters/sec^2)
m = 0.2 ;              % Pendulum bob mass (kg)
[sizes,x0,states]=sysmdl_k([],[],[],0) ;
states
states =
    'sysmdl_k/theta  integrator'
    'sysmdl_k/theta_dot  integrator'
    'sysmdl_k/phi  integrator'
    'sysmdl_k/phi_dot integrator'
```

Figure 8-30 Set system parameters for rotating pendulum model

Since the system is conservative, we expect the input to be zero at equilibrium, so set

    u0 = 0

The output vector is the same as the state vector, so we set

    y0 = [0.5;0;0;5]

We will allow the state and control to vary, but require that the output pendulum deflection be 0.5 rad. Set ix and iu to the empty vector, and set

```
iy = 1
```

The value of the derivative of motor position (ϕ) (the third element of the state vector) will be nonzero at equilibrium, and all the other state derivatives will be zero, so set

```
dx0 = [0;0;5;0]
idx = [1,2,4]
```

The MATLAB statements in Figure 8-31 execute the trim command with these values. The last element of x is the motor angular velocity at equilibrium, computed to be 6.1011 rad/sec. You can easily verify that this value results in a balance between centrifugal force and gravity.

```
x0=[0.5;0;0;5] ;
u0 = 0 ;
y0 = [0.5;0;0;5] ;
ix = [ ] ;
iu = [ ] ;
iy = 1  ;
dx0 = [0;0;5;0] ;
idx = [1,2,4] ;
x = trim('sysmdl_k',x0,u0,y0,ix,iu,iy,dx0,idx)
x =
     0.5000
          0
     0.0000
     6.1011
```

Figure 8-31   Locating the rotating pendulum equilibrium point

8.6   Optimization Toolbox and Simulink

A frequent task in the design of dynamical systems and control systems is the optimization of one or more parameters, often subject to constraints. The MATLAB Optimization Toolbox provides a variety of optimization functions for both unconstrained and constrained problems. The Optimization Toolbox does not provide any Simulink blocks; it is used from within the MATLAB workspace to optimize one or more parameters in a Simulink model. Particularly useful in conjunction with Simulink are `fminu` (unconstrained multivariable optimization), and `constr` (constrained optimization).

The syntax of these commands is

```
[x,options]=fminu(fun,x0,options,'grad',p1,p2,...,pn)
[x,options]=constr(fun,x0,options,vlb,vub,'grad',p1,p2,...,pn)
```

where *fun* is a MATLAB string containing the name of the objective function, and x0 is the initial guess for the parameter vector to be optimized. We will not discuss the syntax of the commands in detail here. For a detailed discussion, refer to the Optimization Toolbox documentation [1], or the MATLAB help system. However, it is worthwhile to discuss the construction of the objective function.

The goal of the optimization functions is to find a parameter vector (x) such that the value of the objective function is minimized. The objective function is a function M-file of the form

```
function f = fun(x)
```

or

```
function f = fun(x,p1,p2,...,pn)
```

where p1, p2,...,pn are optional parameters that are passed unchanged to *fun* by the optimization function. An objective function used with a Simulink model has the following structure:

1. Initialize Simulink parameters based on the values of the elements of x (the input argument passed to *fun* by the optimization function).

2. Run the Simulink model using `sim`, saving the state and possibly the output trajectory or input history in MATLAB variables.

3. Compute f (a scalar) using the saved variables. f is frequently a time integral of a function of the state, input, or output trajectories, but it could also be the extreme value of a trajectory component or the final value of a component.

It's important that `sim` options `SrcWorkspace` and `DstWorkspace` be set to 'current' (see Table 8-3) so that parameter values set in *fun* will be used instead of values assigned to variables of the same names in the base MATLAB workspace. Furthermore, since these options must be set to 'current', all workspace variables used to configure Simulink blocks must be assigned values in the objective function. If it is necessary to use parameters set in the base MATLAB workspace or in an M-file that calls the optimization function, pass the parameters using the optional arguments (p1,p2,...,pn).

Given a suitable objective function, the optimization function may be called from the MATLAB command line or from within an M-file. It is helpful if the initial guess for the parameter vector to be optimized (x0) is as close to the optimal value as possible, as this frequently improves convergence. Additionally, note that the optimization functions locate local minima, so if the minimum point is not unique, there is no guarantee that the desired minimum point will be found.

Example 8-12

To illustrate the use of the Optimization Toolbox, consider the damped pendulum illustrated in Figure 8-32.

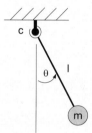

Figure 8-32   Damped pendulum

Suppose we wish to determine the value of the damping coefficient (c) that will minimize the objective function

$$f = \int_0^{50} (\theta^2 + \dot{\theta}^2)dt$$

for an initial pendulum deflection of $\pi/3$ radians, where $m = 1$ kg and $l = 1$ m. The equation of motion of the pendulum can be written

$$\ddot{\theta} + \frac{c}{ml^2}\dot{\theta} + \frac{g}{l}\sin\theta = 0$$

A Simulink model of this system is shown in Figure 8-33.

A function M-file that computes the value of the objective function given c is shown in Figure 8-34. In Figure 8-35, we use fminu to find the optimal value of c, using a starting guess of 5.

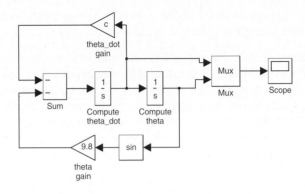

Figure 8-33   Simulink model of damped pendulum

```
function f = pdn_prf(c)
% System parameters used by Simulink model
t0 = 0 ;     % Start time
tf = 50 ;    % End time
h = .1 ;     % Time step size
opts=simset('SrcWorkspace','current') ;
opts=simset(opts,'DstWorkspace','current') ;
[t,x] = sim('sysmdl_m',[t0:h:tf],opts) ;  % Get the trajectory
[nt,nx] = size(x) ;
jp = zeros(1,nt) ; % Preallocate performance integrand
for i = 1:nt
   jp(i) = x(i,:)*x(i,:)' ; % Integrand of objective function
end
f = h*(sum(jp)-(jp(1)+jp(nt))/2) ;   % Trapezoidal integration
```

Figure 8-34   Function M-file to compute damped pendulum objective function

```
» c = fminu('pdn_prf',5)
c =
    9.4892
```

Figure 8-35   Finding the optimal damping coefficient using fminu

8.7 Other Toolboxes Useful with Simulink

The MathWorks and others offer a number of MATLAB toolboxes that are useful in conjunction with Simulink. Some of these are analysis tools, while others provide additional Simulink blocks. The toolboxes that primarily support analysis and design include the Control System Toolbox, the System Identification Toolbox, the Frequency Domain System Identification Toolbox, and the Linear Matrix Inequality Control Toolbox. The Fuzzy Logic Toolbox and the Neural Network Toolbox provide tools for the design of fuzzy logic or neural network controllers, and also provide Simulink blocks that implement the controllers. The Digital Signal Processing Blockset, Fixed Point Blockset, and Nonlinear Control Design Blockset all supply additional blocks that extend the capabilities of Simulink.

The list of products that supplement MATLAB and Simulink continues to grow. A good source of information concerning products offered by The MathWorks and others is the MathWorks Web page at www.mathworks.com.

8.8 Summary

In this chapter, we have discussed the use of Simulink analysis tools. First, we showed how to identify the structure of a model's state vector. Next, we showed how to run Simulink models from the MATLAB workspace using `sim`. Then, we used the linearization tools to find linear models of nonlinear systems, and used the linear models for control system design. We also discussed using `trim` to locate equilibrium points. Finally, we discussed the Optimization Toolbox, and showed how to use it with a Simulink model.

8.9 References and Further Reading

1. Grace, Andrew, *Optimization Toolbox User's Guide*, Natick, Mass., The MathWorks, Inc., 1992, pp. 3-16 to 3-19.

2. Khalil, Hassan K., *Nonlinear Systems*, 2nd ed., Upper Saddle River, N.J., Prentice Hall, 1996. An excellent text on the analysis and design of nonlinear systems.

3. Ogata, Katsuhiko, *Modern Control Engineering*, Englewood Cliffs, N.J., Prentice Hall, 1990. This book presents a thorough coverage of the standard techniques for the analysis and design of controls for continuous systems.

4. Ogata, Katsuhiko, *Designing Linear Control Systems with MATLAB*, Englewood Cliffs, N.J., Prentice Hall, 1993, pp. 50–67. This book presents brief

tutorials and MATLAB implementations of several important linear systems design techniques, including pole placement, state observers, and linear quadratic regulators.

5. Shahian, Bahram, and Hassul, Michael, *Control System Design Using MATLAB*, Englewood Cliffs, N.J., Prentice Hall, 1993. This book provides an introduction to MATLAB programming, and uses MATLAB to solve many of the standard problems in classical control and modern control theory.

6. Scheinerman, Edward C., *Invitation to Dynamical Systems*, Upper Saddle River, N.J., Prentice Hall, 1996, p. 134. This text provides a good introduction to the analysis of nonlinear systems.

7. Vidyasagar, M., *Nonlinear Systems Analysis*, 2nd ed., Englewood Cliffs, N.J., Prentice Hall, 1993. This book presents a detailed coverage of the analysis of nonlinear systems.

Callbacks

In this chapter we'll show how you can use callbacks with Simulink models. Callbacks are MATLAB commands that are automatically executed when certain events occur. Using callbacks, you can build graphical user interfaces to Simulink models. You can also use callbacks to add graphical animations.

9.1 Introduction

A *callback* is a MATLAB command that is executed when a certain event, such as opening a model or double-clicking a block, occurs. For example, normally, when you double-click a block, the block's dialog box is displayed. But consider the Scope block. Double-clicking it invokes a callback that displays the scope. In this chapter, we will discuss writing and installing callback functions.

Callbacks are closely related to MATLAB Handle Graphics. For example, when you create a menu using Handle Graphics, each menu choice generally is associated with a callback—a MATLAB command that is automatically executed when the menu choice is selected. The callback can be a simple MATLAB statement. So, if a menu choice were **Close Figure**, a suitable callback might be the MATLAB command `close(gcf)`. More often, however, callbacks are associated with M-files you write to accomplish a task corresponding to a menu choice. Since the use of callbacks is so closely related to MATLAB Handle Graphics, to get the most out of callback functions and Simulink, you'll need a solid understanding of MATLAB programming and Handle Graphics, both of which are beyond the scope of this book. In addition to the MATLAB documentation from The MathWorks [1], we recommend the text by Hanselman and Littlefield [2].

9.2 Callback Function Overview

Simulink callbacks can be associated with a model or with a particular block within a model. Table 9-1 lists the callbacks that can be associated with a model, and Table 9-2 lists the callbacks that can be associated with a particular block.

Table 9-1 Model callback parameters

Parameter name	When executed
CloseFcn	Before model is closed. Use this callback to do any needed housecleaning when a model is closed. For example, if the model uses a custom graphical user interface, all interface windows should be closed before closing the model.
PostLoadFcn	After model is loaded. One use of this callback is to automatically start a custom graphical user interface once a model is loaded.
PostSaveFcn	After model is saved.
PreLoadFcn	Before model is loaded. This callback can be used to initialize MATLAB variables used to configure model or block parameters.
PreSaveFcn	Before model is saved.
StartFcn	Before simulation starts. This callback is executed after MATLAB workspace variables are read.
StopFcn	After the simulation stops. This callback is executed after output is written to the MATLAB workspace or files. One use of StopFcn is to automatically produce a plot when the simulation stops.

9.2.1 Installing Callbacks

Callbacks are installed using the MATLAB command set_param. The syntax is

```
set_param(object, parameter, value)
```

object is a MATLAB string containing the name of the model or the path to a block. If the callback is associated with model behavior (Table 9-1), *object* is the name of the model. For example, if the model is stored in file car_mod.mdl, *object* should contain the string 'car_mod'. If the callback is associated with a block, the Simulink path to the block is used. For example, if the block of interest is named Gain_1, in subsystem Controller of car_mod, *object* should contain the string 'car_mod/Controller/Gain_1'.

parameter is a MATLAB string containing the callback parameter (the name given to the event of interest) from Table 9-1 or Table 9-2.

Table 9-2 Block callback parameters

Parameter name	When executed
CloseFcn	When the block is closed using the close_system command. This callback is executed only when the close_system command is issued for the particular block, not for the model as a whole. Additionally, the callback will be executed whenever close_system is issued for a particular block, whether the block's dialog box is open or not.
CopyFcn	After a block is copied. This callback is recursive for subsystems. Thus, if the callback has been defined for a block in a subsystem, and the subsystem is copied, the callback is executed.
DeleteFcn	Before a block is deleted. Use this callback to close any open user interface windows associated with the block. This callback is recursive for subsystems.
InitFcn	Before the block diagram is compiled and before block parameters are evaluated. This callback could be used to obtain data to set block parameters.
LoadFcn	After model is loaded. This callback is recursive for subsystems.
ModelCloseFcn	Before model is closed. This callback is recursive for subsystems. Use this callback to do any block-specific housecleaning before closing a model. For example, if there is a graphical user interface associated with the block, use this callback to close it. This is preferable to closing the interface using the model CloseFcn callback because it eliminates the need to search for multiple instances of a block-specific interface, and the need to reconfigure the model callback when a block is added or renamed.
OpenFcn	When the block is opened. This callback is executed when you double-click a block, and replaces the default behavior of opening the block's dialog box or opening a subsystem window.

Table 9-2   Block callback parameters (Continued)

Parameter name	When executed
ParentCloseFcn	Before closing a subsystem containing the block. This callback is also executed when a subsystem containing the block is created using **Edit:Create Subsystem**. This callback is the subsystem analog to the Model-CloseFcn callback. It is a good practice to define this callback to behave the same as ModelCloseFcn.
PreSaveFcn	Before the model is saved. This callback is recursive for subsystems.
PostSaveFcn	After the model is saved. This callback is recursive for subsystems.
StartFcn	After the block diagram is compiled and before the simulation starts.
StopFcn	When the simulation stops for any reason.
UndoDelete	When a block deletion is undone. If there is a CopyFcn, there should probably also be an UndoDelete.

value is a MATLAB string containing the callback. So, for example, if the callback is a function M-file stored as set_gain.m, value would contain the string 'set_gain'.

Example 9-1

Consider the Simulink model shown in Figure 9-1, which we've stored as callb_1.mdl. The value of the Constant block is set to In_val. We wish for MATLAB to prompt the user for the value of In_val when the model is opened.

A suitable callback is the MATLAB statement

```
In_val = input('Enter the value: ') ;
```

which we saved in M-file initm_1.m

To install the callback so that it is executed when the model is opened, open the model, then enter the following command at the MATLAB prompt:

```
set_param('callb_1','PreLoadFcn','initm_1')
```

Save the model, then close it. The next time the model is opened, the prompt

```
» Enter the value:
```

is displayed. The value entered is assigned to In_val.

If we wanted the user to be prompted for the value of In_val at the start of each simulation instead of when the model is opened, we could install the callback using the command:

```
set_param('callb_1','InitFcn','initm_1')
```

Figure 9-1 Simple model initialized using a callback

9.3   Model Construction Commands

Simulink provides several MATLAB commands to create and edit Simulink models. These commands provide the capability to create and save a new model, to add and delete blocks, to add and delete signal lines, and to get and set model and block parameters. Several of these commands useful in conjunction with callbacks are listed in Table 9-3 and discussed below.

9.3.1   Finding the Name of the Current Block

Use gcb to find the Simulink path to the current block. For example,

```
current_block = gcb ;
```

This function is useful when you create a graphical user interface associated with a Simulink block, as it provides a convenient and positive means to associate a Handle Graphics figure and a Simulink block. The following MATLAB code fragment will get the path name to the current block, create a figure, and store the name of the current block in the new figure's UserData:

```
current_block = gcb ;
h_fig = figure('Position', [left bottom width height]) ;
set(h_fig, 'UserData', current_block) ;
```

Table 9-3 Simulink model building commands useful with callbacks

Command	Description
bdroot(*object*)	Return the name of the Simulink model associated with *object*. *object* is a MATLAB string containing the full Simulink path name of a block or subsystem. bdroot is used with callbacks to get the name of the model with which the current block (the block associated with the currently executing callback) is associated.
gcb	Return the full Simulink path to the current block.
gcs	Return the full Simulink path to the current system or subsystem.
get_param(*obj, param*)	Get the current value of a parameter associated with a system, subsystem, or block.
set_param(*obj, param,value*)	Set the value of a parameter associated with a particular system, subsystem, or block.

9.3.2   Finding the Name of the Current Model

Use bdroot to get the name of the current model as follows:

```
current_model = bdroot(gcb) ;
```

9.3.3   Finding the Name of the Current System

Use gcs to find the name of the current system or subsystem. For example,

```
cur_sys = gcs ;
```

Note that if a block is at the top level of a model, the commands gcs and bdroot(gcb) produce the same result. If the block is in a subsystem, the two commands produce different results.

9.3.4   Setting Parameter Values

The set_param command, described earlier in the context of defining callbacks, can be used to set a large number of model and block parameters. A complete list of these parameters is in Appendix B. More than one parameter for a particular object (system, subsystem, block) can be set using one set_param command. For example, the following command will set the `Tag` parameter to the string `Block A` and `Gain` parameter to 10 for a gain block:

```
set_param(gcb,'Tag','Block A','Gain','10') ;
```

Note that parameter `Gain` is set to the character string `'10'` and not the number 10. To set parameter `Gain` to the vector [10 20 30], you could use the following command:

```
set_param(gcb,'Gain','[10 20 30]') ;
```

`set_param` can be executed while a simulation is in progress. Thus, if a graphical user interface changes the value of gain for a Gain block, the gain is changed immediately. This capability permits you to build interactive simulations.

SimulationCommand

A particularly useful parameter is `SimulationCommand`. This parameter may be set to the following values: `start`, `stop`, `pause`, `continue`. Setting the value of `SimulationCommand` has the same effect as selecting the corresponding choice from the model window menu bar. For example, suppose model `examp_1.mdl` is currently open. Entering the command

```
set_param('examp_1','SimulationCommand','start')
```

at the MATLAB prompt is equivalent to choosing **Simulation:Start** from the model window menu bar.

9.3.5   Reading Parameter Values

`get_param` is similar to `set_param`. However, `get_param` can return only the value of one parameter at a time. Note that when `get_param` is used to read numeric data, the parameter is returned as a string. Thus, if immediately after entering the `set_param` command above, we enter the command

```
g = get_param(gcb,'Gain')
```

the following result will be displayed:

```
g =
[10 20 30]
```

but g is a character string, not a matrix. To get the values the elements of g, use the command:

```
gv = str2num(g)
```

which will result in:

```
gv =
     10     20     30
```

SimulationStatus

In callback functions that control a simulation, parameter SimulationStatus can be very useful. This parameter will be set to one of the following: stopped, initializing, running, paused, terminating, or external (only if used with Real-Time Workshop). For example, if model examp_1.mdl is open but not running, entering, at the MATLAB prompt, the command

```
get_param('examp_1','SimulationStatus')
```

will result in the response

```
ans =
stopped
```

9.4   Graphical User Interfaces with Callbacks

Using Simulink callbacks, it is easy to build graphical interfaces to Simulink models. An excellent example of this capability is the Slider Gain block in the Linear block library. This block is a simple Gain block with a callback that produces the slider interface (Figure 9-2). In this section we will describe the process for building a graphical user interface using Simulink callbacks and discuss the relevant programming issues.

Figure 9-2   Slider Gain user interface window

9.4.1   Graphical User Interface Callback

A MATLAB Handle Graphics user interface can be built using a single M-file that installs the callbacks and responds to each callback generated by the Simulink model and by the user interface itself. The user interface can be installed such that it is opened by double-clicking an associated block in the

Simulink model. A user interface opened by double-clicking a block should respond to the following events:

1. The user interface is opened by double-clicking the associated Simulink block (callback OpenFcn). This callback should contain the MATLAB code to build the interface figure and initialize it. The code should verify that there is not already an instance of the figure open and associated with the same Simulink block.

2. The block associated with the callback is deleted (callback DeleteFcn). Close the interface figure if it is open.

3. The model containing the block is closed (callback ModelCloseFcn). Close the figure if it is open.

4. The subsystem containing the block is closed (callback ParentCloseFcn). If you do not want to close the user interface in this situation, this event can be ignored.

5. A control is selected in the user interface window. There will be a callback associated with each control. These callbacks are installed when the user interface window is opened.

Additionally, it is a good practice to include in the callback M-file statements to install the callbacks. Once this code is executed, the callbacks will become a permanent part of the model when the model is saved. Even though the installation code won't be needed again, it serves as a useful record of exactly how the callbacks were configured.

A convenient means to attach a graphical user interface to a Simulink model is to add an empty subsystem to the model. Install an OpenFcn callback for the subsystem block so that when the user double clicks on the subsystem block, the user interface window is opened. You can mask the subsystem to produce a custom block icon, and also to provide local storage, as will be discussed shortly.

A template for a suitable M-file is shown in Figure 9-3. Notice that each callback has the form

```
'M-file action'
```

where M-file is the name of the callback M-file and action is a case in the switch-case code block. This syntax is identical to that used with the MATLAB eval command, and in fact eval is useful as a quick means to test the callback M-file.

```
function clbktplt(varargin)
% Callback function template
% Install this callback by invoking it with the command
% clbktplt('init_block')
% at the MATLAB prompt with the appropriate model file
% open and selected.
%
% To use the template, save a copy under a new name. Then replace
% clbktplt with the new name everywhere it appears.
action = varargin{1}  ;
switch action,
  case 'init_block',
    init_fcn ;                        % Block initialization function,
                                      % located in this M-file
  case 'create_fig',
    if(findobj('UserData',gcb))   % Don't open two for same block
      disp('Only open one instance per block can be opened')
    else
      % Here, put all commands needed to set up the figure and its
      % callbacks.
      left =    100 ; % Figure position values
      bottom = 100 ;
      width =   100 ;
      height = 100 ;
      h_fig = figure('Position',[left bottom width height], ...
                     'MenuBar','none') ;
      set(h_fig,'UserData',gcb) ; % Save name of current block in
                                  % the figure's UserData. This is
                                  % used to detect that a clbktplt
                                  % fig is open for the current
                                % block, so that only one instance
                                % of the figure is open at a time.
    end
  case 'close_fig',               % Close if open when model is closed.
    h_fig = findobj('UserData',gcb) ;
    if(h_fig)                     % Is figure for current block open?
      close(h_fig) ;              % If so, close it.
    end
```

Figure 9-3 Callback function template

```
  case 'rename_block',    % Change the name in the figure UserData.
    h_fig = findobj('UserData',gcb) ;
    if(h_fig)                       % Is the figure open?
      set(h_fig,'UserData',gcb) ; % If so, change the name.
    end
  case 'UserAction1',      % Place cases for various user actions
                          % here. These callbacks should be defined
                          % when the figure is created.
end
%**********************************************************************
%*                       init_fcn                                    *
%**********************************************************************
function init_fcn()
% Configure the block callbacks
% This function should be executed once when the block is created
% to define the callbacks. After it is executed, save the model
% and the callback definitions will be saved with the model. There
% is no need to reinstall the callbacks when the block is copied;
% they are part of the block once the model is saved.
sys = gcs ;
block = [sys,'/InitialBlockName'] ; % Replace InitialBlockName with
                                    % the name of the block when it is
                                      % created and initialized. This
                                        % does not need to be changed k
                                      % when the block is copied, as the
                                      % callbacks won't be reinstalled.
set_param(block,'OpenFcn',        'clbktplt create_fig',...
                'ModelCloseFcn','clbktplt close_fig', ...
                'DeleteFcn',     'clbktplt close_fig', ...
                'NameChangeFcn','clbktplt rename_block') ;
```

Figure 9-3   Callback function template (Continued)

9.4.2 Programming Issues

There are several programming issues to consider when writing callback M-files. These issues are discussed next.

Avoid embedded names

Don't embed block or subsystem names in the callback M-file. Instead use gcb and gcs and store the names in MATLAB variables.

Current system and block

MATLAB commands gcb and gcs are reliable only during the execution of Simulink callbacks. These commands are not reliable during the execution of callbacks associated with user interface controls such as pushbuttons and sliders, as there is no guarantee that the block or even the system associated with a user interface control is the current block or system. For example, gcb returns the Simulink path to the block most recently clicked on, even if that block is in another open Simulink model.

Most user interface callbacks must access various parameters of the corresponding Simulink model, so it is necessary to store the name of the model, system, or block in local storage that is accessible to the callback function, and which is independent of the current system or block.

Local data storage

In addition to the need to store the names of the block or system associated with a callback, it is often necessary to store local data such as parameter values. While it is possible to store this data using global variables, that's not a good idea as it adds the risk of unintended side effects. There are two good places to store the information: UserData and masked block dialog box parameters.

Every Simulink block has a UserData parameter that can store any MATLAB variable. UserData is not stored with the model, so it can't be used to store default data. The UserData for a Simulink block is available as long as the model is open, so it is a convenient place to store data such as the current value of model parameters. Set Simulink block UserData using the MATLAB command

```
set_param(gcb,'UserData',value) ;
```

and read block UserData using

```
value = get_param(block,'UserData') ;
```

value can be a single scalar, a matrix, or even a cell array or structure.

Each MATLAB Handle Graphics object (figure, axis, and user interface control (slider, pushbutton, etc.)) has its own UserData. These UserData variables are set with MATLAB Handle Graphics command set, and read with get. It is convenient to use these UserData variables to store the system and block associated with an instance of a user interface. If the user interface is created by the block callback `OpenFcn`, save the path to the Simulink block in the figure's `UserData`:

```
set(gcf,'UserData',gcb) ;
```

The `UserData` for Handle Graphics objects is available only as long as the object exists. For example, the `UserData` for a figure is available as long as the figure is open. If it is closed, the `UserData` is destroyed. In the callback M-file template in Figure 9-3, this fact is used as a mechanism to determine whether there is already an instance of a user interface figure associated with a particular block. Since user interface windows may be opened and closed during a Simulink session, store local data in these `UserData` variables only if this data is to be reinitialized each time the interface is opened.

Masked block dialog box parameters are an alternative to the block's `UserData` for storing user interface local data. This can be very useful, as variables defined in this manner are available to both the callback function and to any blocks in the masked subsystem. The variable name associated with each dialog box prompt is treated as a parameter of the masked block (the subsystem), and may be set using `set_param` and read using `get_param`. As with other block parameters, the values must be entered in the dialog box fields as strings.

Example 9-2

Consider the Mask Editor Initialization page prompt definition shown in Figure 9-4.

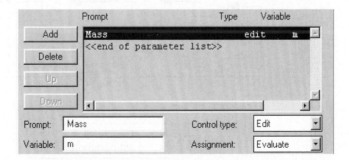

Figure 9-4   Mask Editor Initialization page prompt definition

To set the value of the variable m associated with prompt **Mass**, the following statements may be entered at the MATLAB prompt or in an M-file:

```
x = 10.0 ;
x_string = num2str(x) ;
set_param('examp/subsys_a','m',x_string) ;
```

To read the contents of the field, use the following statement:

```
y=str2num(get_param('examp/subsys_a','m')) ;
```

Example 9-3

Consider the Simulink model shown in Figure 9-5. This system models a spring, mass, dashpot system. Double-clicking on the block labeled SetParams opens the dialog box shown in Figure 9-6. The contents of the three text fields in the dialog box are used to compute the value of gain for the two Gain blocks. The gain values are updated when the OK button is pressed. The parameters can be changed either before or during the execution of a simulation.

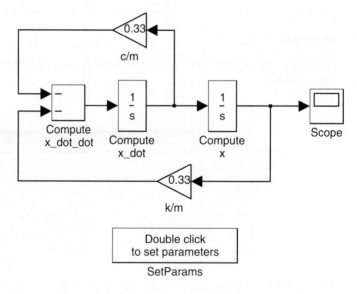

Figure 9-5   Simulink model with graphical user interface

The block labeled SetParams is an empty masked subsystem. The block was created by dragging a Subsystem block from the Connections block library,

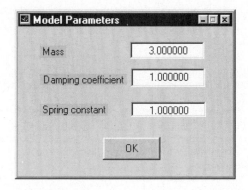

Figure 9-6   Spring, mass, dashpot graphical user interface

then converting the block into a masked subsystem using **Edit:Create Mask**. The label was created using the single command

```
disp('Double click\nto set parameters')
```

in the **Drawing commands** field on the Icon page of the Mask Editor. The Initialization page of the Mask Editor (Figure 9-7) has fields **Mass**, **Damping coefficient**, and **Spring constant**. The OpenFcn parameter for the masked block is set to open to the dialog box shown in Figure 9-6, so the user does not have direct access to the masked block's dialog box fields. Instead, the callback function uses these dialog box fields to store the current values of mass, damping coefficient, and spring constant. Since these values are stored in the masked block's dialog box, the parameters are saved with the model, and the most recently saved version of the parameters will be loaded in the Model Parameters dialog box fields when the model is next opened.

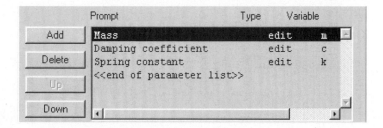

Figure 9-7   Mask Editor Initialization page

Figure 9-8 shows the callback function M-file that installs and responds to the callbacks. This M-file was based on the template shown in Figure 9-3.

```
function sys_set(varargin)
%*****************************************************************
%*                        sys_set                              *
%*****************************************************************
% Callback function for the SetParam Masked subsystem block
% This callback is installed by invoking it with the command
% sys_set('init_block')
% at the MATLAB prompt, with the appropriate model file open and
% selected. There is an additional callback associated with the
% sys_set figure'sOK button, 'sys_set OK_pressed'. This callback
% sets the Gain blocksaccording to the current values of mass,
% damping, and spring constant.
action = varargin{1}  ;
switch action,
  case 'init_block',
    init_fcn ;                % Call init_block, located in this M-file
  case 'create_fig',
    if(findobj('UserData',gcb)) % Don't open two for same block
    else
      create_fig ;
    end
  case 'close_fig',                % Close if open when model is closed
    h_fig = findobj('UserData',gcb) ;
    if(h_fig)                % Is the figure for current block open?
      close(h_fig) ;        % If so, close it.
    end
  case 'rename_block',    % Change the name in the figure UserData.
    h_fig = findobj('UserData',gcb) ;
    if(h_fig)                        % Is the figure open?
      set(h_fig,'UserData',gcb) ; % If so, change the name.
    end
  case 'OK_pressed',              % OK button in sys_set figure
    ok_pressed ;
end
%*****************************************************************
%*                        init_fcn                             *
%*****************************************************************
function init_fcn()
% Configure the subsystem block callbacks
sys = gcs ;
block = [sys,'/SetParams'] ;
set_param(block,'OpenFcn',        'sys_set create_fig',...
                'ModelCloseFcn','sys_set close_fig', ...
                'DeleteFcn',     'sys_set close_fig', ...
                'NameChangeFcn','sys_set rename_block') ;
set_param(block,'k','1') ;    % Load initial values in the dialog
set_param(block,'m','1') ;    % box fields.
set_param(block,'c','1') ;
%*****************************************************************
%*                        create_fig                           *
%*****************************************************************
```

Figure 9-8   Spring, mass, dashpot callback M-file

```
function create_fig()
% We'll check UserData for the Subsystem block. This UserData
% will contain the most recent values of mass, damp, spring.
% Since UserData is not saved with the model, this will be
% blank initially. We could save the default data in a .mat
% file, but we'll just let everything default to 1
mds = get_param(gcb,'UserData') ;
mass = str2num(get_param(gcb,'m')) ;
damp = str2num(get_param(gcb,'c')) ;
spring = str2num(get_param(gcb,'k')) ;
mass_str = sprintf('%f',mass) ;        % Put values in strings
damp_str = sprintf('%f',damp) ;
spring_str = sprintf('%f',spring) ;
% Create the user interface figure and ui controls
h_fig = figure('Position',[555 406 250 169],'Tag','sys_set',...
               'MenuBar','none','NumberTitle','off', ...
               'Resize','off', ...
               'Name','Model Parameters') ;
h_mass_label = uicontrol('Parent',h_fig, ...
'Units','points', ...
'Position',[18 99.75 23.25 10], ...
'String','Mass', ...
'Style','text', ...
'Tag','mass_label');
h_damp_label = uicontrol('Parent',h_fig, ...
'Units','points', ...
'Position',[18 76.25 76.5 10], ...
'String','Damping coefficient', ...
'Style','text', ...
'Tag','damp_label');
h_spring_label = uicontrol('Parent',h_fig, ...
'Units','points', ...
'Position',[18 50.25 60 10], ...
'String','Spring constant', ...
'Style','text', ...
'Tag','spring_label');
h_mass_text = uicontrol('Parent',h_fig, ...
'Units','points', ...
'BackgroundColor',[1 1 1], ...
'Position',[97.5 99 64.5 14.25], ...
'String',mass_str, ...
'Style','edit', ...
'Tag','mass_string');
h_damp_text = uicontrol('Parent',h_fig, ...
'Units','points', ...
'BackgroundColor',[1 1 1], ...
'Position',[98.25 75 64.5 15.75], ...
'String',damp_str, ...
'Style','edit', ...
'Tag','damp_string');
h_spring_text = uicontrol('Parent',h_fig, ...
```

Figure 9-8   Spring, mass, dashpot callback M-file (Continued)

```
'Units','points', ...
'BackgroundColor',[1 1 1], ...
'Position',[98.25 49.5 65.25 12.75], ...
'String',spring_str, ...
'Style','edit', ...
'Tag','spring_string');
h_OK_button = uicontrol('Parent',h_fig, ...
'Units','points', ...
'Callback','sys_set OK_pressed', ...
'Position',[73.5 12.75 50.25 19.5], ...
'String','OK', ...
'Tag','OK_button', ...
'UserData',gcs );              % Save current system in OK button
set(h_fig,'UserData',gcb) ; % userdata Save name of current block
                             % in the figure's UserData. This is
                             % used to detect that a sys_set fig
                             % is already open for the current block,
                             % so that only one instance of the figure
                             % is open at a time.
%*****************************************************************
%*                     ok_pressed                              *
%*****************************************************************
function ok_pressed()
% When the OK button is pressed get the current parameter values
% and update the gain values
h_fig = gcbf ;
h_mass = findobj(h_fig,'Tag','mass_string') ;
h_OK_button = findobj(h_fig,'Tag','OK_button') ;
mass_string = get(h_mass,'String') ;
mass = str2num(mass_string);
h_damp = findobj(h_fig,'Tag','damp_string') ;
damp_string = get(h_damp,'String') ;
damp = str2num(damp_string);
h_spring = findobj(h_fig,'Tag','spring_string') ;
spring_string = get(h_spring,'String') ;
spring = str2num(spring_string);
% We could put close(h_fig) here to close figure when OK pressed
cm_str = sprintf('%f',damp/mass) ; % Set the gain blocks
km_str = sprintf('%f',spring/mass) ;
% Note that the set_param statements that follow are looking for
% 2 particular named gain blocks. If the names of those blocks
% change, these two set_param statements must also change.
cur_sys = get(h_OK_button,'UserData') ;
cur_block = get(h_fig,'UserData') ;
set_param([get_param(cur_sys,'Name'),'/c//m'],'Gain',cm_str) ;
set_param([get_param(cur_sys,'Name'),'/k//m'],'Gain',km_str) ;
% Store values for mass, damping, spring in masked block
% dialog box fields that are not directly accessible to the user
set_param(cur_block,'m',sprintf('%f',mass)) ;
set_param(cur_block,'c',sprintf('%f',damp)) ;
set_param(cur_block,'k',sprintf('%f',spring)) ;
```

Figure 9-8   Spring, mass, dashpot callback M-file (Continued)

In addition to handling Simulink model events (open block, delete block, etc.), there is a callback (case `'OK_pressed'`) that responds to clicking the OK button in the Model Parameters dialog box. This callback is defined for the OK button when the graphical user interface is opened.

Example 9-4

In this example we will build a block that produces a graphical user interface to start and stop a simulation. Consider the Simulink model shown in Figure 9-9(a). Double-clicking on the block StartStop opens the Start/Stop control window shown in Figure 9-9(b). Whenever the simulation is not running, the label on the button is Start. Pressing the button will cause the simulation to begin. When the simulation starts, the label changes to Stop. Pressing the button when the label is Stop will cause the simulation to stop.

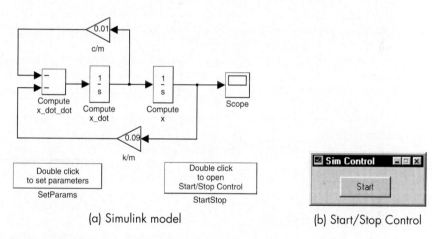

(a) Simulink model   (b) Start/Stop Control

Figure 9-9   Model with Start/Stop control

The block labeled StartStop is an empty masked subsystem created as described in Example 9-3. Figure 9-10 shows the M-file that installs and responds to the callbacks.

```
function strtstpm(varargin)
%*********************************************************************
%*                           strtstpm                              *
%*********************************************************************
% Callback function for the StartStop subsystem block
% This callback is installed by invoking it with the command
% strtstpm('init_block')
% at the MATLAB prompt, with appropriate model file open and
selected.
% There is an additional callback associated with each button
action = varargin{1}  ;
switch action,
  case 'init_block',
    init_fcn ;                % Call init_block, located in this M-
file
  case 'create_fig',
    if(findobj('UserData',gcb)) % Don't open two for same block
      % Do nothing
    else
      create_fig ;
    end
  case 'close_fig',            % Close if open when model is closed
    h_fig = findobj('UserData',gcb) ;
    if(h_fig)                  % Is the figure for current block
open?
      close(h_fig) ;           % If so, close it.
    end
  case 'rename_block',    % Change the name in the figure
UserData.
    h_fig = findobj('UserData',gcb) ;
    if(h_fig)                      % Is the figure open?
      set(h_fig,'UserData',gcb) ; % If so, change the name.
    end
  case 'Start_pressed',                  % Start button
    Start_Pressed ;
case 'Stop_pressed',                     % Stop button
    Stop_Pressed ;
  case 'start_sim',                      % Something caused sim to
start
    Sim_Starting ;
  case 'stop_sim',                       % Something caused sim to
stop
    Sim_Stopping ;
end
```

Figure 9-10   Start/Stop control callback M-file

```
%*********************************************************************
%*                           init_fcn                               *
%*********************************************************************
function init_fcn()
% Configure the subsystem block callbacks
sys = gcs ;
block = [sys,'/StartStop'] ;
set_param(block,'OpenFcn',        'strtstpm create_fig',...
                'ModelCloseFcn','strtstpm close_fig', ...
                'DeleteFcn',     'strtstpm close_fig', ...
                'NameChangeFcn','strtstpm rename_block', ...
                'StartFcn',      'strtstpm start_sim',...
                'StopFcn',       'strtstpm stop_sim') ;
%*********************************************************************
%*                          create_fig                              *
%*********************************************************************
function create_fig()
% Create the user interface figure and ui controls
h_fig = figure('Position',[555 406 145 44],'Tag','strtstpm',...
               'MenuBar','none','NumberTitle','off', ...
               'Resize','off', ...
               'Name','Sim Control') ;
h_Start_button = uicontrol('Parent',h_fig, ...
'Units','points', ...
'Callback','strtstpm Start_pressed', ...
'Position',[27 4.75 50.25 19.5], ...
'String','Start', ...
'Tag','Start_button', ...
'UserData',bdroot );          % Save current system in Start
button userdata
set(h_fig,'UserData',gcb) ; % Save name of current block in
                            % the figure's UserData. This is
                            % used to detect that a strtstpm fig
                            % is already open for the current
block,
                            % so that only one instance of the
figure
                            % is open at a time.
sim_stat = get_param(bdroot,'SimulationStatus') ;
if(strcmp(sim_stat,'running') | strcmp(sim_stat,'paused'))
  Sim_Starting ;
end
```

Figure 9-10 Start/Stop control callback M-file (Continued)

```
%******************************************************************
%*                        Start_Pressed                          *
%******************************************************************
function Start_Pressed()
% When the Start button is pressed start the simulation
h_fig = gcbf ;
h_Start_button = findobj(h_fig,'Tag','Start_button') ;
cur_sys = get(h_Start_button,'UserData') ;
set_param( cur_sys, 'SimulationCommand', 'start' );
%******************************************************************
%*                        Stop_Pressed                           *
%******************************************************************
function Stop_Pressed()
% When the Stop button is pressed Stop the simulation
h_fig = gcbf ;
h_Start_button = findobj(h_fig,'Tag','Start_button') ;
cur_sys = get(h_Start_button,'UserData') ;
set_param( cur_sys, 'SimulationCommand', 'stop' );
%******************************************************************
%*                        Sim_Starting                           *
%******************************************************************
function Sim_Starting()
% Something started the sim. Make the Start_Stop button read Stop
h_fig = findobj('UserData',gcb) ;
h_Start_button = findobj(h_fig,'Tag','Start_button') ;
set(h_Start_button,'Callback','strtstpm Stop_pressed', ...
'String','Stop') ;
%******************************************************************
%*                        Sim_Stopping                           *
%******************************************************************
function Sim_Stopping()
% Something stopped the sim. Make the Start_Stop button read
Start
h_fig = findobj('UserData',gcb) ;
h_Start_button = findobj(h_fig,'Tag','Start_button') ;
set(h_Start_button,'Callback','strtstpm Start_pressed', ...
'String','Start') ;
```

Figure 9-10   Start/Stop control callback M-file (Continued)

9.5 Callback-Based Animations

The techniques discussed previously for associating graphical user interfaces with Simulink models can be extended to create animations. Using the techniques discussed in this section, you can build custom Simulink blocks that produce graphical output devices such as meters, or that use a graphical representation of a physical system to show the state of a simulation. An animation differs from a graphical user interface in that an animation receives the data it displays from the Simulink model as the model executes, while an interface responds to user input. There are several approaches to developing Simulink animations. In addition to the technique discussed here, animations can be built using S-Functions or using the Animation Toolbox, both of which are discussed in later chapters.

A callback-based animation consists of a masked subsystem and a callback M-file. A template animation subsystem is shown in Figure 9-11. The Zero-Order hold is used to cause the graphical output to update at specified intervals. Increasing the sample time will cause the display to update less frequently, and cause the simulation to execute faster. The MATLAB Function block dialog box MATLAB Function field contains the command

```
anmclbk('Update_Anm',cb_var,u(1))
```

anmclbk is the name of the callback function M-file. Update_Anm is the first argument to function anmclbk, and corresponds to the variable action in the template M-file, used to select the case to update the animation figure. cb_var is the name of the first variable in the animation subsystem initialization page. We use this variable to store the handle of the animation figure when the figure is opened by double-clicking the animation block. When, during the course of the simulation, function anmclbk is called by a particular instance of the animation block, this second argument will contain the handle of the corresponding animation figure. If there is no figure corresponding to this handle (the figure either was not opened or has been closed), the callback M-file does nothing and returns. If there is a figure with that handle, the code to update the figure according to the value of the third argument (u(1)) is executed. Using this mechanism, there can be multiple instances of the animation block open at the same time, even in the same Simulink model.

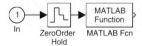

Figure 9-11   Animation subsystem template

The callback function M-file template in Figure 9-3 can be used to create a callback-based animation in conjunction with the animation subsystem template shown in Figure 9-11. There should be one additional `case` corresponding to action `'Update_Anm'`, containing the code to update the figure.

Example 9-5

In this example we will build a Simulink block that produces a "progress bar" that shows the progress of a simulation. The masked subsystem is shown in Figure 9-12, and the progress bar figure is shown in Figure 9-13.

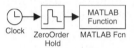

Figure 9-12 Progress bar masked subsystem

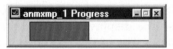

Figure 9-13 Progress bar

The callback function M-file is shown in Figure 9-14. When the user double-clicks on the Progress Bar icon, function `create_fig` is executed. In addition to building the progress bar figure, this function obtains the current simulation start and stop times from Simulink model parameters `StartTime` and `Stop-Time` and saves these values in the progress bar (handle `h_bar`) `UserData`. Each time the callback function is called during the simulation by the MATLAB Function block, the start and stop times are read from the progress bar `User-Data`, and with the third calling argument (current simulation time) used to update the figure.

```
function prog_bar(varargin)
% Install this callback by invoking it with the command
% prog_bar('init_block')
% at the MATLAB prompt with the appropriate model file open and selected.
%
action = varargin{1}  ;
switch action,
  case 'init_block',
    init_fcn ;                      % Block initialization function,
                                    % located in this M-file
```

Figure 9-14 Progress bar callback function M-file

```
  case 'create_fig',
    if(findobj('UserData',gcb))   % Don't open two for same block
      disp('Only open one instance per block can be opened')
    else
      % Set up the figure and its callbacks
      create_fig ;
    end
  case 'close_fig',            % Close if open when model is closed.
    h_fig = findobj('UserData',gcb) ;
    if(h_fig)                  % Is the figure for current block open?
      close(h_fig) ;           % If so, close it.
    end
  case 'rename_block',    % Change the name in the figure UserData.
    h_fig = findobj('UserData',gcb) ;
    if(h_fig)                       % Is the figure open?
      set(h_fig,'UserData',gcb) ; % If so, change the name.
    end
  case 'UpdateTime',
    if(ishandle(varargin{2}))   % Only do update if block is open
      do_update(varargin{2},varargin{3}) ;
    end
end
%*****************************************************************
%*                          init_fcn                            *
%*****************************************************************
function init_fcn()
% Configure the block callbacks
% This function should be executed once when the block is created
% to define the callbacks. After it is executed, save the model
% and the callback definitions will be saved with the model. There is no need
% to reinstall the callbacks when the block is copied; they are part of the
% block once the model is saved.
sys = gcs ;
block = [sys,'/Progress'] ;
set_param(block,'OpenFcn',        'prog_bar create_fig',...
                'ModelCloseFcn','prog_bar close_fig', ...
                'DeleteFcn',      'prog_bar close_fig', ...
                'NameChangeFcn','prog_bar rename_block') ;
set_param(gcb,'Tag','prog_bar') ;
%*****************************************************************
%*                          reate_fig                           *
%*****************************************************************
function create_fig()
% Create the progress bar figure
h_fig = figure('Position',[200 200 200 30], ...
                'MenuBar','none','NumberTitle','off', ...
                'Resize','off', ...
                'Name',[gcs,' Progress']) ;
```

Figure 9-14   Progress bar callback function M-file (Continued)

```
set(h_fig,'UserData',gcb) ; % Save name of current block in
                            % the figure's UserData. This is
                            % used to detect that a prog_bar fig
                            % is already open for the current block,
                            % so that only one instance of the figure
                            % is open at a time.
axis([0,1,0,1]) ;
hold on ;
h_axis = gca ;
set(h_axis,'Xtick',[]) ;
set(h_axis,'Ytick',[]) ;
h_bar = fill([0,0.005,0.005,0],[0,0,1,1],'r') ; % Make the bar red
StartTime = str2num(get_param(gcs,'StartTime')) ;
StopTime  = str2num(get_param(gcs,'StopTime'))  ;
set(h_bar,'UserData',[StartTime StopTime]) ;
% Put the progress bar handle in the masked block data field
% so that it can be passed to this function during the simulation.
set_param(gcb,'MaskValueString',num2str(h_bar,25)) ;
%*****************************************************************
%*                         do_update                           *
%*****************************************************************
function do_update(h_bar,current_time)
% Update the progress bar to the current simulation time
UserData = get(h_bar,'UserData') ;
start_time = UserData(1) ;
stop_time = UserData(2)  ;
x_val = (current_time - start_time)/(stop_time - start_time) ;
set(h_bar,'Xdata',[0,x_val,x_val,0]) ;
```

Figure 9-14   Progress bar callback function M-file (Continued)

9.6   Summary

In this chapter we have discussed Simulink callbacks and have shown how they can be used to create graphical user interfaces and to build custom animations.

9.7   References and Further Reading

1. Using MATLAB Graphics, Version 5, Natick, Mass., The MathWorks, Inc., 1996.

2. Hanselman, Duane C., and Littlefield, Bruce R., *Mastering MATLAB 5: A Comprehensive Tutorial*, Upper Saddle River, N.J., Prentice Hall, 1998.

S-Functions

In this chapter we'll show how you can use S-Functions to build custom Simulink blocks. S-Functions allow you to incorporate existing code into a Simulink model. They can also be used in situations where it's easier to describe a subsystem algorithmically than in block diagram notation. You can write S-Functions either as MATLAB function M-files or by using the C programming language via the MATLAB MEX-file mechanism.

10.1 Introduction

S-Functions allow you to define custom Simulink blocks using either MATLAB or C language code. S-Functions are useful in several situations. If there is existing MATLAB or C language code that models a portion of a system, it may be desirable to reuse that code in a Simulink model. For example, suppose you wish to try several different control system designs for a plant for which you have developed a dynamics model using an M-file. You can include the dynamics model in an S-Function, then use standard Simulink blocks to model the control system. S-Functions are also useful where it is easier to describe a portion of a dynamical system algorithmically than to describe it graphically via block diagram notation. S-Functions also might improve the efficiency of a simulation, particularly in models involving algebraic loops (see Chapter 12 for a discussion of algebraic loops). Finally, S-Functions provide a straightforward mechanism for adding animations to a Simulink model, a capability to be discussed in Chapter 11.

In this chapter, we will start with a general description of S-Function structure. Next we will discuss M-file S-Functions and provide examples of M-file S-Functions that have no states, that have continuous states, and that have discrete states. Last, we will discuss C S-Functions and provide C examples of the same three example subsystems.

10.2 S-Function Block

An S-Function is included in a Simulink model using the S-Function block in the Nonlinear block library. Figure 10-1(a) shows a simple model that includes an S-Function. The block dialog box (Figure 10-1(b)) has two fields. **S-function**

name contains the filename of the S-function, without an extension. This field must not be empty. **S-function parameters** contains any parameters required by the S-Function. If parameters are present, they must be in the form of a list, with the elements separated by commas, and without brackets. For example, suppose the S-Function requires three parameters: 1.5, a matrix [1,2;3,4], and the string "miles". A suitable entry in **S-function parameters** would be:

```
1.5,[1,2;3,4],'miles'
```

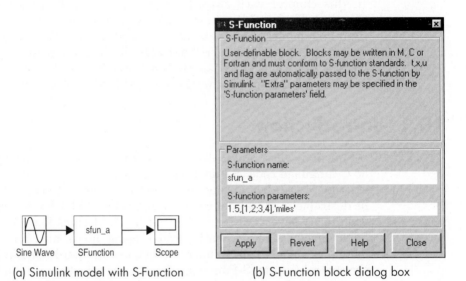

(a) Simulink model with S-Function   (b) S-Function block dialog box

Figure 10-1   Simple model with S-Function block

10.3   S-Function Overview

An S-Function represents a general Simulink block with input vector $\boldsymbol{u}$, output vector $\boldsymbol{y}$, and state vector $\boldsymbol{x}$ consisting of continuous states $\boldsymbol{x}_c$ and discrete states $\boldsymbol{x}_d$. Every S-Function must include code to set the initial values of all elements of the state vector, and to define the sizes of the input vector, the output vector, and the continuous and discrete components of the state vector. Also, every S-Function must be able to compute the output

$$\boldsymbol{y} = \boldsymbol{g}(\boldsymbol{x}, \boldsymbol{u}, t, \boldsymbol{p}) \tag{10-1}$$

update the discrete states

$$\boldsymbol{x}_d(k+1) = \boldsymbol{f}_d(\boldsymbol{x}, \boldsymbol{u}, t, \boldsymbol{p}) \tag{10-2}$$

and compute the derivatives of the continuous states

$$\dot{\boldsymbol{x}}_c = \boldsymbol{f}_c(\boldsymbol{x}, \boldsymbol{u}, t, \boldsymbol{p}) \qquad (10\text{-}3)$$

Here, t is the current value of simulation time and $\boldsymbol{p}$ is the optional list of parameters specified in S-Function block dialog box field **S-function parameters**. If an S-Function has variable sample time, it must also compute the time of the next sample hit.

The size of each of these vectors is completely arbitrary, and in particular, may be zero. So, for example, it is common for an S-Function to have inputs and outputs, but no states (behavior exhibited by Gain blocks and most blocks in the Nonlinear block library). An S-Function could also be used to create a custom source or sink, or a block with only continuous states (integrators) or only discrete states (delays).

In equations (10-1) to (10-3), the functions have access to all elements of the state vector. If there are n continuous states and m discrete states, the first n elements of the state vector $\boldsymbol{x}$ are the current values of the continuous states $(\boldsymbol{x}_c)$ and the remaining m components of $\boldsymbol{x}$ are the current values of the discrete states $(\boldsymbol{x}_d)$. Simulink may call the S-Function to evaluate equations (10-1) and (10-3) at any value of simulation time (t), but equation (10-2) is evaluated only at sample times. If there are multiple sample times, the S-Function must include logic that determines which components of $\boldsymbol{x}_d$ to update.

The S-Function state vector contains only the states defined by the S-Function—not all of the states in the model. Thus, if an S-Function implements a scalar integrator, its state vector will have one state. If it implements a transfer function of a third-order system, the state vector will have three components.

10.4 M-file S-Functions

An M-file S-function is a function M-file with a prescribed set of calling arguments. The first executable statement in the M-file is the function statement:

```
function [sys,x0,str,ts] = sfunc_name(t,x,u,flag,p1,p2,...,pn)
```

where *sfunc_name* is the name of the S-Function. For example, if an S-Function is stored in file sfun1.m, *sfunc_name* would be sfun1 (the same as the filename, without the .m extension). The input arguments are defined in Table 10-1, and the output arguments in Table 10-3.

The MathWorks includes a template M-file S-Function in sfuntmpl.m, located in the matlab/toolbox/simulink/blocks directory in the standard Simulink installation. It is advisable to use the template as the starting point for

Table 10-1 S-Function input arguments

Argument	Definition
t	Current value of simulation time.
x	Current value of S-Function state vector. If there are n continuous states and m discrete states, the first n components of x are the continuous states, and the remaining m are the discrete states.
u	Current value of input vector.
flag	Flag set by Simulink each time the S-Function is called. The S-Function must test the value of flag and perform the action indicated in Table 10-2.
p1,...,pn	List of optional parameters. The number of parameters should be the same as the number of parameters in S-Function dialog box field **S-function parameters**.

Table 10-2 S-Function flag definition

Flag value	Action required of the S-function
0	Initialize the sizes structure, and assign the value of the sizes structure to sys. Set x0 (initial conditions) and ts (matrix of sample times and offsets). Set str = [ ].
1	Compute the values of the derivatives of the continuous states. Set sys to the value of the derivative vector (that is, the derivative of the continuous portion of the S-Function state vector). sys is the only output argument.
2	Update the discrete states. Set sys to the new value of the discrete portion of the S-Function state vector. If there are multiple sample times, all components of the discrete state vector must be set each time flag is 2, including those that don't change. sys is the only output argument.
3	Compute outputs. Set sys to the value of the output vector. sys is the only output argument.
4	Compute the next sample time. Set sys to the value of the next sample time. sys is the only output argument.
9	Perform any necessary end-of-simulation tasks. There are no output arguments.

Table 10-3 S-Function output argument definitions

Argument	Definition
sys	Multipurpose output argument. The definition of sys depends on the value of flag.
x0	Initial value of S-Function state vector. x0 contains the initial value of both the continuous and discrete states. x0 is needed only if flag is 0.
str	str is a placeholder output argument. It should be set to an empty matrix. str is needed only if flag is 0.
ts	Matrix of sample time, offset pairs. The matrix must have two columns. There must be at least one row. ts is needed only if flag is 0.

building an S-Function, as this will eliminate some typing, and allow you to start with an S-Function that follows The MathWorks conventions.

An S-Function M-file must test the value of input argument flag, and perform the corresponding operation indicated in Table 10-2. The approach taken in The MathWorks template (and here) is to use a switch-case block that calls internal functions based on the value of flag. flag has six possible values. We will discuss the required behavior of the S-Function for each possible value.

10.4.1 Initialization (flag = 0)

Initialization entails four operations. The first is to set up a sizes structure, and to assign this structure to the multipurpose return argument sys. Create a sizes structure using the statement

```
sizes = simsizes ;
```

Next, assign values to each member of sizes. Each member of sizes must be assigned a value, even if the value is zero. Table 10-4 lists the members of the sizes structure.

Once the sizes structure is defined, assign it to output sys using the statement

```
sys = simsizes(sizes) ;
```

The second initialization step is to set the initial condition vector x0. For example, if there are two continuous states with initial values of 1.0, and two discrete states with initial value 0.0, use the statement

```
x0 = [1.0,1.0,0.0,0.0] ;
```

Table 10-4 Sizes structure

Member	Definition
sizes.NumContStates	Number of continuous states. For example, if there are two continuous states, set sizes.NumContStates = 2 ;
sizes.NumDiscStates	Number of discrete states.
sizes.NumOutputs	Number of outputs.
sizes.NumInputs	Number of inputs.
sizes.DirFeedthrough	Set to 1 if there is direct feedthrough, otherwise 0. Direct feedthrough means that the block output (Equation (10-1)) is a function of the input. A block for which the output is an algebraic function of the input (a Gain block, trigonometric function, etc.) has direct feedthrough. A block for which the output is a function only of the states does not have direct feedthrough. Simulink uses the value of this flag to determine whether there are any algebraic loops. For more information on algebraic loops, see Chapter 12. A block that has a variable sample time has direct feedthrough.
sizes.NumSampleTimes	Number of sample time, offset pairs. Must be at least 1, even for purely continuous S-Functions.

The third initialization step is to set str using the statement

    str = [] ;

The final initialization step is to create the sample time, offset matrix, ts. There must be one row in ts for each sample time, offset pair, and there must be at least one row, even for continuous S-Functions. For a continuous S-Function, use the statement

    ts = [0,0] ;

As another example, suppose there are two discrete sample times. The first has a period of 0.5 sec and no offset, so the sample times are at 0.0, 0.5, 1.0, ... The second has a period of 0.25 sec with a 0.1 sec offset, resulting in sample times of 0.1, 0.35, 0.60, ... In this case, set

    ts = [0.5,0 ; 0.25, 0.1] ;

If the sample time is to be inherited, set the sample time to −1. The sample time will usually be inherited from the block connected to the S-Function block input. In certain situations, Simulink will detect that a longer sample time will not affect the simulation results, and the sample time (if inherited) will be set accordingly.

If the sample time is to be variable, set the value of sample time to −2. In this case, the S-Function will be called with flag = 4 to compute the time of the next sample hit.

10.4.2   Continuous State Derivatives (flag = 1)

If flag is 1, assign to sys the value of the derivative of the continuous portion of the state vector. Note that if there are also discrete states, the size of sys will not be the same as the size of x, as x includes both the continuous and discrete states.

Example 10-1

Suppose an S-Function models the nonlinear system

$$\dot{x}_1 = x_2$$
$$\dot{x}_2 = x_1 - 3x_2^2 + u_1$$

The following statements will set sys appropriately:

```
sys(1) = x(2) ;
sys(2) = x(1) - 3*x(2)^2 + u(1) ;
```

10.4.3   Discrete State Updates (flag = 2)

If flag is 2, assign to sys the updated value of the discrete part of the state vector. If there are multiple sample times (including hybrid systems which have a sample time of 0 for the continuous states), the S-Function must test for a sample time hit and only update those components of the discrete portion of the state vector for which the current simulation time is a sample time hit. But note that all components of the discrete portion of the state vector must be assigned a value.

Example 10-2

First, consider the single-rate first-order discrete subsystem

$$x_1(k+1) = x_1(k) + u_1(k)$$

Use the following statement to set the new value of sys if flag is 2:

```
sys = x(1) + u(1) ;
```

Now, consider a second-order discrete subsystem with two sample times. The first discrete component is updated every 0.3 sec, and the second component every 0.5 sec, both with zero offset. The first state is to be updated according to the equation

$$x_1(k+1) = x_1(k) + 0.5x_2(k)$$

and the second state is to be updated according to the equation

$$x_2(k+1) = x_2(k) + u_1(k)$$

The following statements test the simulation time and update sys appropriately if the current time is a sample time hit.

```
period_1 = 0.3 ;
offset_1 = 0.0 ;
period_2 = 0.5 ;
offset_2 = 0.0
sys = x ;
if abs(round(t-offset_1)/period_1-((t-offset_1)/period_1))< 1.0e-8
   sys(1) = sys(1) + 0.5*x(2) ;
end
if abs(round(t-offset_2)/period_2-((t-offset_2)/period_2))< 1.0e-8
   sys(2) = sys(2) + u(1) ;
end
```

Notice that we did not use an if..else control structure when testing for sample time hits. If we had done that, the S-Function would produce incorrect results whenever both sample times hit simultaneously.

10.4.4 Block Outputs (flag = 3)

If flag is 3, assign to sys the value of the S-Function output (Equation (10-1)).

Example 10-3

Suppose the output of a second-order system is

$$y = x_1 + x_2$$

The following statement will set sys appropriately when flag is 3.

$$\text{sys} = x(1) + x(2) ;$$

10.4.5 Next Sample Time (flag = 4)

If flag is 4, assign to sys the value of the next sample time. The S-Function will be called with flag = 4 only if the sample time is variable (set to −2).

10.4.6 Terminate (flag = 9)

When the simulation is complete for any reason (**Stop time** reached, **Simulation:Stop** selected), the S-Function is called with flag set to 9. The S-Function should perform any necessary end-of-simulation tasks. There is no need to assign a value to sys.

10.4.7 Programming Considerations

Local data storage

Frequently, S-Functions require local data storage. Since an S-Function is a MATLAB function M-file, local variables must be initialized each time the S-Function is called. It is possible to preserve data between calls using global variables, but that is not a good idea. If global variables are used, there can be only one instance of a particular S-Function in a model. Otherwise, multiple instances of the S-Function would share the same storage locations. The preferred approach is to use the UserData parameter for the S-Function block that references the S-Function. Using the block UserData, there may be multiple instances of a particular S-Function in a model, because each instance of the S-Function block has its own UserData. UserData can be a scalar, a matrix, or even a cell array or structure. Therefore, there is no limit to the amount or types of data that can be stored in a block UserData parameter.

Example 10-4

Suppose that an S-Function needs to store the value of time and the state vector for use the next time the S-Function is called. The following statements will save the data:

```
u_dat.time = t ;
u_dat.state = x ;
set_param(gcb,'UserData',u_dat) ;
```

The most recent values may be read from the block UserData using the statement

```
old_data = get_param(gcb,'UserData') ;
```

Dynamic sizing

Many Simulink blocks can accept inputs of varying dimension. For example, a Gain block with scalar gain can accept scalar or vector input signals, and the vector input signals can be of any dimension. To configure an S-Function to adapt to different size input vectors, set sizes.NumInputs to –1. The S-Function can determine the size of the input vector when flag is 1, 2, 3, or 4 using the statement

```
size_input = size(u) ;
```

If the size of the output vector or the number of continuous or discrete states is dependent on the size of the input vector, set the appropriate member of sizes to –1 as well. The dimension of any of these vectors specified to be –1 is defined to be the same as the size of the input vector.

Hybrid and multirate S-Functions

S-Functions can be hybrid (containing both discrete and continuous states). Discrete S-Functions can have multiple sample times. There are occasions where these capabilities are useful. In general, however, it is preferable to build S-Functions that have a single purpose. This makes the S-Functions easier to develop and maintain, and also makes the S-Functions more likely to be reusable for other projects.

10.4.8 M-file S-Function Examples

Three example M-file S-Functions are presented next. These examples show how to create algebraic, continuous, and discrete M-file S-Functions. Several other helpful examples can be found in the matlab/toolbox/simulink/sim-demos directory of the standard MATLAB/Simulink installation.

Example 10-5

This example demonstrates an S-Function that has no states. The S-Function represents the algebraic equation

$$y = u_1 + u_2^2$$

The S-Function will have two inputs, one output, and no states. Since the input is passed directly to the output, the S-Function has direct feedthrough. A Simulink model that uses the S-Function is shown in Figure 10-2. S-Function block dialog box field **S-function name** contains s_xmp1. The S-Function listing is shown in Figure 10-3.

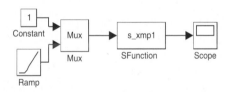

Figure 10-2 Simulink model with no states

```
function [sys,x0,str,ts] = s_xmp1(t,x,u,flag)
%    S-file example 1
%    This is an S-file subsystem with no states. It performs
%    the algebraic function y = u(1) + u(2)^2. There are two
%    inputs and one output.
%
%    Based on sfuntmpl.m, supplied with Simulink
%    Copyright (c) 1990-96 by The MathWorks, Inc.
%
switch flag,
  case 0,              % Initialization
    [sys,x0,str,ts]=mdlInitializeSizes;
```

Figure 10-3 M-file S-Function with no states

```
  case 1,                % Compute derivatives of continuous states
    sys=mdlDerivatives(t,x,u);
  case 2,
    sys=mdlUpdate(t,x,u);
  case 3,
    sys=mdlOutputs(t,x,u);  % Compute output vector
  case 4,                   % Compute time of next sample
    sys=mdlGetTimeOfNextVarHit(t,x,u);
  case 9,                   % Finished. Do any needed
    sys=mdlTerminate(t,x,u);
  otherwise                 % Invalid input
    error(['Unhandled flag = ',num2str(flag)]);
end
%****************************************************************
%*                     mdlInitializeSizes                     *
%****************************************************************
function [sys,x0,str,ts]=mdlInitializeSizes()
% Return the sizes of the system vectors, initial conditions,
% and the sample times and offets.
sizes = simsizes;   % Create the sizes structure
sizes.NumContStates  = 0;
sizes.NumDiscStates  = 0;
sizes.NumOutputs     = 1;
sizes.NumInputs      = 2;
sizes.DirFeedthrough = 1;
sizes.NumSampleTimes = 1;   % at least one sample time needed
sys = simsizes(sizes);      % load sys with the sizes structure
x0  = [];     % Specify initial conditions for all states
str = [];     % str is always an empty matrix
ts  = [0 0]; %initialize the array of sample times
%****************************************************************
%*                     mdlDerivatives                         *
%****************************************************************
function sys=mdlDerivatives(t,x,u)
% Compute derivatives of continuous states
sys = [];   % Empty since this S-file has no continuous states
%****************************************************************
%*                     mdlUpdate                              *
%****************************************************************
function sys=mdlUpdate(t,x,u)
% Compute update for discrete states. If necessary, check for
% sample time hits.
```

Figure 10-3 M-file S-Function with no states (Continued)

```
sys = [];     % Empty since this model has no discrete states.
%**************************************************************
%*                      mdlOutputs                          *
%**************************************************************
function sys=mdlOutputs(t,x,u)
% Compute output vector given current state, time, and input
sys = [u(1) + u(2).^2];
%**************************************************************
%*                  mdlGetTimeOfNextVarHit                  *
%**************************************************************
function sys=mdlGetTimeOfNextVarHit(t,x,u)
% Return the time of the next hit for this block.  Note that
% the result is absolute time.  Note that this function is only
% used when you specify a variable discrete-time sample time
sampleTime = [];
%**************************************************************
%*                     mdlTerminate                         *
%**************************************************************
function sys=mdlTerminate(t,x,u)
% Perform any necessary tasks at the end of the simulation
sys = [];
```

Figure 10-3 M-file S-Function with no states (Continued)

Example 10-6

This example illustrates using an S-Function to model a continuous system. It also illustrates the process of using a masked subsystem to supply parameters to an S-Function.

Consider the inverted pendulum model from Example 8-9, shown in Figure 8-14. The equations of motion of the cart and pendulum are

$$(M + m)\ddot{x} - ml\dot{\theta}^2\sin\theta + ml\ddot{\theta}\cos\theta = u$$

$$m\ddot{x}\cos\theta + ml\ddot{\theta} = mg\sin\theta$$

where g is the acceleration due to gravity. In Example 8-9, we manipulated the equations of motion such that $\ddot{x}$ and $\ddot{\theta}$ each appears in only one equation. An alternative approach is to rewrite the equations of motion in the form of a

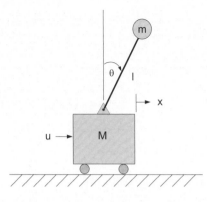

Figure 10-4   Cart with inverted pendulum

linear system, and solve the linear system for $\ddot{x}$ and $\ddot{\theta}$. In matrix notation, the equations of motion can be written

$$\begin{bmatrix} (M+m) & ml\cos\theta \\ m\cos\theta & ml \end{bmatrix} \begin{bmatrix} \ddot{x} \\ \ddot{\theta} \end{bmatrix} = \begin{bmatrix} ml\dot{\theta}^2\sin\theta + u \\ mg\sin\theta \end{bmatrix}$$

There are three parameters in the equations of motion: the cart mass (M), the pendulum mass (m), and the pendulum length (l). An S-Function that implements the equations of motion is shown in Figure 10-5. The function statement includes the three parameters.

The state derivatives are computed by solving the linear system for $\ddot{x}$ and $\ddot{\theta}$. Next, the value of the state vector time derivative is assigned to sys as follows:

$$\begin{bmatrix} \dot{x}_1 \\ \dot{x}_2 \\ \dot{x}_3 \\ \dot{x}_4 \end{bmatrix} = \begin{bmatrix} x_2 \\ \ddot{x} \\ x_4 \\ \ddot{\theta} \end{bmatrix}$$

The S-Function output is the state vector.

This S-Function can be used to build a subsystem to replace the inverted pendulum subsystem shown in Figure 8-15. To build the new subsystem, proceed as follows. Make a copy of the model in Example 8-9 and delete the Cart Model subsystem.

Drag a Subsystem block to the model window from the Connections block library. Open the Subsystem block, and drag Inport and an Outport blocks to the subsystem window. Also drag an S-Function block to the subsystem window. Connect the blocks as shown.

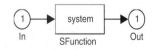

S-Functions   Chapter 10

```
function [sys,x0,str,ts] = s_xmp2(t,x,u,flag,M,m,l)
%    S-file example 2
%    This is an S-file subsystem that models a cart with
%    inverted pendulum. The cart and pendulum masses and
%    pendulum length are parameters that must be set in
%    the block dialog box.
%
%    Based on sfuntmpl.m, supplied with Simulink
%    Copyright (c) 1990-96 by The MathWorks, Inc.
%
switch flag,
  case 0,          % Initialization
    [sys,x0,str,ts]=mdlInitializeSizes;
  case 1,          % Compute derivatives of continuous states
    sys=mdlDerivatives(t,x,u,M,m,l) ;
  case 2,
    sys=mdlUpdate(t,x,u);
  case 3,
    sys=mdlOutputs(t,x,u);  % Compute output vector
  case 4,                   % Compute time of next sample
    sys=mdlGetTimeOfNextVarHit(t,x,u);
  case 9,                   % Finished. Do any needed
    sys=mdlTerminate(t,x,u);
  otherwise                 % Invalid input
    error(['Unhandled flag = ',num2str(flag)]);
end
%****************************************************************
%*                    mdlInitializeSizes                       *
%****************************************************************
function [sys,x0,str,ts]=mdlInitializeSizes
% Return the sizes of the system vectors, initial
% conditions, and the sample times and offets.
sizes = simsizes;   % Create the sizes structure
sizes.NumContStates  = 4;
sizes.NumDiscStates  = 0;
sizes.NumOutputs     = 4;
sizes.NumInputs      = 1;
sizes.DirFeedthrough = 0;
sizes.NumSampleTimes = 1;   % at least one sample time
sys = simsizes(sizes);      % load sys with the sizes structure
x0  = [0,0,0,0];    % Specify initial conditions for all states
```

Figure 10-5   S-Function model of cart with inverted pendulum

```
str = [];       % str is always an empty matrix
ts  = [0 0]; %initialize the array of sample times
%**********************************************************
%*                      mdlDerivatives                    *
%**********************************************************
function sys=mdlDerivatives(t,x,u,M,m,l)
% Compute derivatives of continuous states
g = 9.8 ;
Mass = [(M+m),m*l*cos(x(3));m*cos(x(3)),m*l] ;
x_dot_dot = Mass\[m*l*x(4)^2*sin(x(3))+u ; m*g*sin(x(3))] ;
sys = [x(2),x_dot_dot(1),x(4),x_dot_dot(2)] ;
%**********************************************************
%*                      mdlUpdate                         *
%**********************************************************
function sys=mdlUpdate(t,x,u)
% Compute update for discrete states. If necessary, check for
% sample time hits.
sys = [];       % Empty since this model has no discrete states.
%**********************************************************
%*                      mdlOutputs                        *
%**********************************************************
function sys=mdlOutputs(t,x,u)
% Compute output vector given current state, time, and input
sys = x ;
%**********************************************************
%*                      mdlGetTimeOfNextVarHit            *
%**********************************************************
function sys=mdlGetTimeOfNextVarHit(t,x,u)
% Return the time of the next hit for this block.  Note that
% the result is absolute time.  Note that this function is
% only used when you specify a variable discrete-time sample
% time [-2 0] in the sample time array in sampleTime = 1;
sys = [] ;
%**********************************************************
%*                      mdlTerminate                      *
%**********************************************************
function sys=mdlTerminate(t,x,u)
% Perform any necessary tasks at the end of the simulation
sys = [];
```

Figure 10-5 S-Function model of cart with inverted pendulum (Continued)

Open the S-Function block dialog box and configure the Parameters as shown.

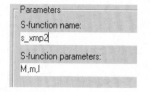

Close the Subsystem block dialog box and the subsystem window.

Rename the Subsystem block Cart Subsystem.

Select the Cart Subsystem block, then choose **Edit:Mask Subsystem** from the model window menu bar.

Select the Initialization page and define the prompts and associated variables as shown. Note that the variables (M,m,l) are used in the S-Function block dialog box as the parameters sent to the S-Function.

Prompt	Type	Variable
Cart mass:	edit	M
Pendulum mass:	edit	m
Pendulum lenght:	edit	l
<<end of parameter list>>		

Connect the output of the Sum block to the input of the new masked subsystem, and the output of the new masked subsystem to the Demux block. Configure the Gain blocks as shown in Figure 10-6. This model will produce results identical to the model in Example 8-9.

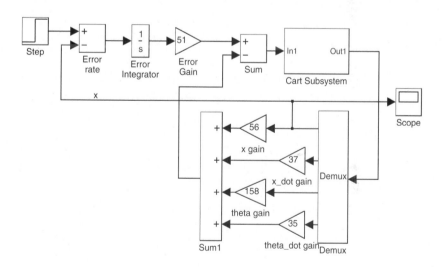

Figure 10-6   Inverted pendulum model using an S-Function

Example 10-7

In this example, we will use an S-Function to model a discrete PID controller. The example will also illustrate the use of local storage in an M-file S-Function. Consider the discrete PID controller used in the automobile model in Example 6-6. An S-Function that implements an equivalent controller is shown in Figure 10-7.

The discrete PID controller has one discrete state associated with the discrete integrator, and no continuous states. The S-Function requires parameters for proportional gain (K_p), integral gain (K_i), and discrete gain (K_d). As in Example 6-6, upper (L_{upper}) and lower (L_{lower}) limits will be set on the integrator output to eliminate windup. Sample time will also be an input parameter.

Recall from Example 6-6 that the input to the controller is the difference between the desired plant output (in this case automobile speed) and the actual value. The controller output is the sum of the proportional term, the integral term, and the derivative term. For consistency with S-Function notation, we will represent the input error signal with the variable u and the controller output signal with the variable y. The integral term requires an approximation to

$$y_i = K_i \int_0^t u(\tau)d\tau$$

The state update equation will approximate the integral using forward Euler integration. Thus, the state update is

$$x(k+1) = x(k) + Tu(k)$$

where T is the sample time. The state variable (x) is the current approximate value of the integral. To implement the saturation limits, $x(k + 1)$ is constrained to be between L_{upper} and L_{lower}.

As in Example 6-6, the derivative of the error will be approximated numerically as

$$\dot{u} \approx \frac{u(k) - u(k-1)}{T}$$

so it is necessary to store the value of the input from the previous sample. During initialization (flag = 0), the block UserData value is set to 0. Each time the output is computed (flag = 3), the previous value of the input is read from the block UserData and stored in variable approve. Then, the current value of the input (u) is stored in the block UserData parameter for use on the next sample hit.

```
function [sys,xO,str,ts] = s_xmp3(t,x,u,flag,Kp,Ki,Kd, ...
                         L_upper,L_lower,T_samp)
%    S-file example 3
%    MATLAB S-file implementation of discrete PID controller.
%
%    Based on sfuntmpl.m, supplied with Simulink
%    Copyright (c) 1990-96 by The MathWorks, Inc.
%
switch flag,
  case 0,                    % Initialization
    [sys,xO,str,ts]=mdlInitializeSizes(T_samp) ;
  case 1,                    % Derivatives of continuous states
    sys=mdlDerivatives(t,x,u) ;
  case 2,
    sys=mdlUpdate(t,x,u,L_upper,L_lower,T_samp);
  case 3,
    sys=mdlOutputs(t,x,u,Kp,Ki,Kd,T_samp);  % Output vector
  case 4,                                   % Next sample time
    sys=mdlGetTimeOfNextVarHit(t,x,u);
  case 9,                    % Finished. Do any needed
    sys=mdlTerminate(t,x,u);
  otherwise                  % Invalid input
    error(['Unhandled flag = ',num2str(flag)]);
end
%**********************************************************
%*                    mdlInitializeSizes                 *
%**********************************************************
function [sys,xO,str,ts]=mdlInitializeSizes(T_samp)
% Return the sizes of the system vectors, initial
% conditions, and the sample times and offets.
sizes = simsizes;    % Create the sizes structure
sizes.NumContStates  = 0;
sizes.NumDiscStates  = 1;
sizes.NumOutputs     = 1;
sizes.NumInputs      = 1;
sizes.DirFeedthrough = 1;
sizes.NumSampleTimes = 1;
sys = simsizes(sizes);       % load sys with sizes structure
xO  = [0];    % Specify initial conditions for all states
str = [];     % str is always an empty matrix
ts  = [T_samp 0]; %initialize the array of sample times
set_param(gcb,'UserData',0) ;
```

Figure 10-7   S-Function version of discrete PID controller

```
%**********************************************************
%*                     mdlDerivatives                     *
%**********************************************************
function sys=mdlDerivatives(t,x,u,M,m,l)
% Compute derivatives of continuous states
sys = [];
%**********************************************************
%*                      mdlUpdate                         *
%**********************************************************
function sys=mdlUpdate(t,x,u,L_upper,L_lower,T_samp)
% Compute update for discrete states. If necessary, check
% for sample time hits.
x_new = [x(1) + T_samp*u(1)] ;
x_new = min(max(x_new,L_lower),L_upper) ; % Prevent wind-up
sys = x_new ;
%**********************************************************
%*                      mdlOutputs                        *
%**********************************************************
function sys=mdlOutputs(t,x,u,Kp,Ki,Kd,T_samp)
% Compute output vector given current state, time, input
u_prev = get_param(gcb,'UserData') ;
set_param(gcb,'UserData',u(1)) ;      % Get input at
                                      % previous sample
u_deriv = (u(1) - u_prev)/T_samp ;    % Save current input
sys = Kp*u(1) + Ki*x(1) + Kd*u_deriv ;
%**********************************************************
%*                mdlGetTimeOfNextVarHit                  *
%**********************************************************
function sys=mdlGetTimeOfNextVarHit(t,x,u)
% Return the time of the next hit for this block.
sys = [] ;
%**********************************************************
%*                     mdlTerminate                       *
%**********************************************************
function sys=mdlTerminate(t,x,u)
% Perform any necessary tasks at the end of the simulation
sys = [];
```

Figure 10-7   S-Function version of discrete PID controller (Continued)

The output of the controller is the sum of the proportional term ($K_p u$), the integral term ($K_i x$), and the derivative term ($K_d \dot{u}$).

This S-Function is installed in the automobile model in a manner identical to that used in the previous example for the cart subsystem. The S-Function block **S-function parameters** field should contain

```
Kp,Ki,Kd,L_upper,L_lower,T_samp
```

Enclose the S-Function block in a masked subsystem, and add the prompts and associated variables shown in Table 10-5 to the Initialization page for the masked subsystem.

Table 10-5 Prompt definitions for discrete PID subsystem

Prompt	Variable
Proportional gain:	Kp
Integral gain:	Ki
Derivative gain:	Kd
Upper saturation limit:	L_upper
Lower saturation limit:	L_lower
Sample period:	T_samp

10.5 C Language S-Functions

C language S-Functions are built using the MATLAB MEX-file mechanism. C language S-Functions perform the same tasks as M-file S-Functions, but the flag mechanism is not used. Instead, a C S-Function is a single C source file that contains a set of functions with specified names. Simulink automatically calls the functions as the simulation progresses. Table 10-6 shows the simulation operations required and the names of the C functions that are called to perform these tasks.

Every C S-Function file must contain all of the functions listed in Table 10-6, even though some of the functions may do nothing. The functions may appear in the file in any order. The structure of a C S-function file is illustrated in Figure 10-8. The structure is discussed in detail in the sections that follow. A template C S-Function is in the simulink/src subdirectory in file sfuntmpl.c.

The calling arguments to the S-Function routines have consistent definitions, listed in Table 10-7.

Table 10-6 C language S-Function routines

Functions called	Action required of the S-function
mdlInitializeSizes	Initialize the sizes structure using the ssSet macros.
mdlInitializeSampleTimes	Initialize the sample times and offsets.
mdlInitializeConditions	Set the subsystem state vector initial conditions.
mdlDerivatives	Compute the values of the derivatives of the continuous states.
mdlUpdate	Update the discrete states.
mdlOutputs	Compute outputs.
mdlGetTimeOfNextVarHit	Compute next sample time.
mdlTerminate	Perform any necessary end-of-simulation tasks.

```
/* **************************************************** */
/*                      s_tpl                           */
/* This template illustrates the structure of a         */
/* C S-Function file                                    */
/* Based on MathWorks template file                     */
/* Copyright (c) 1990-96 by The MathWorks, Inc.         */
/* All Rights Reserved                                  */
/* **************************************************** */
#define S_FUNCTION_NAME s_tpl
#include "simstruc.h"
#include "math.h"
static void mdlInitializeSizes(SimStruct *S)
{
   /* Use ssSet macros to intialize the sizes struct    */
}
static void mdlInitializeSampleTimes(SimStruct *S)
{
   /* Use ssSet macros to initialize sample times and   */
   /* offsets                                           */
}
static void mdlInitializeConditions(double *x0,
                                    SimStruct *S)
```

Figure 10-8 C S-Function file structure

```
{
    /* Set the initial conditions of the S-Function    */
    /* vector, pointed to by x0                         */
}
static void mdlOutputs(double *y, double *x, double *u,
                       SimStruct *S, int tid)
{
    /* Compute the output vector, pointed to by y       */
}
static void mdlUpdate(double *x, double *u, SimStruct *S,
                      int tid)
{
    /* Update the discrete states                       */
}
static void mdlDerivatives(double *dx, double *x,
                           double *u,  SimStruct *S,
                           int tid)
{
    /* Compute the derivatives of continuous states,    */
/* pointed to by dx                                     */
}
static void mdlTerminate(SimStruct *S)
{
    /* Perform any end-of-simulation tasks              */
}
#ifdef
#include "simulink.c"
#else
#include "cg_sfun.h"
#endif
```

Figure 10-8   C S-Function file structure (Continued)

10.5.1   C File Header

The header of the C source file in Figure 10-8 declares the name of the S-Function (using the #define), and uses #include statements to supply declarations for the C math library and the S-Function data structures. The format of the #define statement is

```
#define S_FUNCTION_NAME s_fun_name
```

where *s_fun_name* is the name of the C S-Function file, and also the name of the S-Function being built. In the example in Figure 10-8, the C source file is named s_tpl.c.

Table 10-7 S-Function routine calling arguments

Argument	Definition
dx	Pointer to state derivative vector. The length of dx is the same as the number of continuous states.
S	Pointer simulation structure. S is defined in simstruc.h. Although it is possible to access the members of S directly, the preferred method is to use the simulation structure macros, such as ssSetNumContStates(S, n).
tid	Task identifier for use with certain real-time operating systems. For standard Simulink models, tid should be treated as a placeholder argument.
u	Pointer to S-Function block input vector.
x	Pointer to S-Function block state vector. x is composed of the continuous states followed by the discrete states.
x0	Pointer to S-Function initial condition vector. *x0 must be initialized by function mdlInitializeConditions.
y	Pointer to S-Function block output vector.

The #define and the inclusion of simstruc.h are always required. math.h is usually required, but it is possible to build an S-Function that does not need the math library.

10.5.2 Initializing the sizes Struct

Simulink will call function mdlInitializeSizes during simulation initialization with a pointer (S) to a simulation structure. A separate instance of the simulation structure is maintained for each instance of each S-Function in a model. Function mdlInitializeSizes initializes the size elements of the simulation structure using a set of macros defined in simstruc.h. The macros that must be included are defined in Table 10-8. Each macro has two arguments: a pointer to the simulation structure (S) and an integer set to the size parameter being set. For example, to set the number of continuous states to 2, use the following C code:

```
ssSetNumContStates(S, 2) ;
```

C S-Functions can be written to use dynamically sized inputs by setting the number of inputs to the value DYNAMICALLY_SIZED. If the number of inputs is declared to be dynamically sized, the number of continuous states, discrete states, and outputs may also be declared to be dynamically sized. For example,

Table 10-8 Sizes initialization macros

Macro name	Purpose
ssSetNumContStates	Set the number of continuous states.
ssSetNumDiscStates	Set the number of discrete states.
ssSetNumOutputs	Set the number of elements in the output vector.
ssSetNumInputs	Specify the number of elements in the input vector.
ssSetDirectFeedThrough	Set to 1 if there is direct feedthrough, 0 if there is no direct feedthrough.
ssSetNumSampleTimes	Set to the number of sample times. As with M-file S-Functions, there must be at least one sample time.
ssSetNumInputArgs	Specify the number of block parameters. An M-file S-Function obtains the number of parameters from the function statement. In a C S-Function, the number of parameters must be specified.
ssSetNumIWork	Specify the number of integer work vector elements.
ssSetNumRWork	Specify the number of real work vector elements.
ssSetNumPWork	Specify the number of pointer work vector elements.

if an S-Function is to have dynamically sized inputs, and the number of outputs is the same as the number of inputs, the following two statements should appear in function mdlInitializeSizes:

```
ssSetNumInputs(S, DYNAMICALLY_SIZED) ;
ssSetNumOutputs(S, DYNAMICALLY_SIZED) ;
```

At runtime, Simulink will assign storage to the input array and output array based on the size of the S-Function block input signal.

10.5.3   Defining SampleTimes and Offsets

C S-Functions require a separate function to define sample times, in contrast to M-file S-Functions, in which all initialization tasks are performed when flag = 0. Two macros are required in function `mdlInitializeSampleTimes`. The first macro defines sample times, and the second defines corresponding offsets. The number of sample time, offset pairs must be the same as the number set in function `mdlInitializeSizes` using the `ssSetNumSampleTimes` macro.

Setting Sample Times

To set a sample time, use the statement

```
ssSetSampleTime(S, n, T) ;
```

where n represents the ordinal number of the sample time being set (starting at 0), and T is the sample time. So to set the first sample time to 0.5, use the following statement:

```
ssSetSampleTime(S, 0, 0.5) ;
```

The header file `simstruc.h` includes #defines for three special values of sample time. Use `CONTINUOUS_SAMPLE_TIME` if the subsystem is continuous. Use `INHERITED_SAMPLE_TIME` if the sample time is to be inherited from the driving signal. Use `VARIABLE_SAMPLE_TIME` if the sample time is variable. Using these names will make the S-Function easier to understand.

Setting Sample Offsets

To set a sample offset, use the statement

```
ssSetOffsetTime(S, n, offset) ;
```

where n represents the ordinal number of the sample time being set (starting at 0), and offset is the value of the offset. So to set the first sample time offset to 0.2, use the following statement:

```
ssSetOffsetTime(S, 0, 0.2) ;
```

10.5.4   Setting Initial Conditions

C S-Functions require a separate function (`mdlInitializeConditions`) to set initial conditions. The function should assign an initial value to each element of the initial condition vector (x0). For example, if there are two elements of the state vector, the first of which has initial value 0.0, and the second of which has initial value 1.0, the following statements could be used:

```
*x0 = 0.0 ;
*(x0 + 1) = 1.0 ;
```

If the state vector is dynamically sized, use macros `ssGetNumContStates(S)` and `ssGetNumDiscStates(S)` to determine the size of each portion of the state vector. For example, suppose an S-Function is continuous, and all components of the initial condition vector are to be set to 0.0. The following statements will set x0 appropriately:

```
int nCont, i ;
nCont = ssGetNumContstates(S) ;
for(i = 0 ; i < nCont ; i++) *(x0+i) = 0.0 ;
```

Recall that if the S-Function models a hybrid subsystem, the state vector consists of the continuous states followed by the discrete states.

10.5.5 Setting the Output Vector

Function `mdlOutputs` computes the model output vector. The input arguments are the simulation structure (S), and the state and control vectors. If the output vector is dynamically sized, use macro `ssGetNumOutputs(S)` to find the size of the output vector. Use macro `ssGetT(S)` to determine the current simulation time, if needed.

Example 10-8

Suppose we wish to model a subsystem with dynamically sized input vector of dimension m and one continuous state variable. The state variable is defined by the differential equation

$$\dot{x} = \sum_{i=1}^{m} u_i$$

The subsystem output is

$$y_i = u_i x, \qquad 1 \le i \le m$$

The following statements will set the output vector correctly:

```
int m, i;
m = ssGetNumOutputs(S) ;
for(i = 0 ; i < m ; i++) *(y + i) = *(u + i) * (*x) ;
```

10.5.6   Updating the Discrete States

Function `mdlUpdate` must update the discrete states. Referring to Figure 10-8, the function statement is

```
static void mdlUpdate(double *x, double *u, SimStruct *S,int tid)
```

If the S-Function is hybrid, x points to the complete state vector, not just the discrete portion of the state vector. Therefore, care must be taken to ensure that only the discrete portion of x is updated. If the S-Function is multirate or hybrid, use the techniques discussed in Section 10.4.3 to select which components of x to update. Use macros `ssGetNumTotalStates(S)`, `ssGetNumCont-States(S)`, and `ssGetNumDiscStates(S)` as needed to obtain the sizes of the continuous and discrete portions of x. To determine the current value of simulation time, use macro `ssGetT(S)`.

10.5.7   Computing the State Derivatives

Function `mdlDerivatives` must compute the derivatives of the continuous states. Use macro `ssGetNumContStates(S)` if the continuous portion of the state vector is dynamically sized.

Example 10-9

The following statements will compute and set the state derivative defined in Example 10-8:

```
int m, i;
m = ssGetNumInputs(S) ;
*dx = 0 ;
for(i = 0 ; i < m ; i++) *dx += *(u + i)
```

10.5.8   End-of-Simulation Tasks

Function `mdlTerminate` should perform any necessary end-of-simulation tasks. The only input argument to `mdlTerminate` is a pointer to the S-Function simulation structure (S). Pointers to the state vector, input vector, and simulation time may be obtained using macros `ssGetX(S)`, `ssGetU(S)`, and `ssGetT(S)` respectively.

10.5.9   C S-Function File Trailer

The C S-Function file trailer consists of the `#ifdef .. #endif` compiler direc-
tives shown in the last five lines of Figure 10-8. These statements are necessary in order for the MATLAB MEX-file mechanism to work properly.

10.5.10 Programming Considerations

The many functions in the MATLAB MEX application programming interface
are accessible from within C S-Functions. Some of the MEX functions most
useful in C S-Functions are discussed in this section. Refer to the API documentation [1] and the on-line API documentation for much more detailed coverage of MEX programming.

Accessing block parameters

You can access S-Function block parameters in C S-Functions using the
`ssGetArg(S, arg_num)` macro. `arg_num` is the ordinal argument number, with
the first argument 0, the second 1, and so on. `ssGetArg` returns a pointer compatible with MEX API functions `mxGetPr` and `mxGetPi`. `mxGetPr` returns a
pointer to the real part of the parameter and `mxGetPi` returns a pointer to the
imaginary part.

The recommended programming technique is to specify at the top of the S-
Function file a `#define` for each parameter. So, if there are two scalar parameters, you could use the following statements in the C S-Function file header:

```
#define param_1 *mxGetPr(ssGetArg(S,0))
#define param_2 *mxGetPr(ssGetArg(S, 1))
```

Then, in the function that uses the arguments, use the following statements

```
double p1, p2 ;
p1 = param_1 ;
p2 = param_2 ;
```

Persistent local data storage

The S-Function mechanism provides persistent storage for real, integer, and
pointer data. The persistent storage for each instance of an S-Function block in
a Simulink model is unique. Therefore, there is no conflict if there are multiple
instances of an S-Function block in the same model. The persistent storage
variables are called *work vectors*. The size of each work vector (real, integer,
pointer) must be set in `mdlInitializeConditions` using macros ssSetNumR-

Work, ssSetNumIWork, and ssSetNumIWork. For example, to set the number of real work vector elements to 3, use the statement

```
ssSetNumRWork(S, 3) ;
```

Values are stored in the work vectors using ssSetRWorkValue, ssSetI-WorkValue, and ssSetPWorkValue. The syntax is

```
ssSetRWorkValue(S, R_index, value) ;
```

where R_index is the index into the work vector (real in this case), and value is the value being stored. Read data from the work vector using ssGetR-WorkValue, ssGetIWorkValue, and ssGetPWorkValue. The syntax is

```
value = ssGetRWorkValue(S, R_index) ;
```

Example 10-10

Suppose we wish to create an S-Function that produces as its output the maximum value its scalar input has reached thus far during the simulation:

$$y(t) = \max(u(\tau)), \qquad 0 \le \tau \le t$$

In the function mdlInitializeConditions, include the statements

```
ssSetNumRWork(S, 1) ;
ssSetRWorkValue(S, 0, -9.9E20) ;
```

to allocate space for a work vector that will hold a single real number and to initialize the contents of the work vector to a value that is certain to be less than the initial value of the input signal. The output function should be as follows

```
static void mdlOutputs(double *y, double *x, double *u,
                       SimStruct *S, int tid)
{
    double u_max_prev ;
    u_max_prev = ssGetRWorkValue(S, 0) ;
    *y = u_max_prev ;   /* Assume current max is previous max */
    if(*u > u_max_prev)   /* Should maximum be updated? */
      {
        ssSetRWorkValue(S, 0, *u) ;    /* Update maximum */
        *y = *u ;                      /* Update output  */
      }
}
```

Accessing the MATLAB engine

One of the most powerful features of MEX files, including C S-Functions, is that they have access to MATLAB's computational engine. Details on calling MATLAB functions from within MEX functions are provided in the MATLAB API Guide [1] and the on-line MEX documentation (through the MATLAB HelpDesk). To illustrate the concepts needed, we will discuss the procedure for defining a real matrix and using MATLAB to compute its eigenvalues.

To create a matrix, which we'll call A, three statements are required:

```
mxArray *A ;
double *A_dat
A = mxCreateDoubleMatrix(nrows, ncols, mxREAL) ;
```

Assuming that nrows and ncols have previously been set to 2, A is now a real MATLAB matrix with two rows and two columns. Next, assign a pointer to the data in A using the statement

```
A_dat = mxGetPr(A) ;
```

The data in a MATLAB matrix is stored using the FORTRAN columnwise convention. Suppose the matrix A is defined as

$$A = \begin{bmatrix} 1.5 & 3.5 \\ 2.3 & 4.8 \end{bmatrix} \tag{10-4}$$

The following statements will fill A correctly:

```
*A_dat = 1.5 ;
*(A_dat + 1) = 2.3 ;
*(A_dat + 2) = 3.5 ;
*(A_dat + 3) = 4.8 ;
```

To call a MATLAB function, use MEX function mexCallMATLAB. The syntax is

```
mexCallMATLAB(num_ret, ret_array, num_in, in_array, operation) ;
```

num_ret is the number of returned arguments. So, if the MATLAB function is called using a statement of the form [ret_1, ret_2] = MATLAB_functon(A), num_ret would be 2.

ret_array is a pointer to an array of MATLAB matrices. ret_array must be declared in the S-Function. In this example, ret_array should be declared as

```
mxArray *ret_array[1] ;
```

num_in is the number of input arguments, in this case 1.

`in_array` is a pointer to an array of MATLAB matrices. Here, `in_array` is declared

```
mxArray *in_array[1] ;
```

and set to point to A:

```
in_array[0] = A ;
```

The final argument, `operation`, is a string containing the name of the MATLAB function. Here, operation is `"eig"`. If the operation is a basic math operation such as addition, use the symbol for the operation, enclosed in quotes: `"+"`.

The function should end with statements freeing the storage allocated to the array. Function `mxDestroyArray` frees the storage:

```
mxDestroyArray(A) ;
```

Useful Macros in `simstruc.h`

The S-Function header file `simstruc.h` provides a number of macros that provide access to S-Function parameters and variables. Several of the more useful macros are listed in Table 10-9. Refer to the header file for a complete list.

10.5.11 Compiling a C S-Function

Compile a C S-Function by entering the following command at the MATLAB prompt:

```
mex sfun_name.c
```

where `sfun_name.c` is the name of the C source file. The `mex` command will generate the compiler and linker commands necessary to produce the executable S-Function file. Compiler error messages will be displayed in the MATLAB window.

10.5.12 C S-Function Examples

This section provides C S-Function versions of the examples in Section 10.4.8. In each case, the Simulink model is configured the same for the C S-Function as for the M-file S-Function. The only difference is the name of the S-Function file in the S-Function block dialog box.

Table 10-9 Useful `simstruc.h` macros

Macro	Purpose
`ssGetT(S)`	Get current simulation time.
`ssGetU(S)`	Get current input vector.
`ssGetY(S)`	Get current output vector.
`ssGetX(S)`	Get current state vector.
`ssGetNumContStates(S)`	Get the number of continuous states.
`ssGetNumDiscStates(S)`	Get the number of discrete states.
`ssGetNumTotalStates(S)`	Get the total number of states.
`ssGetNumOutputs(S)`	Get the number of outputs.
`ssGetNumInputs(S)`	Get the number of inputs.
`ssIsDirectFeedThrough(S)`	True if there is direct feedthrough.
`ssSetRWorkValue(S, index, value)`	Set the value of an element of the real work vector.
`ssSetIWorkValue(S, index, value)`	Set the value of an element of the integer work vector.
`ssSetPWorkValue(S, index, value)`	Set the value of an element of the pointer work vector. This sets the pointer, not the thing pointed to.
`ssGetRWorkValue(S, index)`	Get an element of the real work vector.
`ssGetIWorkValue(S, index)`	Get an element of the integer work vector.
`ssGetPWorkValue(S, index)`	Get an element of the pointer work vector.

Example 10-11

This example demonstrates an S-Function that has no states. The S-Function represents the algebraic equation

$$y = u_1 + u_2^2$$

The C S-Function is shown in Figure 10-9.

```
/* ******************************************************* */
/*                        s_xmp4                          */
/* C S-File example that computes y = u(1) + u(2)^2       */
/* Based on MathWorks template file                       */
/* Copyright (c) 1990-96 by The MathWorks, Inc.           */
/* All Rights Reserved                                    */
/* ******************************************************* */
#define S_FUNCTION_NAME s_xmp4
#include "simstruc.h"
#include "math.h"
/* ******************************************************* */
/*                   mdlInitializeSizes                   */
/* ******************************************************* */
static void mdlInitializeSizes(SimStruct *S)
{
    /* number of continuous states */
    ssSetNumContStates(    S, 0);
    /* number of discrete states */
    ssSetNumDiscStates(    S, 0);
    /* number of inputs         */
    ssSetNumInputs(        S, 2);
    /* number of outputs */
    ssSetNumOutputs(       S, 1);
    /* direct feedthrough flag */
    ssSetDirectFeedThrough(S, 1);
    /* number of sample times */
    ssSetNumSampleTimes(   S, 1);
    /* number of input arguments */
    ssSetNumSFcnParams(    S, 0);
    /* number of real work vector elements */
    ssSetNumRWork(         S, 0);
```

Figure 10-9 C S-Function with no states

```
    /* number of integer work vector elements*/
    ssSetNumIWork(          S, 0);
    /* number of pointer work vector elements*/
    ssSetNumPWork(          S, 0);
}
/* ********************************************************/
/*              mdlInitializeSampleTimes                 */
/* ********************************************************/
static void mdlInitializeSampleTimes(SimStruct *S)
{
    ssSetSampleTime(S, 0, CONTINUOUS_SAMPLE_TIME);
    ssSetOffsetTime(S, 0, 0.0);
                        }
/* ********************************************************/
/*              mdlInitializeConditions                  */
/* ********************************************************/
static void mdlInitializeConditions(double *x0,
                                    SimStruct *S)
{
}
/* ********************************************************/
/*                   mdlOutputs                          */
/* ********************************************************/
static void mdlOutputs(double *y, double *x, double *u,
                  SimStruct *S, int tid)
{
  *y = *u + pow(*(u+1),2.0) ;    /* y = u(1) + u(2)^2  */
}
/* ********************************************************/
/*                   mdlUpdate                           */
/* ********************************************************/
static void mdlUpdate(double *x, double *u, SimStruct *S,
                  int tid)
{
}
/* ********************************************************/
/*                   mdlDerivatives                      */
/* ********************************************************/
static void mdlDerivatives(double *dx, double *x,
                        double *u, SimStruct *S,
                        int tid)
```

Figure 10-9   C S-Function with no states (Continued)

```
{
}
/* ********************************************************* */
/*                       mdlTerminate                    */
/* ********************************************************* */
static void mdlTerminate(SimStruct *S)
{
}
#ifdef
#include "simulink.c"
#else
#include "cg_sfun.h"
#endif
```

Figure 10-9   C S-Function with no states (Continued)

Example 10-12

This example models the cart with inverted pendulum in a manner identical to Example 10-6. It demonstrates two important capabilities. Referring to Figure 10-10, notice the #defines in the C file header. These #defines illustrate using S-Function block dialog box parameters in a C S-Function. Second, this S-Function illustrates the procedure for using the MATLAB engine from within the S-Function.

```
/* ********************************************************* */
/*                          s_xmp5                       */
/*    This is a C version of the S-file subsystem that   */
/*    models a cart with inverted pendulum. The cart     */
/*    and pendulum masses and pendulum length are        */
/*    parameters that must be set in the block dialog    */
/*    box.                                                */
/*                                                        */
/* Based on MathWorks template file                       */
/* Copyright (c) 1990-96 by The MathWorks, Inc.           */
/* All Rights Reserved                                    */
/* ********************************************************* */
```

Figure 10-10 C S-Function model of cart with inverted pendulum

```
#define S_FUNCTION_NAME s_xmp5
#include "simstruc.h"
#include "math.h"
#define M_macro *mxGetPr(ssGetArg(S,0))
#define m_macro *mxGetPr(ssGetArg(S,1))
#define l_macro *mxGetPr(ssGetArg(S,2))
/* *********************************************** */
/*                 mdlInitializeSizes               */
/* *********************************************** */
static void mdlInitializeSizes(SimStruct *S)
{
    ssSetNumContStates(    S, 4);
    ssSetNumDiscStates(    S, 0);
    ssSetNumInputs(        S, 1);
    ssSetNumOutputs(       S, 4);
    ssSetDirectFeedThrough(S, 0);
    ssSetNumSampleTimes(   S, 1);
    ssSetNumSFcnParams(    S, 3);
    ssSetNumRWork(         S, 0);
    ssSetNumIWork(         S, 0);
    ssSetNumPWork(         S, 0);
}
/* *********************************************** */
/*            mdlInitializeSampleTimes              */
/* *********************************************** */
static void mdlInitializeSampleTimes(SimStruct *S)
{
    ssSetSampleTime(S, 0, CONTINUOUS_SAMPLE_TIME);
    ssSetOffsetTime(S, 0, 0.0);
}
/* *********************************************** */
/*            mdlInitializeConditions               */
/* *********************************************** */
static void mdlInitializeConditions(double *x0, SimStruct *S)
{
   int i ;
   for(i = 0 ; i < 4 ; i++) *(x0+i) = 0.0 ;
}
/* *********************************************** */
/*                   mdlOutputs                     */
/* *********************************************** */
static void mdlOutputs(double *y, double *x, double *u,
                     SimStruct *S, int tid)
```

Figure 10-10 C S-Function model of cart with inverted pendulum (Continued)

```
{
  int i ;
  for(i = 0 ; i < 4 ; i++) *(y+i) = *(x+i) ; /* y = x */
}
/* *****************************************************/
/*                        mdlUpdate                    */
/* *****************************************************/
static void mdlUpdate(double *x, double *u, SimStruct *S,
                      int tid)
{
}
/* *****************************************************/
/*                     mdlDerivatives                  */
/* *****************************************************/
static void mdlDerivatives(double *dx, double *x, double *u,
                           SimStruct *S, int tid)
{
    static double g = 9.8 ;     /* Acceleration due to gravity */
    double M, m, l ;            /* Model parameters */
    /* MATLAB matrix to contain the mass matrix */
    mxArray *Mass ;
    /* pointer to the data part of the matrix */
    double *Mass_v ;
    /* Store right hand side of dynamic equation */
    mxArray *x_dot_dot_rhs ;
    double *x_dot_dot_rhs_v ;  /* pointer to the data */
    mxArray *input_array[2], *out_array[1] ;
    double *x_dot_dot ;
    M = M_macro ; /* Obtain the values of the parameters */
    m = m_macro ;
    l = l_macro ;
    /* Create mass matrix */
    Mass = mxCreateDoubleMatrix(2, 2, mxREAL) ;
    Mass_v = mxGetPr(Mass) ;
    /* Load the values in mass matrix */
    *Mass_v = M + m ;
    *(Mass_v+1) = m*cos(*(x+2)) ;
    *(Mass_v+2) = m*l*cos(*(x+2)) ;
    *(Mass_v+3) = m*l ;
    /* Create rhs */
    x_dot_dot_rhs = mxCreateDoubleMatrix(2, 1, mxREAL) ;
    x_dot_dot_rhs_v = mxGetPr(x_dot_dot_rhs) ;
    *x_dot_dot_rhs_v = m*l*pow(*(x+3),2.0)*sin(*(x+2)) + *u ;
```

Figure 10-10 C S-Function model of cart with inverted pendulum (Continued)

```c
      *(x_dot_dot_rhs_v+1) = m*g*sin(*(x+2)) ;
       /* Set up for call to MATLAB */
      input_array[0] = Mass ;
      input_array[1] = x_dot_dot_rhs ;
      /* Solve system */
      mexCallMATLAB(1, out_array, 2, input_array, "\\") ;
      x_dot_dot = mxGetPr(out_array[0]) ;
      /* Fill derivative vector */
      *dx = *(x+1) ;
      *(dx+1) = *x_dot_dot ;
      *(dx+2) = *(x+3) ;
      *(dx+3) = *(x_dot_dot+1) ;
      /* Free the memory allocated by MATLAB */
      mxDestroyArray(out_array[0]) ;
      /* Free the memory used for Mass and rhs */
      mxDestroyArray(Mass) ;
      mxDestroyArray(x_dot_dot_rhs) ;
}
/* *******************************************************/
/*                        mdlTerminate                 */
/* *******************************************************/
static void mdlTerminate(SimStruct *S)
{
}
#ifdef MATLAB_MEX_FILE
#include "simulink.c"
#else
#include "cg_sfun.h"
#endif
```

Figure 10-10 C S-Function model of cart with inverted pendulum (Continued)

Example 10-13

This example presents a C S-Function (Figure 10-11) that implements the discrete PID controller discussed in Example 10-7. This example uses S-Function block parameters to configure the controller. It also uses an S-Function work vector to store the value of the block input from the previous sample, for use in approximating the derivative of the input signal (the speed error).

```
/*                            s_xmp6                          */
/* ***********************************************************/
/*   This is a C version of the S-file subsystem that        */
/*   implements a discrete PID controller.                   */
/*                                                           */
/* Based on MathWorks template file                          */
/* Copyright (c) 1990-96 by The MathWorks, Inc.              */
/* All Rights Reserved                                       */
/* ***********************************************************/
#define S_FUNCTION_NAME s_xmp6
#include "simstruc.h"
#include "math.h"
#define Kp_macro      *mxGetPr(ssGetArg(S,0))
#define Ki_macro      *mxGetPr(ssGetArg(S,1))
#define Kd_macro      *mxGetPr(ssGetArg(S,2))
#define L_upper_macro *mxGetPr(ssGetArg(S,3))
#define L_lower_macro *mxGetPr(ssGetArg(S,4))
#define T_samp_macro  *mxGetPr(ssGetArg(S,5))
/* ***********************************************************/
/*                    mdlInitializeSizes                     */
/* ***********************************************************/
static void mdlInitializeSizes(SimStruct *S)
{
    ssSetNumContStates(    S, 0);
    ssSetNumDiscStates(    S, 1);
    ssSetNumInputs(        S, 1);
    ssSetNumOutputs(       S, 1);
    ssSetDirectFeedThrough(S, 1);
    ssSetNumSampleTimes(   S, 1);
    ssSetNumSFcnParams(    S, 6);
    ssSetNumRWork(         S, 1);
    ssSetNumIWork(         S, 0);   /* integer work vec */
    ssSetNumPWork(         S, 0);   /* pointer work vec */
}
/* ***********************************************************/
/*              mdlInitializeSampleTimes                     */
/* ***********************************************************/
static void mdlInitializeSampleTimes(SimStruct *S)
{
    double T_samp ;
    T_samp = T_samp_macro ;
    ssSetSampleTime(S, 0, T_samp);
```

Figure 10-11 C S-Function implementation of discrete PID controller

```
    ssSetOffsetTime(S, 0, 0.0);
}
/* ******************************************************/
/*                mdlInitializeConditions              */
/* ******************************************************/
static void mdlInitializeConditions(double *x0,
                                       SimStruct *S)
{
   *x0 = 0.0 ;
   ssSetRWorkValue(S, 0, 0.0) ; /* Initialize to zero */
}
/* ******************************************************/
/*                     mdlOutputs                      */
/* ******************************************************/
static void mdlOutputs(double *y, double *x, double *u,
                     SimStruct *S, int tid)
{
  double Kp, Ki, Kd, T_samp, u_prev, u_deriv ;

  Kp = Kp_macro ;
  Ki = Ki_macro ;
  Kd = Kd_macro ;
  T_samp = T_samp_macro ;
  u_prev = ssGetRWorkValue(S, 0) ;
  ssSetRWorkValue(S, 0, *u) ; /* Reset to current input */
  u_deriv = (*u - u_prev)/T_samp ;
  *y = Kp*(*u) + Ki*(*x) + Kd*u_deriv ;
}
/* ******************************************************/
/*                      mdlUpdate                      */
/* ******************************************************/
static void mdlUpdate(double *x, double *u, SimStruct *S,
                    int tid)
{
   double T_samp, L_upper, L_lower ;
   T_samp = T_samp_macro ;
   L_upper = L_upper_macro ;
   L_lower = L_lower_macro ;
   *x = *x + T_samp*(*u) ;          /* Compute update */
   if(*x > L_upper) *x = L_upper ;  /* Apply limits */
   if(*x < L_lower) *x = L_lower ;
}
```

Figure 10-11 C S-Function implementation of discrete PID controller (Continued)

```
/* ************************************************** */
/*                    mdlDerivatives                 */
/* ************************************************** */
static void mdlDerivatives(double *dx, double *x,
                           double *u, SimStruct *S,
                           int tid)
{
}
/* ************************************************** */
/*                    mdlTerminate                   */
/* ************************************************** */
static void mdlTerminate(SimStruct *S)
{
}
#ifdef MATLAB_MEX_FILE
#include "simulink.c"
#else
#include "cg_sfun.h"
#endif
```

Figure 10-11 C S-Function implementation of discrete PID controller (Continued)

10.6 Summary

In this chapter, we have described using S-Functions to build custom Simulink blocks. We discussed the functions each S-Function must perform and the general structure of an S-Function. Next, we discussed M-file S-Functions in detail, and presented examples using S-Functions with no states, with continuous states, and with discrete states. Last, we discussed C S-Functions, and presented similar examples.

10.7 Reference

1. *Application Programming Interface Guides,* Version 5, Natick, Mass., The MathWorks, Inc., 1996.

11

Graphical Animations

In this chapter we will discuss two methods you can use to add graphical animations to a Simulink model. First, we'll discuss using MATLAB Handle Graphics in an S-Function to build an animation. Next, we will show how to use the Animation Toolbox.

11.1 Introduction

Graphical animations can make it easier to visualize a process being simulated. For example, one of the demonstrations included with Simulink is a model of a cart with an inverted pendulum. As the simulation progresses, the cart and pendulum move to graphically depict the state of the simulation. This animation makes it much easier to visualize the motion of the system.

In Chapter 9, we showed how you can build graphical animations using callbacks. This chapter presents two alternatives that are easier to use: S-Function-based animations and the Animation Toolbox. Each of the three methods of building graphical animations has advantages and disadvantages. The callback approach discussed earlier is the most powerful of the three techniques, as it permits you to include custom controls in the animation window, and also allows you to build an animation block that can be open or closed during a simulation. An S-Function-based animation is easier to build, but doesn't conveniently support adding custom controls. The Animation Toolbox is the easiest and fastest method of building a graphical animation. The Animation Toolbox does not allow you to add custom controls to the animation window, and it requires some additional effort on the part of the user.

11.2 S-Function Animations

S-Function-based animations are S-Functions that have no states and no outputs. Therefore, they are custom sinks. An animation S-function has two main parts: initialization and update. During initialization, the figure window is created and the animation objects are prepared. During updates, the properties of the animation objects are changed to cause the objects to move or change in some other way as a function of the S-Function block input.

11.2.1　Animation S-Function Initialization

The initialization phase of an S-Function animation consists of S-Function initialization, as discussed in Chapter 10, and figure initialization. The sample time should be set to some small value such that the animation is acceptably smooth, but does not cause the simulation to run too slowly. You can find a suitable value with a little experimentation. A good initial guess might be (**Start time – Stop time**)/100. Don't set the sample time to 0 (continuous system), because it will cause the animation to appear very erratic.

It is necessary to have some mechanism to determine whether an animation figure associated with the current S-Function block is already open. The approach used here is to store the path to the current block (from the gcb command) in the figure UserData parameter. It is safe to use gcb here because during execution of an S-Function, gcb will always return the path to the S-Function block. The figure initialization logic starts by determining whether the figure associated with the current block is already open. Suitable MATLAB statements are:

```
if(findobj('UserData',gcb))
  % Do nothing, figure is already open
else
  % initialize figure
end
```

If the figure is not already open, create it using the figure statement, for example

```
h_fig = figure('Position',[x_pos, y_pos, width, height], ...
```

Next, store the path to the current S-Function block in the figure UserData so that the test for existence of the figure just described will work correctly. The following statement will set the UserData:

```
set(h_fig,'UserData',gcb) ;
```

Next, draw the animation figure using MATLAB graphics commands. (For a good tutorial on MATLAB graphics, see Hanselman and Littlefield [2]). Save the handles of graphics elements that will move or change in some other way as the simulation progresses. For example, suppose an element is defined by vectors x_array and y_array. Plot the points and save the handle using the statement

```
hd1 = plot(x_array, y_array) ;
```

The last step in figure initialization is to save the handles of the elements that will change during the simulation. The technique used here to save these elements is to group them into a single MATLAB variable, and store that variable in the S-Function block UserData. The UserData can store any MATLAB variable, including cell arrays and structures, so there is no restriction on the type or amount of working data you can store. Suppose there are two graphics elements that are to be animated, and their handles are named hd1 and hd2. The following statements will store them in a structure

```
t_data.hd1 = hd1 ;
t_data.hd2 = hd2 ;
set_param(gcb,'UserData',t_data) ;
```

11.2.2 Animation S-Function Updates

The animation S-Function will be treated as a discrete block because we set the sample time to a positive number. Simulink will execute the S-Function at the sample times with flag = 2. The update function should first read from the S-Function block UserData the handles of the graphics objects that will change. For example, if the handles are stored in a structure variable as indicated above, they can be read as follows:

```
t_data = get_param(gcb,'UserData') ;
hd1 = t_data.hd1 ;
hd2 = t_data.hd2 ;
```

Next, compute new values for the properties of the objects that change and update the properties using the set command:

```
set(handle, PropertyName, PropertyValue) ;
```

where *handle* is the handle of the object, *PropertyName* is a MATLAB string containing the name of the object property to be changed, and *PropertyValue* is the new property value.

Example 11-1

In this example, we will build a graphical animation of a disk rolling back and forth in a semi-circular trough. Figure 11-1 illustrates the problem.

Assuming the disk rolls without slipping, the equation of motion of this system is

$$\ddot{\theta} = \frac{-g\sin\theta}{1.5(R-r)}$$

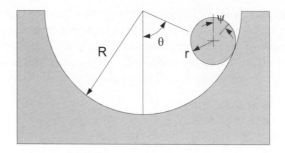

Figure 11-1   Disk rolling in a trough

where g is the acceleration due to gravity. The kinematic relationship between ψ and θ is

$$\psi = \theta \frac{(R-r)}{r}$$

Figure 11-2 illustrates a Simulink model of the equation of motion of this system, with an animation S-Function block to show the motion of the disk. We assume that $R = 12, r = 2, g = 32.2$.

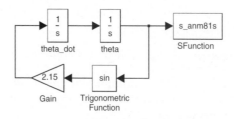

Figure 11-2   Simulink model of disk rolling in a trough

The animation S-Function is shown in Figure 11-3, and the animation figure is shown in Figure 11-4.

```
function [sys,x0,str,ts] = s_anm81s(t,x,u,flag)
%   S-file animation example 1
%   This example demonstrates building an animation
%   using a single S-file with no callbacks.
%
%   Based on sfuntmpl.m, supplied with Simulink
```

Figure 11-3   Rolling disk animation S-File

```
%    Copyright (c) 1990-96 by The MathWorks, Inc.
%
switch flag,
  case 0,                 % Initialization
    [sys,x0,str,ts]=mdlInitializeSizes;
  case 1,                 % Derivatives
    sys=mdlDerivatives(t,x,u);
  case 2,
    sys=mdlUpdate(t,x,u);
  case 3,
    sys=mdlOutputs(t,x,u);  % Compute output vector
  case 4,                 % Compute time of next sample
    sys=mdlGetTimeOfNextVarHit(t,x,u);
  case 9,                 % Finished. Do any needed
    sys=mdlTerminate(t,x,u);
  otherwise               % Invalid input
    error(['Unhandled flag = ',num2str(flag)]);
end
%***********************************************************
%*                    mdlInitializeSizes                  *
%***********************************************************
function [sys,x0,str,ts]=mdlInitializeSizes()
% Return the sizes of the system vectors, initial
% conditions, and the sample times and offets.
sizes = simsizes;   % Create the sizes structure
sizes.NumContStates  = 0;
sizes.NumDiscStates  = 0;
sizes.NumOutputs     = 0;
sizes.NumInputs      = 1;
sizes.DirFeedthrough = 0;
sizes.NumSampleTimes = 1;
sys = simsizes(sizes);
x0  = [];         % There are no states
str = [];         % str is always an empty matrix
                  % Update the figure every 0.25 sec
ts  = [0.25 0]; %initialize the array of sample times.
% Initialize the figure
% The handles of the disk and index mark are stored
% in the block's UserData.
if(findobj('UserData',gcb))
  % Figure is open, do nothing
```

Figure 11-3   Rolling disk animation S-File (Continued)

```
else
  h_fig = figure('Position',[200 200 400 300], ...
                 'MenuBar','none','NumberTitle','off', ...
                 'Resize','off', ...
                 'Name',[gcs,' Rolling Disk']) ;
  set(h_fig,'UserData',gcb) ; % Save name of current block
                              % in the figure's UserData.
                              % This is used to detect
                              % that a rolling disk figure
                              % is already open for the
                              % current block, so that
                              % only one instance of the
                              % figure is open at a time
                              % for a given instance of the
                              % block.
  r = 2 ;
  R = 12 ;
  q = r ;
  thp = 0:0.2:pi ;
  xp = R*cos(thp);
  yp = -R*sin(thp) ;
  xp = [xp,-R,-(R+q),-(R+q),(R+q), (R+q),R] ;
  yp = [yp,0,0,-(R+q),-(R+q),0,0] ;
  cl_x = [0,0] ;
  cl_y = [0,-R] ;
  % Make the disk
  thp = 0:0.3:2.3*pi ;
  xd = r*cos(thp);
  yd = r*sin(thp) ;
  hd = fill(xp,yp,[0.85,0.85,0.85]); % Draw trough
  hold on ;                          % So it won't get erased
  set(hd,'erasemode','none');
  axis('equal');axis('off');
  hd0 = plot(cl_x,cl_y,'k--');    % Draw the centerline
  set(hd0,'erasemode','none');
  % During this initialization pass, create the disk
  % (hd2) and the index mark (hd3).
  theta = 0 ;
  xc = (R-r)*sin(theta);    % Find center of disk
  yc = - (R-r)*cos(theta) ;
  psi = theta*(R-r)/r ;
```

Figure 11-3   Rolling disk animation S-File (Continued)

```
  xm_c = r*sin(psi) ;     % Relative position of index mark
  ym_c = r*cos(psi) ;
  xm = xc + xm_c ;        % Translate mark
  ym = yc + ym_c ;
  hd2 = fill(xd+xc, yd+yc, ...
             [0.85,0.85,0.85]) ; % Draw disk and mark
  hd3 = plot([xc,xm],[yc,ym],'k-');
  set_param(gcb,'UserData',[hd2,hd3]) ;
end
%***********************************************************
%*                      mdlDerivatives                    *
%***********************************************************
function sys=mdlDerivatives(t,x,u)
% Compute derivatives of continuous states
sys = [];   % Empty since no continuous states
%***********************************************************
%*                      mdlUpdate                         *
%***********************************************************
function sys=mdlUpdate(t,x,u)
% Compute update for discrete states.
sys = [];     % Empty since this model has no states.
% Update the figure
r = 2 ;
R = 12 ;
q = r ;
userdat = get_param(gcb,'UserData') ;
hd2 = userdat(1) ;
hd3 = userdat(2) ;
theta = u(1) ;        % The sole input is theta
xc = (R-r)*sin(theta);    % Find center of disk
yc = - (R-r)*cos(theta) ;
psi = theta*(R-r)/r ;
xm_c = r*sin(psi) ;  % Find relative position of index
ym_c = r*cos(psi) ;
xm = xc + xm_c ;        % Translate mark
ym = yc + ym_c ;
thp = 0:0.3:2*pi ;
xd = r*cos(thp);
yd = r*sin(thp) ;
% Move the disk and index marks to new positions
set(hd2,'XData',xd+xc);
```

Figure 11-3   Rolling disk animation S-File (Continued)

```
set(hd2,'YData',yd+yc);
set(hd3,'XData',[xc,xm]);
set(hd3,'YData',[yc,ym]);
%**********************************************************
%*                    mdlOutputs                          *
%**********************************************************
function sys=mdlOutputs(t,x,u)
% Compute output vector
sys = [];
%**********************************************************
%*                    mdlGetTimeOfNextVarHit              *
%**********************************************************
function sys=mdlGetTimeOfNextVarHit(t,x,u)
sys = [];
%**********************************************************
%*                    mdlTerminate                        *
%**********************************************************
function sys=mdlTerminate(t,x,u)
% Perform any necessary tasks at the end of the simulation
sys = [];
```

Figure 11-3   Rolling disk animation S-File (Continued)

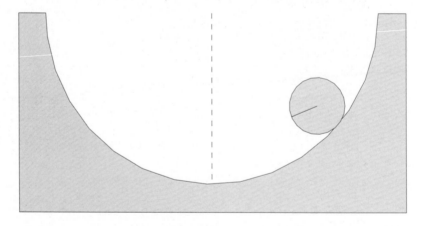

Figure 11-4   Rolling disk animation figure

11.3   Animation Toolbox

The Animation Toolbox is an extension to Simulink that permits you to create an animation graphically, in a manner similar to building a simulation in Simulink. To build an animation, you copy graphic objects to a figure window, and then set properties of the objects using object dialog boxes.

11.3.1   Obtaining the Animation Toolbox

The Animation Toolbox is available on The MathWorks Web site. The toolbox is free, but it requires Simulink. To install the Animation Toolbox, first download it to your computer using a Web browser or file transfer protocol (FTP) program. Add the directory in which you stored the toolbox files to the MATLAB path so that Simulink can find the toolbox files.

11.3.2   Using the Animation Toolbox

To add an Animation block to a model, open the Simulink model `animblk.mdl` in the Animation Toolbox directory, and drag the Animation block to your model window. The Animation block can accept scalar or vector inputs. Double-click the Animation block, opening the animation figure window shown in Figure 11-5.

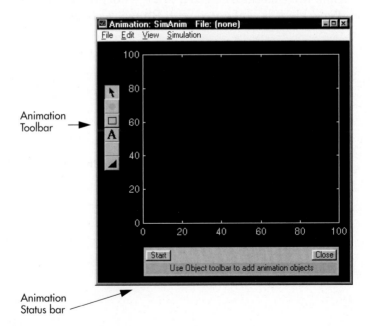

Figure 11-5   Animation Toolbox figure window

The animation figure window consists of three areas: the Animation Toolbar, the Animation Status bar, and the animation figure. The Animation Toolbar consists of a set of icons representing the available animation objects: dot, rectangle, text, line, and patch. The Animation Status bar displays the animation status and provides buttons to control the simulation and close the animation figure. When the simulation is running, the Animation Status bar contains a Stop button, a checkbox to show trails, and a button to clear the trails. The animation figure is the area in which the animation is created and displayed.

To construct an animation, click one of the icons in the Animation Toolbar, then click the animation figure at the desired location of the object represented by the icon. An object dialog box will pop up. Enter the object configuration data in the dialog box, then choose **Apply** and close the dialog box. Repeat for each object in the animation. Use the various choices on the **View** menu to configure the display. You can run the simulation using the Animation Status bar **Start** button or **Simulation:Start** from the model window menu bar.

Example 11-2

To illustrate the process of building an animation using the Animation Toolbox, consider the Simulink model shown in Figure 11-6. The model consists of two Sine Wave blocks connected to a Mux to produce a vector signal. The lower Sine Wave block is configured with **Phase** set to `pi/2`.

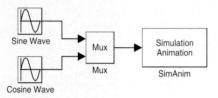

Figure 11-6 Simulink model with Animation block

Double-click the Animation block, opening the animation figure window.

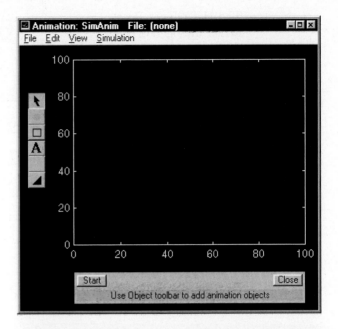

Click the dot icon, then click the figure.

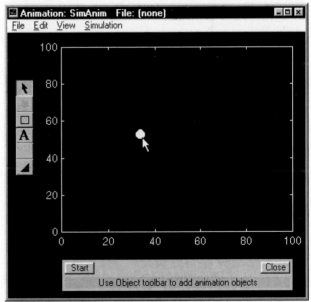

The Dot Object Properties dialog box will automatically be displayed. Configure the block dialog box fields as shown, then press **OK** and close the dialog box.

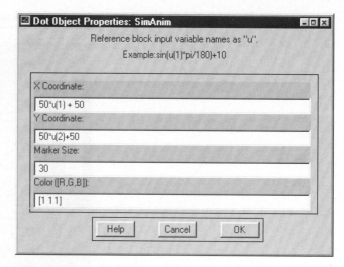

Run the simulation by clicking on the **Start** button. The dot should move in a circle.

11.3.3   Animation Object Properties

Each of the properties fields in the object dialog boxes can contain expressions consisting of constants, variables currently defined in the MATLAB workspace, and elements of the input vector (u). In addition to making the location of an object a function of the input, you can also make the color or size of an object a function of the input.

11.3.4   Configuring an Animation

The **View** menu contains several options that are useful in tailoring the appearance of an animation figure.

Figure Properties

The **View** menu provides options to show or hide several figure properties. You can turn the axes on or off, turn a grid on or off, and display or hide a border. There are also options to show or hide the Status bar and the Toolbar.

Figure Scale

View:AutoScale allows you to control whether or not the animation figure automatically scales. The autoscale feature can be useful in determining appropriate axis limits. Once you've found acceptable limits, the appearance of the animation can be improved by setting **AutoScale** to off and then using the **View:Change Axis Limits** to fine-tune the limits.

11.3.5 Modifying an Animation

After running a simulation you can add objects to an animation figure or modify the objects in the figure. Before modifying the figure, choose **Simulation:Reset** from the animation window menu bar. To modify an existing object, double-click the object.

11.3.6 Setting Initial Inputs

You can set the initial values of animation block input variables (u(1),u(2), etc.) by selecting **Simulation:Set Initial Inputs**. This will open the dialog box shown in Figure 11-7. Enter the initial values of the inputs as a vector. This capability is useful because the Animation block does not have access to the inputs until the simulation begins. Inititializing the inputs prevents a large start-up transient in the animation figure. Setting the inputs in this dialog box has no effect on the inputs themselves; these values do not propagate backwards from the Animation block. The initial values default to zero.

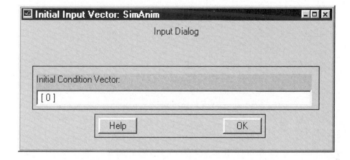

Figure 11-7 Animation initial inputs dialog box

11.3.7 Saving and Loading Animation Files

The **File** menu of the animation figure window provides options to save or load an animation. The information that the Animation Toolbox needs to generate an animation figure is stored in the form of a MATLAB .mat file.

When you open an animation figure window by double-clicking an Animation block, and if the last time you accessed that block you saved an animation associated with that block, there will be a prompt asking whether you wish to use the previous animation or start a new one.

11.4 Summary

In this chapter we have explained two methods for adding graphical animations to Simulink models. First, we showed how you can use S-Function-based animations to create custom animation blocks. We then explained how to use the Animation Toolbox, which is available from The MathWorks Web site.

11.5 References and Further Reading

1. *Using MATLAB Graphics,* Version 5, Natick, Mass., The MathWorks, Inc., 1996.

2. Hanselman, Duane C., and Littlefield, Bruce R., *Mastering MATLAB 5: A Comprehensive Tutorial*, Upper Saddle River, N.J., Prentice Hall, 1998.

Numerical Issues

In this chapter we will discuss two numerical issues you should consider when building Simulink models. First, we will consider choosing the best differential equation solver for a particular model, which can frequently improve the speed and accuracy of a simulation. Then we will explain algebraic loops, how Simulink deals with them, and how you can eliminate them if necessary.

12.1 Introduction

Simulink's block diagram metaphor for programming frees you from many of the details of writing a computer program to model a dynamical system. However, when you build a Simulink model, you are programming, and, as with all programming tasks, there are numerical issues you should keep in mind. We will discuss two of these issues in this chapter: choosing a differential equation solver and dealing with algebraic loops.

12.2 Choosing a Solver

Simulink provides several differential equation solvers. The majority of the solvers are the result of recent numerical integration research, and are among the fastest and most accurate methods available. Detailed descriptions of the algorithms are available in the paper by Shampine [4], available from The MathWorks.

It is generally best to use the variable-step solvers, as they continuously adjust the integration step size to maximize efficiency while maintaining a specified accuracy. Simulink's variable-step solvers can completely decouple the integration step size and the interval between output points, so it is not necessary to limit the step size to get a smooth plot or to produce an output trajectory with a predetermined fixed step size. The available solvers are listed in Table 4-2, repeated here for convenience in Table 12-1.

Solver selection considerations

There is no universal "best" differential equation solver. Choosing the best solver for a particular system requires an understanding of the system

Table 12-1 Simulink Solvers

Solver Type	Characteristics
ODE45	Excellent general-purpose single-step solver. Based on the Dormand-Prince fourth-fifth order Runge-Kutta pair. ODE45 is the default solver, and is usually a good first choice.
ODE23	Uses the Bogacki-Shampine second–third-order Runge-Kutta pair. Sometimes works better than ODE45 in the presence of mild stiffness. Generally requires a smaller step size than ODE45 to get the same accuracy.
ODE113	Variable-order Adams-Bashforth-Moulton solver. Since ODE113 uses the solutions at several previous time points to compute the solution at the current time point, it may produce the same accuracy as ODE45 or ODE23 with fewer derivative evaluations, and thus perform much faster. Not suitable for systems with discontinuities. See Kincaid and Cheney [2] for a good explanation of Adams-Bashforth-Moulton solvers.
ODE15S	Variable-order multistep solver for stiff systems. Based on recent research using numerical difference formulas. If a simulation runs extremely slowly using ODE45, try ODE15S.
ODE23S	Fixed-order single-step solver for stiff systems. Because ODE23S is a single-step method, it is sometimes faster than ODE15S. If a system appears to be stiff, it is a good idea to try both stiff solvers to determine which performs the best.
Discrete	Special solver for systems that have no continuous states.
ODE5	Fixed step size version of ODE45.
ODE4	Classic fourth-order Runge-Kutta formulas using a fixed step size.
ODE3	Fixed step version of ODE23.
ODE2	Fixed step size second-order Runge-Kutta method, also known as Heun's method.
ODE1	Euler's method using a fixed step size.

dynamics. Let's look briefly at the characteristics of each of the methods, and mention systems for which each is probably the best choice.

ODE45 and ODE23 are Runge-Kutta methods. These methods approximate the solution function (in the case of Simulink, the solution function is the state trajectory of the Simulink model) by numerically approximating a Taylor series of a fixed number of terms, the *order* being defined as the highest derivative in the series. The principal error in a Taylor series approximation of a function is known as *truncation error*, and is due to the truncation of the Taylor series to a finite number of terms. ODE45 and ODE23 estimate the truncation error by computing the value of the state variables at the end of an integration step using two Taylor series approximations of different orders (4 and 5 or 2 and 3). The difference in the two computed values is a reliable indicator of the total truncation error. If the error is too large, the integration step size is reduced, and the integration step is repeated. If the error is too small (more accuracy than needed), the step size is increased for the next integration step. An important characteristic of algorithms such as ODE45 and ODE23 is that they select the intermediate points in the integration step such that both Taylor series approximations use the same derivative function evaluations.

ODE113 is a variable-order Adams method (namely, an Adams-Bashforth-Moulton method), a multistep predictor-corrector algorithm. The predictor step approximates the derivative function as a polynomial of degree $n - 1$, where n is the order of the method. The coefficients of the predictor polynomial are computed using the previous $n - 1$ solution points and the derivatives at the points. A trial next solution point is computed by extrapolation. Next, a corrector polynomial is fit through the previous n points and the newly computed trial solution point, and this polynomial is evaluated to recompute the trial solution point. The corrector portion of the algorithm can be repeated to refine the solution point. The difference between the predictor solution and the corrector solution is a measure of the integration error, and is used to adjust the integration step size. ODE113 also adjusts the degree of the approximating polynomials to balance accuracy and efficiency. Multistep methods such as ODE113 tend to work very well for systems that are smooth. They don't work well for systems with discontinuities because the polynomial approximation assumes a smooth function.

ODE15S is a variable-order multistep algorithm specifically designed to work well with stiff systems. A stiff system is one which has both very fast dynamics and very slow dynamics (widely separated eigenvalues). An example would be a system that has a sharp start-up transient followed by a relatively slow steady-state response. Special techniques, such as ODE15S, are required to accurately model such systems. These algorithms contain extra logic to detect transitions in a system's dynamics. The extra computational work expended in adapting to rapidly changing dynamics makes the stiff solvers inefficient for systems that are not stiff.

ODE23S is a single-step stiff system solver based on the Rosenbrock formulas. This method is of fixed order, and since there is no order adjustment logic, it is sometimes faster than ODE15S.

The discrete solver is a special method that is applicable only to systems that have no continuous states. Although all of Simulink's solvers are suitable for such systems, the discrete solver is the fastest choice for these systems.

The Solver options section contains four fields to control integration step size adjustment for the variable step size integrators. Two fields, **Max step size** and **Initial step size**, permit you to reduce the likelihood of the solver missing important system behavior. To allow Simulink to use its default values for these parameters, enter auto in the respective fields. The other two fields allow you to set the absolute and relative tolerances used in the step size adjustment logic.

The default **Max step size** is

$$h_{max} = \frac{t_{stop} - t_{start}}{50} \tag{12-1}$$

which is generally satisfactory. There may be certain situations in which it is desirable to enter a fixed value for **Max step size**. For example, if the duration of the simulation is extremely long, the default maximum step size may be too large to guarantee that no important behavior will be missed. If the system is known to be periodic, the performance of the step size adjustment logic may be slightly improved by limiting the maximum step size to a fraction (The Math-Works suggests 1/4) of the period. It is not advisable to set the maximum step size so as to limit the spacing between points in the output trajectory, as it is much more economical computationally to use the Output options section of the solver page for that purpose.

If **Initial step size** is set to auto, Simulink will compute the initial step size based on the state derivatives at the start of the simulation. If the system dynamics are believed to contain a sharp transient soon after t_{start}, set **Initial step size** to a value small enough to permit the solver to detect the transient. In most other situations, it is best to allow Simulink's built-in logic to compute the initial step size.

Relative tolerance and **Absolute tolerance** are used to compute the allowable value of integration error estimate (e_i) for each state (x_i) according to the formula

$$e_i \le max(tol_{Rel}|x_i|, tol_{Abs}) \tag{12-2}$$

where tol_{Rel} and tol_{Abs} are **Relative tolerance** and **Absolute tolerance**, respectively. The two tolerances for a hypothetical state are depicted graphically in Figure 12-1. In the region in which the magnitude of the state is large, tol_{Rel} determines the error bound. In the region where the magnitude of the state is small, tol_{Abs} determines the error bound. If the integration error estimate for any state exceeds its limit, the integration step size is reduced. If the error limits for every state exceed the estimates by some value that depends on the particular solver used, the integration step size for the subsequent step is increased.

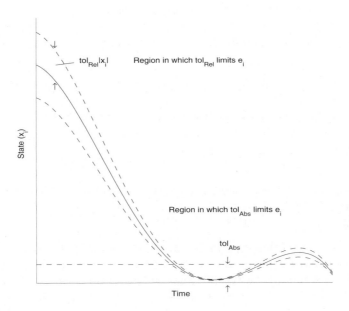

Figure 12-1   Solver error tolerance computation

The fixed step size solvers are all fixed-order single step methods. These methods might be preferable if the system dynamics are sufficiently well understood that a nearly optimal integration step size is known. In such a situation, the elimination of step size and order adjustment might significantly speed up the simulation. It is not advisable to use a fixed step size integrator to force Simulink to produce an output trajectory with a fixed spacing between points, as the Output options section of the Solver page allows you to do that much more economically. If a fixed step size integrator is chosen, there is a single field, **Fixed step size**, to enter the step size. This field may contain a value for step size, or may be set to auto to allow Simulink to automatically choose the fixed step size.

Example 12-1

A stiff system is a system that has both fast dynamics and slow dynamics. Typically, the primary interest is in the slow dynamics, but ignoring the fast dynamics can cause the simulation to produce incorrect results. Consider the unforced second-order system

$$\ddot{x} + 100\dot{x} + 0.9999x = 0$$

Assume that the system starts at rest with $x = 1$. Taking the Laplace transform,

$$s^2X(s) - sx(0) - \dot{x}(0) + 100(sX(s) - x(0)) + 0.9999X(s) = 0$$

Substituting $x(0) = 1$, $\dot{x}(0) = 0$, and solving for $X(s)$,

$$X(s) = \frac{s + 100}{s^2 + 100s + 0.9999}$$

Taking the inverse Laplace transform, we get the time response:

$$x(t) = -0.0001e^{-99.99t} + 1.0001e^{-0.01t}$$

The response of this system has two components. The first component starts at a very small magnitude (–0.0001) and decays rapidly. The second component starts at a magnitude 10,000 times as large, and decays 10,000 times as slowly. So, the slow response dominates the behavior of the system.

Now, let's see what happens when we model this system. Figure 12-2 shows a Simulink model of the system. Set the **Initial condition** of the velocity Integrator to 0, and **Initial condition** of the displacement Integrator to 1. Set **Start time** to 0, and **Stop time** to 500. Select (check) **Simulation:Parameters** dialog box Workspace I/O page field **Save to workspace**, **Time**, and leave **States** and **Output** unselected.

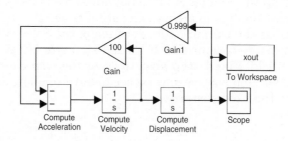

Figure 12-2   Simulink model of stiff second-order system

Next, let's experiment with the different solvers to see the effect of the stiff-ness. First, run the simulation using ODE15S. The simulation runs in a few seconds. The tout (produced as a result of selecting **Save to workspace, Time**) and xout (produced by the To Workspace block) vectors sent to the MATLAB workspace each have about 100 elements. Figure 12-3 shows the simulation results plotted using the MATLAB plot command.

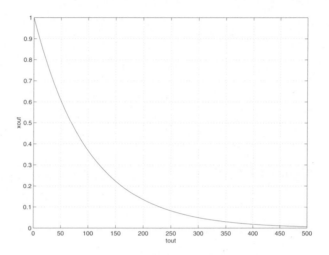

Figure 12-3 Stiff system results using ODE15S

Running the simulation using ODE45 takes a much longer time, but produces a plot that appears identical to Figure 12-3. This time, however, the vectors tout and xout have approximately 15,000 elements each. The following MATLAB statements will produce a plot showing the change in the trajectory between successive points from point 14000 to 14100:

```
» t=tout(14000:14100);
» x=xout(14001:14101)-xout(14000:14100);
» plot(t,x)
```

The plot appears in Figure 12-4. Inspecting the plot, you can see that there is a high-frequency component to the output trajectory resulting from the fast dynamics. This component is of very small magnitude (10^{-6}).

Finally, recall that we said that ignoring the fast dynamics can produce incorrect results. The stiff solver required about 100 time points, or on average 5 sec between time points. Run the simulation using the fixed step solver ODE4 and a 5-sec step size. The simulation diverges, causing Simulink to issue an error message.

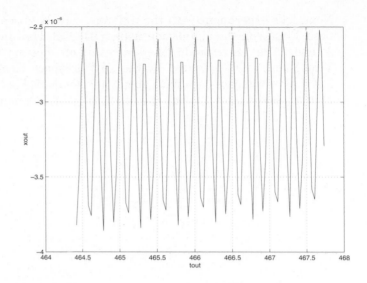

Figure 12-4 Oscillation of stiff system results using ODE45

12.3 Algebraic Loops

Algebraic loops are a programming issue that sometimes requires special care in Simulink modeling. An algebraic loop is a condition in which the output of a block drives the input of the same block. Consider the Simulink model in Figure 12-5. From the model we can compute

$$\dot{x} = u - k_3 k_2 \dot{x} - k_3 k_1 x \tag{12-3}$$

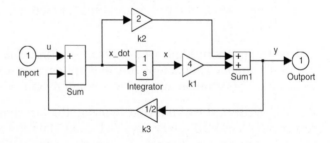

Figure 12-5 First-order system with an algebraic loop

So $\dot{x}$ is a function of x, u, and $\dot{x}$. For each integration step, Simulink must solve the algebraic equation for $\dot{x}$. Simulink can't solve for $\dot{x}$ symbolically, so it uses an iterative numerical technique to solve the algebraic equation. This iterative procedure takes time, and in some cases Simulink fails to arrive at a solution altogether.

In this simple example, the algebraic loop is formed by Gain blocks k2 and k3 and Sum blocks Sum and Sum1. However, algebraic loops are not restricted to Gain and Sum blocks. Any block for which the current value of the output depends, even partially, on the current value of the input can be part of an algebraic loop. Such blocks are said to have *direct feedthrough*. Nearly all of the blocks in the Nonlinear block library have direct feedthrough. Transfer Function and Zero-Pole blocks for which the degree of the numerator is the same as the degree of the denominator, and State-Space blocks with nonzero direct transmittance (D) matrices, also exhibit direct feedthrough.

Algebraic loops are not a problem unique to Simulink. If you attempt to use Equation (12-3) in a program in an algorithmic language such as FORTRAN, C, or even MATLAB, you will have to deal with the fact that $\dot{x}$ appears on both sides of the equation. While the scalar example here is easily dealt with, the situation is not always so simple. For example, modeling the dynamics of robot manipulators can produce complex nonlinear algebraic loops involving several state variables. Simulink's algebraic loop solver can frequently relieve you of the need to worry about algebraic loops, but you should understand the problem and how Simulink approaches it.

12.3.1 Newton-Raphson Method

Simulink attempts to solve algebraic loops using a robust implementation of the Newton-Raphson technique. To illustrate the basic idea of the technique, we will discuss the classic Newton-Raphson method for a scalar problem. For the scalar example above, the algebraic problem can be written

$$\dot{x} = f(x, \dot{x}, u, t) \tag{12-4}$$

where f is in general a nonlinear function. The Newton-Raphson method is an iterative process that attempts to solve the error function

$$\phi = \dot{x} - f(x, \dot{x}, u, t) = 0 \tag{12-5}$$

by minimizing the quadratic

$$P = \phi^2 \tag{12-6}$$

with respect to $\dot{x}$. At each iteration, compute (dropping the arguments of ϕ for convenience)

$$\Delta \dot{x} = -\phi / \frac{\partial \phi}{\partial \dot{x}} \qquad (12\text{-}7)$$

then update the estimate

$$\dot{x}_{new} = \dot{x}_{old} + \Delta \dot{x} \qquad (12\text{-}8)$$

The function ϕ and its partial derivative are evaluated at the current estimate of $\dot{x}$, and the current known values of x, u, and t. If

$$\frac{\partial \phi}{\partial \dot{x}}$$

is constant, that is, if $f(x, \dot{x}, u, t)$ is linear with respect to $\dot{x}$, the Newton-Raphson procedure will converge in exactly one iteration. On the other hand, if $f(x, \dot{x}, u, t)$ is nonlinear with respect to $\dot{x}$, the procedure may require many iterations, and may fail to converge altogether.

12.3.2 Eliminating Algebraic Loops

Simulink will report the detection of an algebraic loop if the **Simulation:Parameters** Diagnostic choice for algebraic loops is set to **warning** or **error**. If an algebraic loop is detected, you have two options: leave the algebraic loop intact, or eliminate it. If the speed of execution of the model is acceptable, leaving the loop intact is probably the better choice. If the speed of execution is not adequate, you must eliminate the algebraic loop.

The most desirable method of eliminating an algebraic loop is to reformulate the model into an equivalent model that does not have an algebraic loop. For example, the model shown in Figure 12-6 has the same input-output behavior as the model in Figure 12-5. However, this model does not have an algebraic loop, and will therefore execute faster.

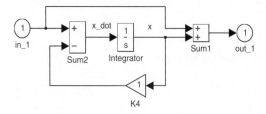

Figure 12-6   First-order system reformulated to eliminate the algebraic loop

It is not always convenient to reformulate a model such that there are no algebraic loops, as the equations of motion of some physical systems lead to algebraic loops. It is always possible in these situations to break an algebraic loop using a memory block. Figure 12-7 shows the model of Figure 12-5 modified such that the algebraic loop is broken using a Memory block. While this approach can always be used to break an algebraic loop, it is not always satisfactory because the delay introduced by a Memory block can degrade the accuracy of the simulation. As we will see in Example 12-2, this approach can change the behavior of the Simulink model so that it no longer accurately represents the physical system.

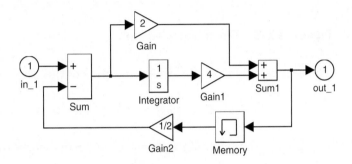

Figure 12-7   Breaking an algebraic loop with a memory block

A final method of eliminating an algebraic loop is to use a MATLAB function block to solve the algebraic problem directly. Although this approach requires that you write MATLAB code to replace some Simulink blocks, it is sometimes the best solution.

Example 12-2

Consider the system of two carts shown in Figure 12-8. Cart 1 moves on the ground, and cart 2 moves relative to cart 1. x_1 and x_2 are the positions of the carts relative to inertial space. The angular displacements of the wheels are θ_1 and θ_2, and the total torque input to the wheels of cart 1 is τ_1, and to the wheels of cart 2 is τ_2.

The wheel angular displacements are related to the cart absolute positions by

$$x_1 = -r_1\theta_1$$
$$x_2 = x_1 - r_2\theta_2$$

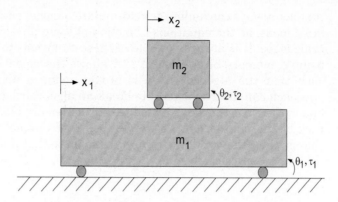

Figure 12-8 Directly coupled carts

The kinetic energy of the system in terms of the wheel angular velocities is

$$T = \frac{1}{2}m_1(-r_1\dot{\theta}_1)^2 + \frac{1}{2}m_2(-r_1\dot{\theta}_1 - r_2\dot{\theta}_2)^2$$

Using a Lagrangian approach, we solve for the wheel torques:

$$\tau_1 = m_1r_1^2\ddot{\theta}_1 + m_2r_1^2\ddot{\theta}_1 + m_2r_1r_2\ddot{\theta}_2$$
$$\tau_2 = m_2r_1r_2\ddot{\theta}_1 + m_2r_2^2\ddot{\theta}_2$$

Solving for the angular accelerations, we get the coupled differential equations

$$\ddot{\theta}_1 = K_{11}(\tau_1 - K_{21}\ddot{\theta}_2)$$
$$\ddot{\theta}_2 = K_{22}(\tau_2 - K_{12}\ddot{\theta}_1)$$

where

$$K_{11} = \frac{1}{(m_1 + m_2)r_1^2}$$

$$K_{21} = K_{12} = m_2r_1r_2$$

$$K_{22} = \frac{1}{m_2r_2^2}$$

A Simulink model that implements the equations of motion is shown in Figure 12-9. We set the parameters using the M-file shown in Figure 12-10.

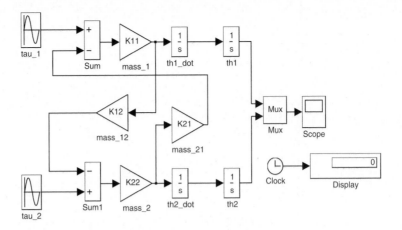

Figure 12-9 Simulink model of directly coupled carts

```
% Set up block parameters for algebraic loop example
m1 = 10 ;
m2 = 5 ;
r1 = 2 ;
r2 = 1.5 ;
K11 = 1/((m1+m2)*r1^2) ;
K12 = m2*r1*r2 ;
K21 = K12 ;
K22 = 1/(m2*r2^2) ;
```

Figure 12-10 MATLAB script to initialize coefficients

The input torques are

$$\tau_1 = \sin(0.1t)$$
$$\tau_2 = \sin(0.2t - 1)$$

Executing the simulation produces an algebraic loop warning in the MATLAB workspace. The output trajectories of the two carts for the first 500 sec is shown in Figure 12-11.

To illustrate the potential for simulation errors when an algebraic loop is broken using a Memory block, consider the revised model in Figure 12-12. The Memory block eliminates the algebraic loop, and causes the simulation to execute significantly faster. Unfortunately, the results of the simulation, shown in Figure 12-13, are incorrect. If the simulation is run with the **Max step size** on the **Simulation:Parameters** Solver page set to a sufficiently small value, correct results are produced. In this example, if the **Max step size** is set to 0.1,

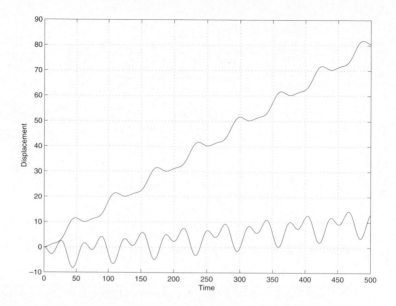

Figure 12-11 Directly coupled cart trajectories

the results are nearly identical to the results shown in Figure 12-11. Of course, limiting **Max step size** slows the simulation, negating the benefit of the Memory block.

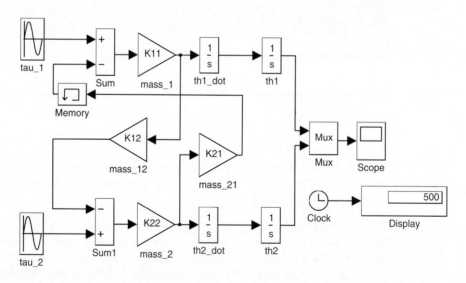

Figure 12-12 Directly coupled cart model with algebraic loop broken

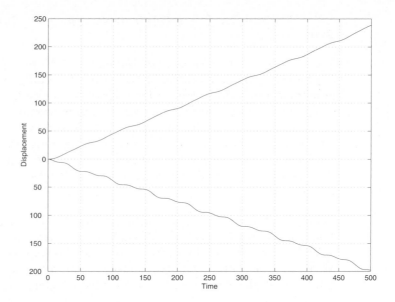

Figure 12-13 Trajectories using the directly coupled cart model with the algebraic loop broken

12.4   Summary

In this chapter, we have discussed two important numerical issues you should consider when building Simulink models. First, we discussed choosing the most appropriate solver, which can improve the speed and accuracy of a simulation. Then, we discussed algebraic loops, how Simulink deals with them, and how you can eliminate them.

12.5   References and Further Reading

1. Hartley, Tom T., Beale, Guy O., and Chicatelli, Stephen P., *Digital Simulation of Dynamic Systems: A Control Theory Approach*, Englewood Cliffs, N.J., Prentice Hall, 1994, pp. 190–238. In addition to covering the most important differential equation solution techniques, this book provides a detailed discussion of solutions to stiff systems.

2. Kincaid, David, and Cheney, Ward, *Numerical Analysis*, Pacific Grove, Calif., Brooks/Cole Publishing Co., 1991, pp. 508–514. This is an excellent,

and very rigorous, text covering many important topics in numerical analysis.

3. Mathews, John H., *Numerical Methods for Mathematics, Science, and Engineering*, Englewood Cliffs, N.J., Prentice Hall, 1992. This is a fine numerical methods reference for scientists and engineers. In particular, Chapter 4 on interpolation and polynomial approximation and Chapter 9 on differential equation solution will assist you in understanding Simulink's solvers. Chapter 2 provides a rigorous treatment of Newton-Raphson methods. Many algorithms are provided, and MATLAB code for the algorithms is available from the MathWorks Web site (www.math-works.com).

4. Shampine, Lawrence F., and Reichelt, Mark W., "The MATLAB ODE Suite," The MathWorks, Inc., Natick, Mass., 1996. This technical paper is available directly from The MathWorks. It provides a detailed discussion of the MATLAB differential equation solvers that are available from within Simulink. It also provides an extensive list of references.

Block Reference

This appendix provides a brief listing of all the blocks in the SIMULINK block libraries. For detailed descriptions of the blocks and their use, refer to the Block Browser.

SIMULINK Block Library

Block	Purpose

Sources

The Sources block library contains blocks that generate signals. The blocks include constants, sine waves, step functions, and a signal generator.

Sinks

The Sinks block library contains blocks that display signals, or save signals for further processing or analysis.

Discrete

The Discrete block library contains blocks that are used to model discrete systems. This library includes blocks that implement time delays, discrete integrators, discrete transfer functions, and zero- and first-order holds.

Linear

The Linear block library contains blocks used to model linear continuous systems. This library includes gain blocks (which can also be used with discrete systems), integrators, transfer function blocks, and a state-space block.

Nonlinear

The Nonlinear block library contains a variety of blocks used to model nonlinearities in both continuous and discrete systems. Examples of nonlinear blocks are logical and relational logic, nonlinear functions, sign and saturation functions, and lookup tables.

Connections

The Connections block library contains a variety of blocks that transfer signals. Examples are goto blocks, input and output ports, and multiplexers and demultiplexers.

Sources Block Library

Block	Purpose
Constant	Generate a constant value. The constant can be a scalar or a vector.
Signal Generator	Generate a periodic signal (sine wave, square wave, or sawtooth wave) or random noise. Configuration parameters are signal amplitude and frequency.
Ramp	Generate a signal for which the time derivative is a constant.
Sine Wave	Generate a sine wave. Amplitude, phase, and frequency can be set.
Step	Generate a step function. Configuration parameters are step time, initial value, and final value.
Chirp Signal	Generate a sinusoidal signal of continuously increasing frequency.
Pulse Generator	Generate a rectangular wave. Configuration parameters are period, amplitude, duty cycle, and start time.
Discrete Pulse Generator	Generate pulses defined by integer multiples of the sample time.
Repeating Sequence	Generate an arbitrary periodic signal. The signal is defined by a table of time points and amplitudes.
Clock	Generate a signal consisting of the current simulation time.

Sources Block Library (Continued)

Block	Purpose
12:34 Digital Clock	Generate a signal consisting of the current simulation time, sampled at a specified period. Equivalent to a combination of a Clock block and a Zero-Order hold, but much more efficient.
untitled.mat From File	Generate a signal by interpolating in a MATLAB matrix stored in a file.
[T,U] From Workspace	Generate a signal by interpolating in a table defined by variables in the MATLAB workspace.
Random Number	Generate a signal containing normally distributed random numbers.
Uniform Random Number	Generate a signal containing uniformly distributed random numbers.
Band–Limited White Noise	Generate a signal containing band-limited white noise of a specified power spectral density (PSD).

Sinks Block Library

Block	Purpose
Scope	Display scalar or vector signals in a method analogous to an oscilloscope.
XY Graph	Produce a graph using two scalar inputs. The signal connected to the top input port is the independent variable (x-axis), and the signal connected to the lower input port is the dependent variable (y-axis).
0 Display	Display the current value of the input signal.

Sinks Block Library (Continued)

Block	Purpose
To File	Save the input signal to a file in MATLAB .mat format. The signal may be scalar or vector.
To Workspace	Store the input signal in a MATLAB matrix accessible in the MATLAB workspace after the simulation stops. The signal may be scalar or vector.
Stop Simulation	Cause the simulation to stop when the input signal is nonzero.

Discrete Block Library

Block	Purpose
Unit Delay	The output signal of the Unit Delay is the input signal delayed by one sample time.
Discrete–Time Integrator	The Discrete-Time Integrator is a discrete approximation to a continuous integrator.
Zero–Order Hold	The output of the Zero-Order Hold is the input at the most recent sample time.
First–Order Hold	The output of the First-Order Hold is a continuously varying signal. At an offset time δ since the last sample ($x(k)$), the output is $$x(k) + \frac{\delta}{T}(x(k) - x(k-1)),$$ where T is the sample period.
Discrete State–Space	Model a linear time-invariant multiple-input, multiple-output discrete system using state-space notation.

Discrete Block Library (Continued)

Block	Purpose
$\dfrac{1}{1+2z^{-1}}$ Discrete Filter	The Discrete Filter block implements a discrete transfer function using the notation (polynomials of z^{-1}) frequently associated with digital filtering.
$\dfrac{1}{z+0.5}$ Discrete Transfer Fcn	The Discrete Transfer Fcn block implements a discrete transfer function using the notation (polynomials of z) frequently associated with control systems.
$\dfrac{(z-1)}{z(z-0.5)}$ Discrete Zero–Pole	Model a discrete transfer function using zero-pole notation.

Linear Block Library

Block	Purpose
1 Gain	The output of a Gain block is the input multiplied by a constant. The Gain block will work with scalar or vector signals, and the value of gain may be a scalar or vector compatible with the input signal.
+ + Sum	The output of the Sum block is the algebraic sum of its inputs. The number of inputs and the sign applied to each input can be set in the block dialog box.
$\dfrac{1}{s}$ Integrator	Compute the time integral of the input signal.
$\dfrac{1}{s+1}$ Transfer Fcn	Implement a continuous transfer function.
$x' = Ax+Bu$ $y = Cx+Du$ State–Space	Model a linear time-invariant multiple-input, multiple-output system or subsystem using state-space notation.

Linear Block Library (Continued)

Block	Purpose
Zero–Pole	Implement a continuous transfer function using zero-pole notation.
Derivative	The output of the Derivative block is the time rate of change of the input.
Dot Product	The Dot Product block accepts two vector signals of the same dimension. The output is the dot product of the current input vectors.
Matrix Gain	The output of the Matrix Gain block is the current input vector multiplied by a compatible matrix. The input vector is treated as a column vector. Therefore, the gain matrix must have the same number of columns as there are elements in the input vector. The number of outputs is the same as the number of rows in the gain matrix, which does not have to be square.
Slider Gain	The Slider Gain is a Gain block for which the value of gain may be set using a slider control. Open the slider control by double-clicking the block. The slider can be moved during a simulation, thus providing a variable input device.

Nonlinear Block Library

Block	Purpose
Abs	Compute the absolute value of the input signal, which may be scalar or vector.
Trigonometric Function	The Trigonometric Function block can be configured to implement standard trigonometric functions such as sine and cosine.
Math Function	The Math Function block can be configured to perform a variety of mathematical functions such as exp, log, and sqrt.

Nonlinear Block Library (Continued)

Block	Purpose
floor Rounding Function	The Rounding Function block can be configured to round, round up (ceil), round down (floor), and round to the nearest integer toward zero (fix).
min MinMax	The MinMax block can be configured to compute the minimum or maximum value of its inputs. The number of input ports can be set in the block dialog box.
× Product	The Product block can be configured with one or more inputs. If there is one input, the output is the product of all elements of the input vector. If there are multiple inputs, the output is the element-by-element product of the vectors at each input port.
[::::] Combinatorial Logic	Implement a truth table.
AND Logical Operator	The Logical Operator can be configured to implement a number of logical operations such as AND and OR.
<= Relational Operator	The Relational Operator block can be configured to implement a number of relational operations such as less than or equal, greater than, etc.
Sign	Implement the signum nonlinearity. The output is 1 if the input is positive, 0 if the input is 0, and -1 if the input is negative.
Rate Limiter	Limit the rate of change of the output signal. When the input is changing, the rate of change of the output will be the same as the rate of change of the input, as long as the rate of change of the input is less than a settable limit. If the rate of change of the input exceeds the limit, the rate of change of the output will be the same as the limit.
Saturation	Implement a saturation nonlinearity. The upper and lower limits of the output signal are configuration parameters. If the value of the input signal is between the limits, the value of the output will be the same as the value of the input.

Nonlinear Block Library (Continued)

Block	Purpose
Quantizer	The Quantizer models an analog to digital converter. Its output is a multiple of the quantization interval, which is a block configuration parameter.
Coulomb & Viscous Friction	Implement a simple model of Coulomb and viscous friction.
Backlash	Implement a backlash nonlinearity.
Dead Zone	A dead zone is a region in which the output is zero. The upper and lower limits of the dead zone are configuration parameters. If the input is below the dead zone, the output is the input minus the lower limit, and if the input is above the dead zone, the output is the input minus the upper limit.
Look–Up Table	Perform linear interpolation in a table specified as a configuration parameter. This block maps a single input to a single output, and maps a vector input to a vector output of the same dimension.
Look–Up Table (2–D)	The 2-D Lookup Table maps two inputs to a single output.
Memory	The output of the Memory block is the value of its input at the beginning of the previous integration step.
Transport Delay	The Transport Delay block simulates a time delay. The output is the input delayed by a specified time.
Variable Transport Delay	The Variable Time Delay block has two inputs. The first input is the signal to be delayed. The second input is the length of the delay. Thus, the length of the delay can change during a simulation.

Nonlinear Block Library (Continued)

Block	Purpose
Hit Crossing	The Hit Crossing block causes the simulation to locate the instant (within machine precision) the input signal reaches a value that may be specified in the block dialog box. The block can be configured with or without an output signal. If there is an output signal, it will have a value of 0 except when the input is equal (within machine precision) to the value specified in the block dialog box. When the input signal is equal to the specified value, the block output is 1.
Fcn — f(u)	The Fcn block may be configured with a function in a C language syntax. This block can accept a vector input, but produces a scalar output. This block can't perform matrix arithmetic; however, it is faster than the MATLAB Fcn block, and is therefore preferable when matrix arithmetic is not needed.
MATLAB Fcn — MATLAB Function	The MATLAB Fcn block implements a function using MATLAB syntax. It can accept vector inputs and produce vector outputs.
S-Function — system	The S-Function block is used to incorporate a block written in MATLAB or C code into a SIMULINK model. The *Student Edition of SIMULINK* does not support S-Functions.
Switch	Switches between two input signals based on the value of a control signal.
Manual Switch	The Manual Switch block switches between the two inputs when you double-click the block.
Multiport Switch	The Multiport Switch can be configured to accept any number of inputs. A control signal determines which input is passed to the output.

Nonlinear Block Library (Continued)

Block	Purpose
Algebraic Constraint	The Algebraic Constraint block allows a SIMULINK model to solve algebraic equations. The model must be configured such that the input to the Algebraic Constraint block is dependent upon the value of the output. A model containing an Algebraic Constraint block will attempt to adjust the value of the block output such that the value of the block input is 0.
Relay	Simulate a relay. The output is one of two specified discrete values, depending on the value of the input.

Connections Block Library

Block	Purpose
In	The Inport block creates an input for a subsystem. An Inport block can also be used to receive an external input (for example, using the `sim` command) to a model.
Out	The Outport block creates an output port for a subsystem. An Outport block can also be used to produce model outputs, to be used, for example, by the linearization or trim commands.
Mux	The Mux block combines a configurable number of scalar input signals to produce a vector output signal.
Demux	The Demux block splits a vector input signal into a configurable number of scalar output signals.
[A] From	A From block works with a Goto block. The output of a From block is the same as the input to the corresponding Goto block. A From block can receive input from only one Goto block, but a Goto block can send a signal to any number of From blocks.
{A} Goto Tag Visibility	The Goto Tag Visibility determines which subsystems can contain From blocks corresponding to a particular Goto block.

Connections Block Library (Continued)

Block	Purpose
[A] Goto	A Goto block sends its input to all corresponding From blocks.
A Data Store Read	The output is the current value of the contents of the corresponding Data Store.
A Data Store Memory	A Data Store Memory is a named memory location written to by Data Store Write blocks, and read from by Data Store Read blocks. A simulation can save data in a Data Store Memory, then access that data later.
A Data Store Write	A Data Store Write block writes to a specified Data Store Memory block. More than one Data Store Write block can write to a particular Data Store Memory, but if two or more Data Store Write blocks attempt to write to the same Data Store Memory on the same simulation step, the results are unpredictable.
Enable	Converts a subsystem into an enabled subsystem.
Trigger	Converts a subsystem into a triggered subsystem. Converts an enabled subsystem into a trigger when enabled subsystem.
Ground	Connect Ground blocks to unused inputs to prevent SIMULINK from producing error messages. For example, if a State-Space block is used to model the unforced behavior of a system, connect a Ground block to its input port.
Terminator	Connect unused block outputs to Terminator blocks to prevent SIMULINK from producing error messages. For example, if you use a Demux block to split a vector signal, but only need to use one component of the vector signal, connect the unneeded output ports of the Demux block to Terminator blocks.
[1] IC	The IC block sets the initial condition of its output to a specified value. After the simulation begins, the block output is the same as its input. This block is useful in algebraic loops, as it can provide an initial guess to the algebraic loop solver for the first time step.

Connections Block Library (Continued)

Block	Purpose
Subsystem	A subsystem can be built in a Subsystem block as an alternative to encapsulating the subsystem using **Edit:Create Subsystem**.
Selector	The selector block accepts a vector input, and produces a vector output that consists of selected elements of the input vector in a selected order.
Width	The output of the Width block is the number of elements in the input vector. Thus, if the input is a five-element vector, the output is 5.

Parameter Reference

This appendix lists the parameters that may be set using the `set_param` command and read using the `get_param` command. To read a parameter, the command syntax is

```
get_param(path, parameter_name) ;
```

where `path` is a MATLAB string containing the path to the object and `parameter_name` is a MATLAB string containing the parameter name from this appendix. For a model, `path` is the model name. For a block, `path` is the path to the block, starting with the model name. For example, the path to a Gain block in system `examp_a` would be `'examp_a/gain'`. The syntax of the `set_param` command is

```
set_param(path, parameter_name, parameter_value) ;
```

Here, `parameter_value` is either a string or numeric expression, depending on the particular parameter. Almost all parameter values are entered as strings. For example, to set the value of gain for the Gain block in system `examp_a` to 5.0, the following statement could be used:

```
set_param('examp_a/gain','Gain','5.0') ;
```

An important exception to this rule is the `UserData` parameter for models, masked subsystems, and blocks. `UserData` can accept any MATLAB variable, including arrays, cell arrays, and structures.

Model Parameters

Table B-1 lists the parameters that are defined for a model as a whole.

Table B-1 Model parameters

Parameter	Meaning
Name	Model name. This is normally the filename without the extension.
Version	SIMULINK version used to modify the model the last time it was saved. This parameter is read-only.

Table B-1 Model parameters (Continued)

Parameter	Meaning
SimParamPage	Name of the page on which to open the **Simulation:Parameters** dialog box. Choices are 'Solver', 'Workspace I/O', 'Diagnostics'.
SampleTimeColors	Sample time colors set to 'on' or 'off'.
WideVectorLines	Wide vector lines set to 'on' or 'off'.
PaperOrientation	Paper orientation for printing the model, set to 'portrait' or 'landscape'.
StartTime	Simulation start time.
Solver	Solver name from list 'ode45', 'ode23', 'ode113', 'ode15s', 'ode23s', 'ode5', 'ode4', 'ode3', 'ode2', 'ode1', 'discrete'
RelTol	Relative tolerance.
AbsTol	Absolute tolerance.
Refine	Refine factor.
MaxStep	Maximum integration step size.
InitialStep	Initial integration step size.
FixedStep	Step size for fixed step size solvers.
MaxOrder	Maximum order for solver ode15s.
OutputOption	Output option from list 'AdditionalOutputTimes', 'RefineOutputTimes', 'SpecifiedOutputTimes'.
OutputTimes	Vector of output times depending on setting of OutputOption.
LoadExternalInput	Load input from MATLAB workspace, 'on' or 'off'.
ExternalInput	Variable names for time and output variables if LoadExternalInput is 'on'.
SaveTime	Save simulation time, 'on' or 'off'.
TimeSaveName	Variable name in which to save time.
SaveOutput	Save simulation output, 'on' or 'off'.

Table B-1 Model parameters (Continued)

Parameter	Meaning
OutputSaveName	Variable name in which to save output.
LoadInitialState	Load initial state from MATLAB workspace, 'on' or 'off'.
InitialState	Variable name from which to load initial state.
SaveFinalState	Save final simulation state vector, 'on' or 'off'.
FinalStateName	Variable name in which to save final state.
LimitMaxRows	Limit the number of rows in model output variables, 'on' or 'off'.
MaxRows	Maximum number of rows in output.
Decimation	Decimation factor.
AlgebraicLoopMsg	Setting for algebraic loop messages, 'none', 'warning', 'error'.
MinStepSizeMsg	Setting for minimum step size violation messages, 'warning', 'error'.
UnconnectedInputMsg	Setting for unconnected input messages, 'none', 'warning', 'error'.
UnconnectedOutputMsg	Setting for unconnected output messages, 'none', 'warning', 'error'.
Unconnected LineMsg	Setting for unconnected signal line messages, 'none', 'warning', 'error'.
ConsistencyChecking	Consistency checking, 'on' or 'off'.
ZeroCross	Zero crossing detection, 'on' or 'off'.

Common Block Parameters

Table B-2 lists parameters that are common to all blocks.

Table B-2 Common block parameters

Parameter	Meaning
Name	Block name.
BlockType	SIMULINK object type. This is `'block'`, and is read-only.
Parent	Name of object that owns the block.
BlockType	Block type. This is the name in the top left corner of the block dialog box (not the block dialog box title bar).
BlockDescription	Text in description field of block dialog box.
InputPorts	Array listing the locations of the block input ports.
OutputPorts	Array listing the locations of the block output ports.
Orientation	Block orientation, `'right'`, `left'`, `'down'`, `'up'`.
ForegroundColor	Block foreground color, `'black'`, `'white'`, etc.
BackgroundColor	Block background color, `'black'`, `'white'`, etc.
DropShadow	Drop shadow, `'on'` or `'off'`.
NamePlacement	Placement of block name, `'normal'`, `'alternate'`.
FontName	Name of font used on block.
FontSize	Size of font in points.
FontWeight	Relative weight of font, `'light'`, `'demi'`, `'bold'`.
FontAngle	From list `'normal'`, `'italic'`, `'oblique'`.
Position	Location of block in model window [left, top, right, bottom]. This parameter must be entered as a vector, rather than as a string.
ShowName	Show the block name, `'on'` or `'off'`.
Tag	Block tag. This is a user-defined variable. It must be a character string if used.
UserData	Any MATLAB variable. Note that UserData is not saved with the model.

Table B-2 Common block parameters (Continued)

Parameter	Meaning
Selected	Selection state of block, 'on' or 'off'.
SourceBlock	If BlockType is 'Reference', this is the corresponding library block.
SourceType	If BlockType is 'Reference', this is the corresponding library block BlockType.

Mask Parameters

Table B-3 lists parameters that are specific to masked blocks.

Table B-3 Masked block parameters

Parameter	Meaning
MaskType	Contents of field **Mask Type**.
MaskDescription	Contents of **Block Description**.
MaskHelp	Contents of **Block Help**.
MaskPromptString	Contents of **Prompt** field. If there are multiple prompts, they are separated with the | symbol.
MaskStyleString	**Type** field from 'Edit', 'Checkbox', 'Popup'. If there are multiple prompts, they are separated with |.
MaskVariables	**Variable** field. If there are multiple prompts, the corresponding variable names are separated with |.
MaskInitialization	Contents of **Initialization commands**.
MaskDisplay	Contents of **Drawing commands**.
MaskIconFrame	**Icon frame**, 'on' or 'off'.
MaskIconOpaque	**Icon transparency**, 'on' or 'off'.
MaskIconRotate	**Icon rotation**, 'on' or 'off'.
MaskIconUnits	**Drawing coordinates**, 'Pixel', 'Autoscale', 'Normalized'.
MaskValueString	Contents of the masked block's dialog box fields, in the form of a string with the field contents separated with |.

Sources Block Library

Table B-4 lists the names of the dialog box fields for blocks in the Sources block library. For details on any block field, refer to the Block Browser.

Table B-4   Sources block library

Block	Dialog Field Names	Notes
Band-Limited White Noise	Cov Ts Seed	Height of PSD of the noise. Sample time. Seed of random number generator.
Chirp Signal	f1 T f2	Initial frequency. Target time. Frequency at target time.
Clock		No dialog box fields.
Constant	Value	
Digital Clock	SampleTime	
Discrete Pulse Generator	Amplitude Period PulseWidth PhaseDelay SampleTime	
From File	FileName	
From Workspace	VariableName	
Pulse Generator	period duty amplitude start	
Ramp	slope start X0	Initial value.
Random Number	Mean Variance Seed SampleTime	
Repeating Sequence	rep_seq_t rep_seq_y	Time values. Output values.

Table B-4 Sources block library (Continued)

Block	Dialog Field Names	Notes
Signal Generator	WaveForm Amplitude Frequency Units	
Sine Wave	Amplitude Frequency Phase SampleTime	
Step	Time Before After	
Uniform Random Number	Minimum Maximum Seed SampleTime	

Sinks Block Library

Table B-5 lists the names of the dialog box fields for blocks in the Sinks block library.

Table B-5   Sources block library

Block	Dialog Field Names	Notes
Display	Format	'short', 'long', etc.
	Decimation	
	Floating	
	SampleTime	
Scope	Floating	'on' or 'off'.
	Open	'on' or 'off'.
	Grid	'on' or 'off'.
	TickLabels	'on' or 'off'.
	ZoomMode	'on' or 'off'.
	TimeRange	'auto' or a vector.
	Ymin	
	Ymax	
	SaveToWorkspace	'on' or 'off'.
	SaveName	Variable name.
	LimitMaxRows	'on' or 'off'.
	MaxRows	
	Decimation	
	SampleInput	'on' or 'off'.
	SampleTime	
Stop Simulation		No dialog box fields.
To File	FileName	
	MatrixName	
	Decimation	
	SampleTime	
To Workspace	VariableName	
	Buffer	
	Decimation	
	SampleTime	
XY Graph	xmin	
	xmax	
	ymin	
	ymax	
	st	Sample time.

Discrete Block Library

Table B-6 lists the names of the dialog box fields for blocks in the Discrete block library.

Table B-6 Discrete block library

Block	Dialog Field Names	Notes
Discrete Filter	Numerator Denominator SampleTime	
Discrete State-Space	A B C D X0 SampleTime	
Discrete Transfer Fcn	Numerator Denominator SampleTime	
Discrete Zero-Pole	Zeros Poles Gain SampleTime	
Discrete-Time Integrator	IntegratorMethod ExternalReset InitialConditionSource InitialCondition LimitOutput UpperSaturationLimit LowerSaturationLimit ShowSaturationPort ShowStatePort SampleTime	'ForwardEuler', etc. 'on' or 'off'. 'on' or 'off'. 'on' or 'off'.
First-Order Hold	Ts	Sample time.
Unit Delay	X0 SampleTime	Initial condition.
Zero-Order Hold	SampleTime	

Linear Block Library

Table B-7 lists the names of the dialog box fields for blocks in the Linear block library.

Table B-7 Linear block library

Block	Dialog Field Names	Notes
Derivative		No dialog box fields.
Dot Product		No dialog box fields.
Gain	Gain	
Integrator	ExternalReset	
	InitialConditionSource	
	IntialCondition	
	LimitOutput	'on' or 'off'.
	UpperSaturationLimit	
	LowerSaturationLimit	
	ShowSaturationPort	'on' or 'off'.
	ShowStatePort	'on' or 'off'.
	AbsoluteTolerance	
Matrix Gain	K	Gain matrix.
Slider Gain	low	
	gain	
	high	
State-Space	A	
	B	
	C	
	D	
	X0	Initial conditions.
Sum	Inputs	List of signs.
Transfer Fcn	Numerator	
	Denominator	
Zero-Pole	Zeros	
	Poles	
	Gain	

Nonlinear Block Library

Table B-8 lists the names of the dialog box fields for blocks in the Nonlinear block library.

Table B-8   Nonlinear block library

Block	Dialog Field Names	Notes
Abs		No dialog box fields.
Algebraic Constraint	z0	**Initial guess.**
Backlash	BacklashWidth InitialOutput	
Combinatorial Logic	TruthTable	
Coulomb & Viscous Friction	offset gain	
Dead Zone	LowerValue UpperValue	
Fcn	Expr	**Expression.**
Hit Crossing	HitCrossingOffset HitCrossingDirection ShowOutputPort	`'on'` or `'off'`.
Logical Operator	Operator Inputs	`'AND'`, `'OR'`, etc. **Number of input ports.**
Look-Up Table	InputValues OutputValues	
Look-Up Table (2-D)	x y t	**Row.** **Column.** **Table.**
Manual Switch	sw action	
Math Function	Operator	`'exp'`, etc.
MATLAB Fcn	MATLABFcn OutputWidth	
Memory	X0 InheritSampleTime	`'on'` or `'off'`.

Table B-8 Nonlinear block library (Continued)

Block	Dialog Field Names	Notes
MinMax	Function Inputs	'min' or 'max'.
Multiport Switch	Inputs	**Number of inputs.**
Product		No dialog box fields.
Quantizer	QuantizationInterval	
Rate Limiter	RisingSlewLimit FallingSlewLimit	
Relational Operator	Operator	
Relay	OnSwitchValue OffSwitchValue OnOutputValue OffOutputValue	
Rounding Function	Operator	
S-Function	System Parameters	
Saturation	UpperLimit LowerLimit	
Sign		No dialog box fields.
Switch	Threshold	
Transport Delay	DelayTime InitialInput BufferSize	
Trigonometric Function	Operator	'sin', 'cos', etc.
Variable Transport Delay	MaximumDelay InstallInput MaximumPoints	**Buffer size.**

Connections Block Library

Table B-9 lists the names of the dialog box fields for blocks in the Connections block library.

Table B-9   Connections block library

Block	Dialog Field Names	Notes
Data Store Memory	`DataStoreName` `InitialValue`	
Data Store Read	`DataStoreName` `SampleTime`	
Data Store Write	`DataStoreName` `SampleTime`	
Demux	`Outputs`	**Number of outputs.**
Enable	`StatesWhenEnabling` `ShowOutputPort`	`'on'` or `'off'`.
From	`GotoTag`	
Goto	`GotoTag` `TagVisibility`	
Goto Tag Visibility	`GotoTag`	
Ground		No dialog box fields.
IC	`Value`	

In	`Port`
	`PortWidth`
	`SampleTime`	

Mux	`Inputs`	**Number of inputs.**

Out	`Port`
	`OutputWhenDisabled`
	`InitialOutput`	

Selector	`Elements` `InputPortWidth`	
Subsystem	`ShowPortLabels`	`'on'` or `'off'`.
Terminator		No dialog box fields.

Table B-9   Connections block library (Continued)

Block	Dialog Field Names	Notes
Trigger	`TriggerType` `ShowOutputPort`	`'on'` or `'off'`.
Width		No dialog box fields.

Index